========================
About the Author
========================

DOUGLAS V. GIBBS is a historian, instructor, radio host, freelance
columnist, and internet blogger. He lives in Murrieta, California with
his wife of 30 years.

The Basic Constitution

An Examination of the Principles
and Philosophies of the
United States Constitution

Douglas V. Gibbs

Constitution Association Press: Murrieta, California

THE BASIC CONSTITUTION.

Copyright © 2014 Douglas V. Gibbs

All rights reserved.

CONSTITUTION ASSOCIATION PRESS, Murrieta, CA

www.douglasvgibbs.com

www.politicalpistachio.com

www.constitutionassociation.com

ISBN-10: 1502361280
ISBN-13: 978-1502361288

*Dedicated to the many students, past, present, and future, of my Constitution Classes -
and to Jane, who came up with the idea of having the classes in the first place.*

Also by Douglas V. Gibbs

25 Myths of the United States Constitution

Concepts of the United States Constitution Series:
#1- Separation of Powers

Coming Soon:

Constitution News Quarterly

A Patriot's Guide Through The U.S. Constitution

25 Myths of The Republican Party

25 Myths of The Democrat Party

A Patriot's Guide Through Madison's Notes of The Federal Convention 1787

A Tyrant's Guide to Killing Liberty

Contents

Introduction

When the average person attempts to read the United States Constitution, for the most part, it seems as if it was written in "legalese." The terminology is foreign to the average reader, and most people, even the most informed, may not know the historical context that accompanies the language used by the Founding Fathers when they crafted the document during the Federal Convention in 1787. We, as Americans, were raised in liberty, so we know when something happening in the political realm seems to be wrong. We may even say, "Hey, that's unconstitutional." But when we make such an accusation, do we really know if our assertion is accurate?

Some scholars claim to understand perfectly the Constitution, the original meaning of the text, and the intentions of its authors. Their interpretation, they purport, is the only truth and the text of the Constitution is too complicated for the average person to understand. They contend that only a lawyer, or a seasoned judge, can fully understand the web that accompanies constitutional law. There are volumes written to explain the document, documentaries that attempt to dissect it, and professors who proclaim it is a living and breathing document that changes with the whims of society a reed bending in the breeze.

The reality is that the Constitution was written with the intent that it could be understood by the average informed citizen. The Preamble begins with the words "We the People," not "We the Lawyers," for a reason.

It is my contention that the Constitution is difficult to understand because those who oppose it have created a new constitution, their constitution. The interpretation they offer is a forgery, a counterfeit of the real thing. The original intent has been lost, hidden behind the complexities of case law, and legal precedent. The volumes of books that claim to clarify the complexities of the Constitution were written to further confuse the original text, to create a legal obstacle course designed to move the average person away from even wanting to investigate the Constitution.

13

Those that oppose the Constitution are like those who printed the Bible in Latin. The elite leadership of the Roman Church made the decision to print the Bible in Latin so that the people could not read it, and so that the people would be dependent upon the priests for their interpretation of scripture.

The Constitution is simple to understand, and simple to learn about, if only a person can shut out the noise, forget the myths they've been conditioned to believe, and place themselves in the shoes of the men who met in Philadelphia, during the summer heat of 1787, shortly after the conclusion of the Revolutionary War.

There are certain principles that need to be learned, but once the average citizen understands those principles, the Constitution becomes comprehensible. The original intent comes alive. The founders cease to be enigmas. We recognize them as men of wisdom, learned problem solvers who understood that a central government can be a dangerous thing, unless it is limited, restrained by a set standard that is put into writing. State Sovereignty, Divine Providence, and the Separation of Powers suddenly makes sense, once the waters of the Constitution are navigated with an open mind, and the reader is accompanied by an unbiased guide who understands the original intent of the Founding Fathers when they labored in the convention at Independence Hall in 1787.

Let's cast off, and sail those waters together. Let us investigate the Constitution from the viewpoint of the founders, understanding that though their world was a very different world than ours, their need for liberty was the same. These were men, who, as it states in the Declaration of Independence, were willing to lay down their lives, lose their fortunes, and pledge to each other their sacred honor for liberty - and they did so with a "firm reliance on the protection of divine Providence."

During the early weeks of the Constitutional Convention, the fighting was so intense that the founders achieved nothing. The sovereignty of the States became an explosive issue as the nationalists squared off with those who warned the Articles of Confederation should not be replaced. The delegates, despite receiving the authority of the Congress of the Confederation to convene, were unable to come to an agreement when it came to the powers that should be reserved to the States. The delegates were making no ground in creating a new government, and the confrontations were becoming more passionate with each passing day. After a few weeks of flaring tempers, and clashing interests, the delegates were no closer to forming a new federal government than they had been from day one.

The elder statesman, seated calmly behind his circular spectacles and coonskin cap, said nothing as the battles ensued. He remained silent as the factions squared off, and insults were traded. The deliberations were in crisis, and Doctor Benjamin Franklin finally had enough!

He explained to the delegation that their crisis was one that could be destructive to their efforts. The inability to come to agreement could force them to abort the effort of writing a new constitution. The subject, he explained, could not be approached as long as the delegates were differing as such.

Franklin recommended a short recess, time away from the deliberations, as well as an appeal to Heaven. "How has it happened, Sir, that we have not hitherto once thought of humbly applying to the Father of lights to illuminate our understandings?"

Franklin reminded the delegates of how during the war with Great Britain, "we were sensible of danger we had daily prayer in this room for the divine protection. Our prayers, Sir, were heard, and they were graciously answered. All of us who were engaged in the struggle must have observed frequent instances of a Superintending providence in our favor. To that kind providence we owe this happy opportunity of consulting in peace on the means of establishing our future national felicity. And have we now forgotten that powerful friend?"

Not known for being a religious man, Franklin's words were a curiosity, but he assured the delegates that his journey to seek God had been a long journey, and now he was reaching an age of understanding. "I have lived, Sir, a long time, and the longer I live, the more convincing proofs I see of this truth- that God governs in the affairs of men. And if a sparrow cannot fall to the ground without his notice, is it probable that an empire can rise without his aid?"

Then he referred to Scripture. "We have been assured, Sir, in the sacred writings, that 'except the Lord build the House they labour in vain that build it.'"

In Franklin's opinion, if they continued on the same course without appealing to divine Providence, the success of the delegates in the convention would be "no better than the Builders of Babel: We shall be divided by our little partial local interests; our projects will be confounded, and we ourselves shall become a reproach and bye word down to future ages. And what is worse, mankind may hereafter from this unfortunate instance, despair of establishing Governments be Human Wisdom and leave it to chance, war and conquest."

Then the request emerged. Franklin stated that the delegates should be "imploring the assistance of Heaven, and its blessings on our deliberations." He recommended that prayers should be uttered before each session of the convention, "and that one or more of the Clergy of the City be requested to officiate in that service."

Roger Sherman of Connecticut, the only founder to sign all four founding documents (Articles of Association, Articles of Confederation, Declaration of Independence, and the United States Constitution) seconded Benjamin Franklin's motion.

Alexander Hamilton, a man who, after studying history, one realizes was a bit of a statist, expressed apprehensions. It is unclear if his apprehensions, and the apprehensions of others, were because of an aversion to bringing God into the convention, or if they simply understood that the delegates did not have the money to hire a clergy to officiate the prayers.

According to James Madison's notes on the Federal Convention, the delegates decided to pray before each session, but at the church down the road. Dr. Franklin's request was also the encouragement of a tradition, later in America's history, that prompted prayers before each session of Congress.

America was formed with a firm reliance on the protection of divine Providence.

Freedom was established, and maintained, by a simple idea, that limited government is the essence of liberty.

George Washington was President of the proceedings, and the chair he used, at the top of the back of it, had an image of a half-sun, somewhere between sunrise or sunset on the horizon. Madison reported Benjamin

Franklin saying regarding that chair, "I have often looked at that behind the president without being able to tell whether it was rising or setting. But now I... know that it is a rising...sun."

America is still rising.

"A well-instructed people alone can be permanently a free people." -- James Madison

"The good sense of the people will always be found to be the best army. They may be led astray for a moment, but will soon correct themselves." -- Thomas Jefferson

"I have so much faith in the general government of the world by Providence that I can hardly conceive a transaction of such momentous importance [as the framing of the Constitution]." -- Benjamin Franklin

"[The adoption of the Constitution] will demonstrate as visibly the finger of Providence as any possible event in the course of human affairs can ever designate it." -- George Washington

Chapter 1

We the People

We the People of the United States, in Order to form a more perfect Union, establish Justice, insure domestic Tranquility, provide for the common defence, promote the general Welfare, and secure the Blessings of Liberty to ourselves and our Posterity, do ordain and establish this Constitution for the United States of America.

History

The formal version of the **Magna Carta** in England was issued on June 19, 1215. There was a minor change in the new document, when the final provision was drafted, replacing the term "any baron" with "any **freeman**" in stipulating to whom the provisions applied. The term would eventually include all Englishmen. The final version's applicability to all members of the English Society served as a starting point for the Constitution's Preamble, where "any freeman" was changed once again, but this time to the first three words of the American document: "We the People."

The English Colonists developed legal codes largely incorporating liberties guaranteed by Magna Carta and the 1689 **English Bill of Rights**. Though the education levels of the colonists varied, and few could afford legal training in England, they were familiar with English **common law**. During one parliamentary debate in the late 18th century, Edmund Burke observed, "In no country, perhaps in the world, is law so general a study."

James Madison and Thomas Jefferson drew inspiration from the doctrines of the British constitution, or in what were called English liberties.

Unlike the Spanish Colonies, which were conquered land ruled over by the Spanish Conquistadors, and authoritarian governors, the English Colonies were granted by **charter**. Rather than bear the burden of empire, which, as Spain discovered, could be expensive, and taxing on a nation's armed forces, the English Crown offered the lands along the Atlantic Coast to investors, entrepreneurs, and families seeking a new start. In the northern colonies, the colonists sought religious freedom. The Pilgrims did not want to keep their membership in the Church of England. As **separatists**, the Pilgrims organized their worship independently, colonizing north of the Puritans at Plymouth Rock.

The English Colonies enjoyed autonomy that the Spanish Colonies did not. To survive in the Spanish Colonies, the colonist exhibited a warrior spirit, conquering the lands and the people who stood in the way, forcing the captured natives into slave labor and marriage for the purpose of accomplishing the tasks necessary for survival, while also being heavily dependent upon supplies from the homeland. The English Colonies were expected to survive by living off the land. They were families, **indentured servants**, and seekers of fortune. They were forced to be self-reliant, personally responsible, and hard working, in order to survive. The English Colonists did not attempt to conquer the natives as the Spanish did, but worked with them, making treaties with the Native Americans, because they needed the native population's help in order to survive. In the English Colonies, freedom was a necessary component of survival, and after failing under **communitarianism**, the colonists found that a **free market** system where colonists kept more of what they worked for, and had the option to trade goods in an open market, worked best for the burgeoning society.

In English America, **freemen** adopted the best of the English system, while adapting it as necessary to the new circumstances in the colonies. The English Colonies was a place where a person could rise by merit, not birth. The thirteen colonies was a place where men could voice their opinions and actively share in self-government. When the British Crown challenged these beliefs, turning to the colonies as a source of revenue to help alleviate the Crown's substantial debts, and the growing expense of keeping troops on American soil, the colonists questioned the government in Britain, challenging the actions of **Parliament**, arguing that without consent or direct representation in Parliament, the acts by the motherland were "taxation without representation," and an act of tyranny against the free Englishmen of the colonies.

The influence of the Magna Carta, and the demand for liberty, existed along the Atlantic Coast long before the War of Independence. As John Adams later wrote to Thomas Jefferson, "The Revolution was in the minds of the people, and this was effected, from 1760 to 1775, in the course of 15 years before a drop of blood was shed at Lexington."

The Americans knew their rights, and they were willing to fight for them. The seal adopted by Massachusetts on the eve of the Revolution summed up the mood. The image was of a militiaman with sword in one hand, and the Magna Carta in the other.

When it was time to form a new government, embodied in a written **social contract** we now know as the Constitution of the United States, the founders determined that like England under the Magna Carta, the government must be limited by subjecting it to the rule of law. The Constitution, once ratified by the States, became the law of the land. The document serves as a written standard where the authority emanates from the people, not from any governmental body. Pursuant to the Constitution, no man, not even the country's leader, was considered to be above the law. The rule of law based on the philosophy of the Laws of Nature and of Nature's God was the basis of constitutional thought in the United States in 1787.

"A government of laws, and not of men." - John Adams

Elder statesman Benjamin Franklin strolled across a grassy lawn from Independence Hall in Philadelphia, after the conclusion of the Federal Convention of 1787, when a woman in a bonnet approached him, asking, "Sir, what have you given us?"

"A republic," Dr. Franklin replied. "If you can keep it."

The new government in the fledgling United States was considered to be one that was doomed to fail. Europeans scoffed at the American experiment in self-government. The Old World argued that without the hand of a divinely appointed, wise, ruling **monarch** in place to guide society, a culture could not succeed. The Grand Experiment was a waste of time, and it would not be long before the rebellious, starving, treasonous, and petulant, English colonists came crawling back to the British Crown, begging to be readmitted to the empire.

In a society with no government, people have no freedom. In a society with too much government, people have no freedom.

Without government there is no law, and without law there are no

21

enforcers of the law. This kind of system is called an anarchy, which is a transitional form of government. In an **anarchy**, there is no freedom because the citizens must constantly protect their property, and their lives.

With government in place, there are laws in place. When there are laws in place, it is necessary to hire enforcers of the law, such as a police force. A society with a government in place can create an environment of freedom that allows citizens the ability to leave their property and engage in activities away from their homes.

Tyranny through a **unitary state** dominates the pages of history. Tyrannical governments obtain their power through violence, and bloodshed in a complete disregard for authorities granted, justice, or the **rule of law**. To maintain their power, tyrants use violence and bloodshed. When tyrannies are finally toppled, the path to dislodging tyrannies normally includes violence and bloodshed.

Violence and death are the common results of powerful central governments with dominant rulers.

Dictators do not normally reveal their plans of tyranny during their rise to power, for the people would never have allowed them to become their leaders if they knew this kind of violence was in their future. Tyrannical leaders render legislative bodies irrelevant, demoting them to nothing more than a **consultative assembly**.

In history, tyranny is the rule, and liberty is the exception. Governments that protect the freedoms of the people, and respect the rights of their citizens, are a rare occurrence. Freedom requires the citizens to be informed and involved. With freedom comes responsibility.

An educated society begins by teaching the younger generations the principles of liberty, and to encourage them to be involved in **civic activities**, and local government. The founders understood we need government, but a **limited government** was required to protect the rights and property of the citizens. However, because of human nature, the founders realized that without making sure the people remained educated about the system they had established, a downward spiral into despotism and tyranny was inevitable.

The **Declaration of Independence** was approved by the Continental

Congress on July 4, 1776, and outlined the reasons why the colonies were seeking independence from Great Britain. The founding document declares that it is the right of the people to alter or abolish their government should it become destructive. It also states these truths are self-evident, and that "all men are created equal, that they are endowed by their Creator with certain **unalienable rights**, that among these are life, liberty, and the pursuit of happiness."

The document penned by Thomas Jefferson includes a list of grievances, most of which are also iterated in the U.S. Constitution. The Declaration calls for fair representation, encourages immigration, calls for a judiciary that is separated from the will of the central leadership, calls for a stop to the presence of a standing army, demands that Great Britain stop the quartering of troops in the houses of the citizens, demands fair trials, and calls for due process, free trade, fair taxation, a protection of rights, and for the Crown to hear the redress of grievances by the colonists.

A key aspect of the Declaration of Independence reveals itself in the final sentence of the document. The call for independence ends with the incredible statement, *"And for the support of this Declaration, with a firm reliance on the protection of divine Providence, we mutually pledge to each other our Lives, our Fortunes and our sacred Honor."*

Political Spectrum

In the battle of Left versus Right, it is important to understand what it all means in the first place. Like-minded individuals naturally tend to gather together when a theater of opinion erupts. Congregating in such a manner, creating political parties, is a part of our human nature. Houses, or chambers, of government are no different. Members of the political assembly who support similar agendas sit together, much in the way social allies tend to hang out together at a dinner party. The classification of "left" and "right" grew out of the tendency of people to group together on one side, or the other.

The early definition of "left" and "right" was different than in today's American Society. Among the most commonly known split between the left and the right in a political assembly occurred in France before the French Revolution. Members of the National Assembly sat on the right or the left of the hall depending on their level of political support in regards to the ruling monarchy. Those in support of the monarchy, and the religious elements that came with the reigning government, would sit on the right. The people on the right were defined as being those holding traditional interests in line with the Church and the monarchy, believing the king ruled by divine right, and that Catholicism must continue to be the state religion, and therefore continue to be a strong influence on governance. The people who sat on the right side of the assembly believed that the Church had a vested interest in the political system, and sought to preserve that system.

Those who sat on the left side of the hall in France during the period preceding the French Revolution did so in support of "enlightenment," which was considered to be in the interests of rationalism and secularism. The left used secular elements to challenge the Church's long-held influence over government, fostering nationalism among its allies, and promoting hope in constructing and shaping the political community. The left desired to change government by overthrowing the Church and the aristocracy by promoting secularism and nationalism. The planners of this glorious new "Enlightened" government became the leaders of France after the French Revolution, orchestrating a Reign of Terror, which was a period of chaos during which thousands were guillotined for being politically incorrect.

The radicals within this new government saw the Catholic Church as the enemy while promoting its Cult of Reason. Like with the monarchy before them, however, it became clear that to control the political and social upheaval, the government in place must also become tyrannical in their own right. Under the rule of **statism**, France remained a nation unable to cultivate liberty, and one that remained under the iron fist of a dictatorial government. For many, this was no surprise. Some of the planners of the change of the form of government in France knew that in order to keep order they would need to "treat the people as cattle."

The French National Assembly established a constitutional monarchy and adopted a new constitution in 1791 that created a Legislative Assembly. The political assembly, as with any other political body, rapidly divided into factions opposing each other. The three factions that formed in the new French Legislative Assembly were the radicals (liberals), moderates (centrists) and conservatives. The radicals (liberals) sat in the left section of the assembly hall, the conservatives sat on the right, and the moderates sat in the center section. Their political identities have some similarities to political movements today in the United States, and had little in common with the pre-revolution arrangement that emphasized itself more on monarchy and religion.

America is much younger than the European nations, and never had a landlord class of titled nobles. In fact, the Constitution specifically prohibits such a system. The Founding Fathers desired to break away from European traditions as much as possible, even abandoning much of British Common Law when defining citizenship. To be a British Subject the rules were weak, and divided loyalties ran rampant throughout the British Empire. The United States as a nation could not tolerate divided loyalties, and placed a stronger standard of natural born citizenship upon the President in order to eliminate the opportunity for the executor of the American Form of Government to harbor divided loyalties between the United States of America, and any other nation. That way, the new American government could break completely free of any European influence, and forge itself into a Republic independent from British influence, and in fact, the authoritarian nature of Europe as a whole.

The political landscape of the United States of America, since there never was a class of nobles, was simple in the young nation. Either you were a Federalist, an anti-Federalist, or somewhere in between. In other words, you believed in a stronger centralized federal government, you believed that the federal role in government should be limited greatly, or you found yourself somewhere between the two political beliefs.

Unlike the Europeans, royalty and religion played no role in determining the nature of American political philosophies. Nearly all of the early American Politicians were deeply religious men, but the political spectrum did not separate factions along religious lines. God played a major role in the principle foundation of the nation, but the founding fathers also determined that no religion could ever take an official role in government. In other words, the establishment of any religion as the official religion of the United States was forbidden. However, the freedom to practice one's religion was not to be infringed upon. Almost all of the signers of the Declaration of Independence were either clergy, or highly involved in their church. 27 of the 56 signers had Christian seminary degrees. The founding fathers fervently prayed in Congress.

Benjamin Franklin is widely regarded to be among the least religious of the founding fathers. However, his speech given to Congress on June 28, 1787 asking that Congress have a prayer every morning before conducting business was overtly religious in nature. Despite modern assumptions, there was not a political battle between The Church and the secularists during the founding of the United States of America.

From the newer models of government in France, and America, the definition of the **Political Spectrum** changed, becoming more about the level of control of government over a society, rather than the presence of a monarchy, or established church. Zero percent of government intrusion on the lives of the people inhabits the far right of the current political spectrum, which is a condition known as **anarchy**. 100% governmental control inhabits the far left extremity of the Political Spectrum, or a **totalitarian government**. The American form of government, or a Constitutional Republic that operates under the rule of law, is at the center of the political spectrum.

Most of the current forms of government present in today's international political arena reside on the left side of the Political Spectrum, drawing their foundations from **socialist** principles. Socialism is authoritarian. Socialism claims to seek to overthrow the Church and aristocracy by promoting atheism and nationalism, much like the enlightened planners of the French Revolution, only replacing the government they thought to be a tyranny with a tyranny of their own. In Russia, the rise of socialism held the basic tenet of replacing the individual's commitment to God with a commitment to love and serve a collective society ruled by an elite few.

When one examines the communist society, which resides on the left side of the Political Spectrum, one finds that if society was ruled over by an equally powerful religious **theocracy**, the basic governmental elements of the ruling doctrine are the same, and just as tyrannical. Therefore, a controlling government based on religion is no different than an atheistic system of communism. Either way, the form of governance is based on a centralized control over the people, and limits on personal individualism, and freedoms.

Economically, **leftism** encourages increased government involvement with the instruments that regulate the economy. Under a leftist economic system, such as in the communist model, the government seizes control of the industries, eliminating private ownership. In the fascist model, however, the authoritarian political entity engages in corporatism, allowing the private enterprises to remain private, yet bundled together in a uniting strength under authoritarian government rule. Because **fascism** (from Italian fascismo, Benito Mussolini's authoritarian political movement in Italy 1922 to 1943) was created to be an adverse reaction to the apparent economic failure of Marxism, and labeled itself as the opposite of communism, fascism is often referred to as being right-wing, and ultra-conservative. If you break down the political structure of fascism, however, it becomes apparent that defining fascism as being on the right side of the political spectrum is problematic. Like socialism, fascism exalts the group above the individual (in fascist states often the nation or race is exalted above the identity of the individual). Like other leftist systems, fascism also calls for a separation of church and state, a national civilian army, and **progressive taxation**. One element of fascism some may argue as being right-wing is the fact that fascism seeks to eliminate labor unions for co-ops. But the co-operatives, in a fascist state, are controlled by the government, and therefore become more leftist than the system before. Though fascism, during the early twentieth century, claimed to be anti-communist, the National Socialism aspect of the ideology places fascism on the left side of the Political Spectrum.

Ultimately, the true definition of the Political Spectrum is dependent upon how government interacts with society. Increased government intrusion moves needle on the spectrum to the left. Increasing limitations on government intrusion moves the needle to the right. In both cases, the extreme of totalitarianism, or anarchy, are equally dangerous. Ultimately, most forms of government, despite the promise of fairness, are often only precursors to another form of government. The Founding Fathers realized this, recognizing that the only form of government that both limits the powers of the federal government, while still giving it adequate authority to protect and preserve **State Sovereignty**, is a Constitutional Republic. They knew that if you pursue leftism too far, an authoritarian government would rise from the movement. If government was limited too much, and the government did not have enough power to enforce law, an authoritarian government would also rise to fill the void.

The Preamble

We the People of the United States, in Order to form a more perfect Union, establish Justice, insure domestic Tranquility, provide for the common defence, promote the general Welfare, and secure the Blessings of Liberty to ourselves and our Posterity, do ordain and establish this Constitution for the United States of America.

The **Preamble** is the introduction of the U.S. Constitution. The opening paragraph of the founding document holds no legal authority. The Preamble serves to establish who is granting the authority to create a new federal government, and the reasons for the decision. We The People of the United States are the grantors. In other words, the States, which were the embodiment of the people, were creating the **federal government**, and granting authorities to it so that it may function in a manner necessary to protect, promote, and preserve the union of States. The concept became known as **federalism**.

The Preamble is designed much like a permission form the doctor's office may present to you to sign, giving the doctor the authority to perform necessary procedures on your body in order to make you well. The form begins with your name (I, patient's name), and then limits the doctor to only the procedures necessary to make you well. The doctor, if he or she believes additional procedures may be necessary, must ask for your permission before performing the additional procedures that are not granted by your original agreement with them.

Like the form in the doctor's office, the Preamble begins with who is granting the authorities. "We the People of the United States" are the grantors of the authorities given to the new federal government. The people, through their States, allow the federal government to exist, and to perform the procedures expressly **granted** in the **United States Constitution**.

If a homeowner hires a contractor to add a room to their house, a contract is created between the homeowner, and the company hired to do the work. The contract establishes the granted authorities to the construction company regarding the room addition, listing the materials and labor necessary and proper to carry out that task. If, later, after the work begins, the homeowner observes the workers tending to the garden, and mowing the lawn, the homeowner would be angry because lawn maintenance was not among the authorities granted to the contractor hired to provide the service of adding a room to the house. In the same way, through the Constitution, the federal government has been granted a list of authorities that are necessary and proper for it to carry out the tasks vested in it. The tasks directly relate to protecting and preserving the union, while also respecting and promoting **State Sovereignty**. The federal government's authorities encompass only the external issues necessary to protect the union, and the sovereignty of the States. Internal issues are not granted to the federal government. Local issues are reserved to the local governments, such as the States, counties, and cities.

The first three words of the Preamble, "We the People," often lead people to believe that we are a **democracy**. Taken in context, the first part of the Preamble is not only "We the People," but "We the People of the United States." In the context of **original intent**, "the people of these States that are united have come together to establish this contract for the following reasons."

The words "United States" appear often in the U.S. Constitution. When those words appear in the text of the Constitution, they mean one of two things. Either, "United States" is a reference to the new federal government, or United States means "these states that are united." In the case of the Preamble, both definitions are used. As we notice the first time united States appears in the Declaration of Independence, "united" is not capitalized. Failing to capitalize "united" in the Declaration of Independence was a reflection of the common opinion of the people of that era. America was not a nationalistic country dominated by a powerful government, but a union of States that are sovereign, autonomous, and individual - like the people. We the People are the individual parts of their States, and the States are individual parts of the union.

Early Americans saw the United States in the plural, rather than as a singular nationalistic entity. The people were citizens of their States first, but realized that the States must be united to survive. The individual States would only be safe if they all worked together as a united country. To ensure the union was protected they proposed forming a central government through a social contract called the United States Constitution. This contract to grant limited authorities to a federal government was designed to ensure that the federal government remained limited so as to not infringe on the individual rights of the sovereign States, and the people who resided in those States.

A limited government is the essence of liberty.

The reasons listed in the Preamble for forming a new government were "*In Order to form a more perfect Union, establish Justice, insure domestic Tranquility, provide for the common defense, promote the general Welfare, and secure the Blessings of Liberty to ourselves and our Posterity.*" In line with classical writing standards, these reasons were listed in order of importance.

The most important reason for the formation of the federal government, the main purpose for the creation of the U.S. Constitution, was "in Order to form a more perfect Union." A union already existed under the

Articles of Confederation. A **confederation**, however, is a weak form of government where nearly all of the power remains with the individual members. A confederation is an association of sovereign member states that, by treaty, or other agreement, have delegated some of their powers to a common institution in order to coordinate policies, without constituting a new state on top of the member states. The government under the Articles of Confederation was formed hastily during the Revolutionary War, and as revealed by **Shays' Rebellion**, proved to be too weak to protect the union not only from threats beyond our shores, but insurrection from within the country. The founders realized that they needed to form a more perfect union, one with more authorities, while still remaining fairly limited in its power and scope. The realization that the Articles of Confederation were too weak, and either needed to be fixed, or replaced, was first discussed in delegation during the **Annapolis Convention** in 1786. During that meeting, the attending State delegates decided to meet again in May of 1787 in a convention of all States, which became the Federal Convention of 1787.

Under the Articles of Confederation, the central government was as weak as a lamb. What America needed was a central government with the strength of a lion. The problem with lions, however, is that they can kill you if not restrained. So, the Founding Fathers had to figure out a way to create a lion strong enough to deal with the external issues, and conflict between the States, while restraining that lion in such a way that the people living under it were safe from its potential tyranny. The lion is the federal government, and the chains and restraints of a set standard that protects We the People from that lion is the United States Constitution.

In the Constitution, the authorities granted to the federal government are limited to protecting, preserving, or promoting the union. The federal government, through the **express powers** granted in the Constitution, was granted authorities including, but not limited to, maintaining an army and navy in order to protect the union, to collect taxes in order to pay for that military and the other necessary functions created for the purpose of preserving the union, to regulate commerce by acting as a mediator between the States so that the flow of commerce flows regularly and in good order so as to encourage a growing economy for the union, establish a uniform rule of naturalization for the purpose of ensuring the union grows through legal immigration, and to establish post offices so that the many parts of the union may remain in contact with each other. The federal government was created for the sake of the issues related to the union. The federal government was not created to manage local issues that have nothing to do with the union, and everything to do with the unique cultures and societal needs of the local communities.

The second reason listed in The Preamble for the creation of the federal government through the ratification of the U.S. Constitution were to "establish Justice." Note that the word "establish" is normally used in situations where whatever is being established never previously existed. The word "establish" being used in the Preamble, then, leads us to believe that there was no justice prior to the writing of the founding document. However, justice systems already existed in each of the States, through State court systems. Therefore, the U.S. Constitution was not written to establish justice in the States, but to establish justice at the federal level where a judicial system had not previously existed. The language used in the Constitution, in this case, provides us with a clue that the original intent of the Founding Fathers was for the Constitution to apply only to the federal government, unless it specifically states otherwise.

Though "establish Justice" is listed second in the list of reasons for creating the federal government, we must not confuse "importance" with "power." To establish justice was a very important reason for creating a federal government, but the federal court system, for fear of it becoming a powerful judicial oligarchy, was also greatly limited. During the debates of the Constitutional Convention in 1787, there was actually a consideration to not establish a federal court system. The delegates realized that tyranny easily flows through an activist judiciary. The rule of law could be easily compromised by a judicial branch not willing to abide by the original intent of the U.S. Constitution, or poisoned by political ideology. For this reason, the powers of the judicial branch are greatly limited by the Constitution. We will go into more detail regarding those limitations when we get to Article III, and the 11th Amendment.

The first two reasons for the writing of the U.S. Constitution, according to the Preamble, was to form a more perfect union through the formation of a federal government, and to establish justice by creating a federal judicial system. Those primary goals reveal to us that the Constitution was not written to grant powers to the States, but for the purpose of creating, yet limiting, a newly formed federal government, which was designed to serve the States by protecting them, and preserving the union they enjoyed. Before the States delegated some of their own powers to the federal government through the Constitution, all of those powers belonged to the States - a political condition known as **Original Authority**. The States, however, only granted "some" of their powers to the federal government, retaining most of the powers for themselves.

The U.S. Constitution, and all language within the document, is directed to the federal government, not to the States, unless specifically indicated otherwise. This is because the States essentially "hired" the federal government to protect and preserve the union. The contract that authorizes the federal government to exist and receive the authorities from the States is the U.S. Constitution. Therefore, it would not be reasonable to assume that the provisions of the Constitution are to be applied to the States as much as it would not be logical to believe that an agreement between you and your doctor tells you what you can and can't do regarding the procedures that are about to be performed on you. The agreement with the doctor is specifically designed to tell the doctor what procedures are allowed, just as the Constitution is specifically designed to tell the federal government what authorities it is allowed to have in order to protect, preserve, and promote the union. In that contract with the doctor there may be instructions that tell you what not to do so as to not undermine healing, such as submersing oneself in water before a wound is fully healed. The same is true in the Constitution. There is a section, Article I, Section 10, that tells the States what they are prohibited from doing. These prohibitions were necessary to ensure the States did not interfere with federal functions.

Since it is We The People of the United States who granted the federal government its powers, that means it is the people's responsibility, through the States, responsibility to ensure the federal government acts in a constitutional manner. The Constitution is nothing more than ink and paper if we don't fight for it.

The union, at the time of the writing of the Constitution, was fragile. The States, as colonies, or as individual states shortly after the American Revolution, did not always coexist in a mutually beneficial manner. The States enjoyed their own unique cultures, religions, and laws. The States clashed over territory, commerce, and a variety of other issues that often included disputed legal issues and definitions. The States were much like siblings, fighting over everything under the sun; but when it came down to brass tacks, they were united when it came to defending each other.

The bickering between the States created an atmosphere that placed the cohesion of the union at risk. Therefore, when it came to creating a more perfect union, it was understood by the framers that the federal government would have to "insure domestic Tranquility" and to "promote the general Welfare."

The federal government was expected to ensure there was tranquility between the States by acting as a mediator in disputes. Part of that task by the federal government was to also promote the general welfare of the republic. In other words, the federal government was tasked with making sure the squabbles were properly resolved, while also protecting the union, so that the welfare of the union would not be in jeopardy.

The term **general Welfare**, as it is presented in the Preamble, is capitalized in a curious manner. Welfare is capitalized, but the word "general" is not. Capitalization in the Constitution was often used for the purpose of emphasis. With that tendency as our guide, we recognize that "Welfare" was the key component when these two words were presented in the Preamble. The Founding Fathers were seeking "Welfare" with a capital "W." The founders tasked the federal government with the duty of ensuring there was Welfare in the nation in a general manner. Or, you could say that they wanted the atmosphere in general to be one of "Welfare," or "all's well," hence, the reason general is not capitalized, and Welfare is, in the Preamble.

Tucked between "insure domestic Tranquility" and "promote the general Welfare" is the phrase: "provide for the common defence." The placement of this phrase in The Preamble reveals that providing for the common defense was almost as important as ensuring peaceful cooperation between the States, and slightly more important than promoting the general Welfare of the republic (and a necessary part of ensuring the general Welfare).

The need to provide for the common defense, one may note, was not listed first in The Preamble as one of the reasons for the creation of the federal government. The Founding Fathers, though they recognized the importance of the federal government to field a military force, as realized from the failure of the government to put down insurrection during Shays' Rebellion under the Articles of Confederation, did not list the need to provide for the common defense at the beginning of the Preamble because a country that places too much importance on a military is doomed to become a police state. Defending this nation was not placed at the bottom of the list of reasons for the writing of the Constitution, either, because a nation that refuses to defend itself ultimately becomes a conquered entity that is subject to the authority of a foreign government. Despite the fear of a powerful military that could be used against the people and the States, providing for the common defense was still indeed one of the primary reasons for creating the federal government in the first place. That is why "provide for the common defence" is listed in the Preamble within the central depths of the body of the paragraph.

The final reason for the writing of the Constitution was to "secure the Blessings of Liberty to ourselves and our Posterity." The presence of the word "Blessings" reminds us that the Founding Father's grateful spirit recognized that the result of the American Revolution, and the inspiration for the new federal government, could have only come from the favors of **Divine Providence**. Liberty, remember, is one of the unalienable rights listed in the Declaration of Independence that has been given to us by The Creator. In fact, that is one of the foundational beliefs of the original intent behind the creation of the federal government. Our rights are granted to us by God, not by government, for if our rights are granted to us by government, government would then be able to take those rights away. This idea of God-granted rights is based on a concept called **Natural Law** penned by John Locke during the 1600s. In the Declaration of Independence, it is referred to as, "Laws of Nature and of Nature's God." Natural Law is the unchanging moral principles regarded as a basis for all human conduct, which is observable law we participate in as related to our natural existence.

The U.S. Constitution was not solely written only to protect our **natural rights**, liberty, and property. Protecting our rights, liberty, and property are among the chief reasons the Constitution was written in the manner that it was, and protecting those natural rights are predictable byproducts when the Constitution is being followed by the government, but those are not the only reasons for the perceived need to compose the founding document, or for the creation of the federal government.

As indicated in the Preamble, the primary reason for the Constitution was "in Order to form a more perfect Union." However, the very formation of that union, and devising a governmental system to protect, preserve and promote that union, was not exclusively for the sake of the union, either. The ultimately desire was to protect the sovereignty of each component of that union - The States. The framers understood that by creating a federal government, the potential for the governmental system to become a tyranny was unleashed. Therefore, in order to protect the rights, liberty and property of the people (more specifically to "secure the Blessings of Liberty to ourselves and our Posterity"), the federal government needed to be limited in its authorities by the rule of law. The law of the land in which the governmental system is limited to, in the case of the United States, is the U.S. Constitution, for the sake of protecting the individuality of the States, and We the People.

Chapter 2

Legislative Powers

Article I, Section 1: *All Legislative Powers herein granted shall be vested in a Congress of the United States, which shall consist of a Senate and House of Representatives.*

Article I establishes the Legislative Branch of the federal government. Article I, Section 1 of the U.S. Constitution establishes the two parts of Congress, and grants all legislative powers to the two Houses of the **Congress of the United States**. When studying the language used in Article I, Section 1, the original intent by the Founding Fathers becomes clear.

The first word in the first section of Article I is the word "all." The definition of *all* is "the whole of a particular thing."

The next words in Article I, Section 1 are **legislative powers**. Legislative powers are the ability to make law, modify law, repeal law, and anything else that has to do with affecting law.

The next word in the clause is "herein." The primary definition of *herein* is "here in this document."

After *herein* is the word **granted**. *Granted* is defined as "to give," "to allow," or more specifically "to legally transfer." If powers are granted, then there must be a "grantor," as well as a grantee. As we learned in our discussion regarding The Preamble, the "grantor" of the authorities enumerated in the Constitution is the States.

"Shall be" is definitive. The Constitution in its first clause reads, "All legislative powers herein granted shall be. . .," *shall be* meaning "it is," or "it will be."

"Vested" is much like "granted." Vested is a legal transfer of something, or in this case, an allowance to have legislative powers at the federal level granted to **Congress**.

The Congress of the United States is the legislative branch of the federal government, and this clause indicates that not only will the Congress be granted all legislative powers given to the federal government, but that the branch of government consists of two houses; a Senate and **House of Representatives**.

All legislative powers, according to this clause, are granted to the Congress by the States for the purpose of making law, modifying law, or repealing law. The powers are herein granted, which means that the laws must fall within the authorities granted by the text of the U.S. Constitution. In other words, laws made must remain consistent with the "powers herein granted."

Based on language used in the first clause of the United States Constitution, when members of the judiciary legislates from the bench, or the President issues an executive order to modify a law, such action is unconstitutional. After all, "all legislative powers" were granted to the Congress, not to the judicial branch, or the executive branch.

Since all legislative powers belong to the Congress, that means any regulations by federal departments that are not in line with laws made by the Congress that are in line with the authorities granted by the Constitution are unconstitutional as well. All legislative powers belong to the Congress, therefore any "legislative actions" by regulatory agencies, which are a part of the executive branch, are not in line with the original intent of the Constitution.

Powers the federal government has were "granted" by the States. "We The People of the United States" granted those powers to the federal government through the Constitution. Therefore, if the federal government acts in a manner that is not consistent with the contract between the States and the U.S. Government, the States have the option to ignore those unconstitutional actions by the federal government. This action of ignoring unconstitutional law is the States' way of being the final arbiters of the Constitution. The term for this kind of action by a State is **nullification**. Thomas Jefferson, in his draft of the Kentucky Resolutions, explained that any unconstitutional law is null and void, and as an illegal law, the States have the right to nullify it.

The concept that only Congress has legislative powers, only the executive branch has executive powers, and the judicial branch only has judicial powers, as described in the first sentence of each of the first three articles of the Constitution, is called **Separation of Powers**. The purpose of this philosophy is to disallow different branches from abusing the powers not granted to that branch, as well as to protect against **collusion**.

The Separation of Powers also exists between the States, and the federal government. Most authorities granted to the federal government are powers the States did not reserve to themselves. Most authorities retained by the States are not authorized to be administered to by the federal government. There are a few authorities that are **concurrent**, meaning that both the federal government, and the States, have some authority over the issue. One issue that is concurrent is immigration, which will be addressed later in this book. Sole authority over a particular power is called **Exclusive Powers**.

Chapter 3

House of Representatives

Article I, Section 2 establishes, and defines, the **House of Representatives**. The members of the House of Representatives are divided among the States proportionally. As it is today, the House of Representatives was the voice of the people in the federal government. Each Representative is chosen to serve for two years, which means every two years every Representative is up for re-election, if they choose to run.

The eligibility of a Representative as explained by Article I, Section 2 requires that the candidate must be at least twenty-five years of age, and been a citizen of the United States for at least seven years. The age is lower than for Senators. Representatives were not expected to be as politically savvy as the Senators, and tended to have less experience. The age requirement simply reflected that. Political knowledge and experience tends to come with age.

Divided allegiance was a serious concern to the Founding Fathers. The requirement that Representatives have been citizens of the United States for at least seven years reflects that concern. Seven years, for a Representative of the people, was assumed to have been long enough for the Representative to have thrown off any allegiances to other nations.

The third clause of Article I, Section 2, includes the **3/5s clause**, which was changed by the 14th Amendment following the American Civil War.

The Southern States used slaves for their agricultural economies. The southern states were needed to ratify the new constitution. As a condition for ratifying the Constitution, the southern states demanded that the slaves be counted as one whole person each. The idea was that if the slaves were counted as whole persons, the apportionment would tip the scales in their favor through increased representation in the new United States House of Representatives. White populations in the southern states were lower in number when compared to the northern

41

states, due to the rural nature of the Slave States to the south.

The Northern States, under the heavy influence of merchants, political elitists, and a group of abolitionists, wanted the slaves counted as "zero" in order to reduce the number of representatives the southern states would receive, which would give the majority to the northern states, thus giving the north more legislative power. With this additional voting power in the House of Representatives, the northern states sought to have greater influence on the federal government through legislation. The plan was to use their legislative power to tyrannically force the southern states into submission, and to eventually abandon slavery.

In the interest of compromise, to convince the southern states to ratify the constitution, while giving the northern states the satisfaction that the southern states did not get exactly what they wanted, the decision was made that slaves would be counted as 3/5 of a whole person for the sake of apportionment. In other words, it was not a declaration that they believed blacks to be less than a person, but simply to affect the census in such a way that too much power through apportionment would not be given to either The North or The South, while also ensuring that the Constitution got ratified.

G.R. Mobley, author of *We the People, Whose Constitution Is It Anyway?*, believes the Founding Fathers missed a great opportunity to abolish slavery. He supports the idea that the 3/5s Clause was an error in judgment by the Founders, and that the authors of the Constitution should have only allowed those States that rejected slavery to be members of the union under the Constitution. By failing to ratify the Constitution the southern slave states would then have been on their own as a separate union. Pressure from the Spanish in Florida, and the threat of invasion by Spanish forces, would have then encouraged the slave states to abolish slavery, so that they may rejoin the union, and enjoy the strength of the union of all thirteen States.

Historically, it is impossible to know if that is exactly how it would have played out. Regardless of the opportunity, the Founders largely believed they had to compromise to ensure every State remained a member of the union, and ensure that they would receive the required nine ratifications of States in order to put the new federal government into motion.

Article I, Section 2, Clause 3, in addition to containing the 3/5s Clause, also establishes the **census**. The census is a required a head count to be taken once every ten years in order to determine the enumeration for establishing the number of Representatives each State shall receive. The clause also indicates that the number of Representatives shall not exceed one for every thirty thousand. This means there cannot be more than one Representative for a district of thirty thousand. However, it does not indicate there must be one Representative per thirty thousand. If that was the case, we would have thousands of Representatives.

Article I, Section 2, Clause 4 states that whenever vacancies happen in the House of Representatives, it is the duty of the Executive Authority to issue Writs of Election to fill such vacancies. What this means is that the Governors of the States have the duty to ensure there is a special election to fill any vacancies that may happen in the House of Representatives.

The House of Representatives chooses for itself its own Speaker of the House, and other officers.

According to Article I, Section 2, Clause 5, the House of Representatives has the sole power of **impeachment**. To impeach is to charge with misconduct. The formal process of impeachment may lead to removal of an official accused of unlawful activity or other offenses deemed to be impeachable offenses. Impeachment is not defined as removal from office, though removal from office is often the result of impeachment proceedings. In history, two presidents have been impeached, but neither were removed from office. The presidents who faced impeachment were Andrew Johnson (serving as President of the United States from 1865 to 1869), and William Jefferson Clinton (1993-2001). President Richard Nixon resigned in 1974 before impeachment proceedings began.

Chapter 4

The United States Senate

Article I, Section 3 established, and defines, the **United States Senate**. The representation of the States in the U.S. Senate is equal, two per State. The Senators serve for six years, which means every two years an election is held for one-third of the Senate seats. The required minimum age of a Senator is thirty years, five years older than that of a Representative. The increased age requirement for Senators reveals the importance of longer life and political experience, as considered by the Founding Fathers. Allegiance to the United States also remained important to the framers in the U.S. Senate, requiring that Senators need to be nine years a citizen of the United States, rather than the seven years as required of Representatives.

Article I, Section 3 originally required that Senators were chosen by the legislatures of the States, rather than voted into office directly by the voters. The appointment of Senators by their State legislatures changed to the vote of the people in 1913 with the ratification of the 17th Amendment. By the State legislatures appointing the Senators, it made the Senate the voice of the States, while the House of Representatives was the voice of the people. By the Houses of Congress being different, it created a natural check and balance, which did not allow the representation of the people to accomplish anything without approval of the voice of the States, and vice versa.

Article I, Section 3, Clause 4 establishes the Vice President as the President of the Senate. The Vice President, though a member of the executive branch, is also connected to the legislative branch. The Vice President may preside over the sessions of the U.S. Senate, and even participate in the debates, but in the end, the Vice President has no vote in the U.S. Senate, except as the tie-breaking vote.

During the early days of our nation the Vice President attended a large number of sessions of the Senate. He served as the voice of the executive branch in the Senate, ensuring the States' representation in

Congress had the opportunity to be exposed to the executive branch's opinions regarding the issues that concerned the States, and the union as a whole.

As with the House of Representatives, the Senate chooses its own officers. One of those officers is the **President pro tempore**, which is the President of the Senate when the Vice President is not present.

The House of Representatives has the sole power of impeachment. Article I, Section 3, Clause 6 gives the U.S. Senate the authority to try all impeachments. No conviction can be reached unless two-thirds of the U.S. Senate membership is present. Impeachment cannot extend further than the removal of the impeached from office, and the disqualification to hold any office in the future. However, a legal case can still be brought against the convicted from other sources, according to the law. Since the U.S. Senators were originally appointed by the legislatures of the individual States, this means that impeachment charges could be brought by the people (House of Representatives), but it took the States (Senate) to hear the case, and make the final determination after all evidence was provided. During impeachment hearings, the Chief Justice presides over the hearing, as provided by Article I, Section 3.

The 17th Amendment changed the dynamics of our governmental system. Note that many functions by the executive branch are subject to the **advise and consent** of the Senate. The Senate ratifies treaties, holds hearings for any appointments the executive branch nominates, and the Senate holds the sole power for holding hearings on impeachments. This is because actions by the federal government are subject to approval by the States. The States granted the federal government its powers in the first place.

The House of Representatives, as the voice of the people, and the Senate, as the voice of the States, and the natural check and balance that is the result of that relationship between those two Houses of Congress, also enables both Houses together to be a valuable check against the executive branch. One of the emanations of that correlation is the ability of Congress to override a veto with a 2/3 vote. The authority to override vetoes was established to enable the People, and the States, when they are in full agreement regarding a proposed bill, to be able to ensure a law is put into place, and to constrain the executive together through the power of combined vote.

Chapter 5

Elections and Assembly of Congress

Article I, Section 4 begins, *"The Times, Places and Manner of holding Elections for Senators and Representatives, shall be prescribed in each State by the Legislature thereof."* This clause establishes that each State may have its own methods for electing members of the Congress. The same applies, as determined in Article II, to presidential elections. If there is a discrepancy, or a question regarding the acceptance of ballots, it is not the job of the courts to make final determination. Article I, Section 4 gives that authority to the State legislatures.

The same clause adds, after giving the State legislatures authority over federal elections, that *"Congress may at any time by Law make or alter such Regulations, except as to the Places of chusing Senators."*

Congress, as discussed earlier, is **bicameral**. The two Houses of Congress are the House of Representatives, and the United States Senate. The House of Representatives, at the time of the writing of the Constitution, was designed to be as it is now, the voice of the people. Representatives have always been elected by a **direct vote**. The United States Senate was the voice of the States, appointed by the State legislatures. The appointment of the Senators by representatives of the people is an example of an **indirect vote**.

As the representation of the people, and the States, Congress was not seen as the greatest potential danger in the federal government. Congress was the voice of the people and the States in the federal government; the eyes of the parents to ensure the **central government** did not grow beyond the authorities granted to it. With Congress representing the oversight by the people, and the States, the oversight powers given to the federal legislature often led to other authorities that allowed Congress to act as a **check and balance** against potentially dangerous government activity. Giving Congress oversight authorities was a way to ensure that Congress participated in the concept of a government "by the consent of the governed."

Though elections were established with the State legislatures prescribing the times, places and manner of holding elections, as a check and balance against that authority, Congress may pass laws to *"make or alter such regulations."*

At the end of the clause giving Congress the authority to act as an oversight regarding the manner in which elections are held, a qualifier is present, expressing, *"except as to the Places of chusing Senators."*

A majority of delegates at the Federal Convention in 1787, by the conclusion of the assembly, were strong supporters of the sovereignty of the States, and the parental nature of the States in relation to the newly formed federal government, and the duty of the States as the final arbiters of the United States Constitution to ensure the new government functioned within the limitations granted to it. A part of that function by the States included the very important fact that the States had a voice in Congress with appointed U.S. Senators. The framers did not want that authority to be tinkered with, so they remind future generations at the end of this clause that though Congress has lawmaking authorities, and oversight authorities, manipulating the dynamics of government where the people, *and* the States, have a voice in the United States Congress is something not to be fiddled with. A similar advisement also appears at the end of Article V., "and that no State, without its Consent, shall be deprived of its equal Suffrage in the Senate."

Oversight powers by the States were seen by the framers as being a right of the States, and as with natural rights of the people, a right is not something that should be able to be taken, but if the holder of the right wishes to give it away, no law can prevent such a foolish action.

The second paragraph of Article I, Section 4 reads, *"The Congress shall assemble at least once in every Year."* The first thought regarding this clause by the typical reader may be, "Of course. How can they get anything done if Congress isn't assembling?"

Another question may be, "Why did the framers feel it to be necessary to insert this clause into the Constitution?"

During the convention in 1787, there were some who felt this clause was "overburdensome." Government was not supposed to dominate their everyday lives. The members of Congress were not professional politicians, nor did they care to be. They had businesses to run, and lives to live. Surely, the attitude of many of the Founding Fathers was, there is not enough business to compel Congress to meet every single year!

Those who supported the concept of an annual meeting reminded the others that Congress was the check the people and the States had available to them in the federal government. It was the duty of Congress to serve as a check against the President, and the federal judiciary. To be an effective check, Congress must meet at least once per year. The clause, it was argued, was for the benefit of the people.

In present day politics, the opposite seems to be the norm. Government is viewed as being broken if they do not act on an endless and constant flow of issues, committees, and crises. Politicians view their position as their job, rather than a service they are providing.

Originally, the required meeting day was the first Monday in December. That was later changed to noon on the third day of January by the 20th Amendment.

Chapter 6

Congressional Procedure

Article I, Section 5 requires Congress to have a minimum number of members present in order to do business. That majority constitutes a **quorum**, and if the Congress deems it necessary, the present members may set fines for members who do not show up. The Houses of Congress may remain in session, during which no formal business is conducted because the House does not have a quorum, so as to prevent executive actions that may be carried out during recess. This kind of session is called a **pro forma session**.

In Article II, Section 2, the President is given the authority to make **recess appointments**, when Congress is not in session. Normally, the United States Senate has **advise and consent** authority over appointments, which means that appointments of personnel to fill vacancies are possible for the President to grant, but such appointments requires the approval of the United States Senate (voice of the States). If the Senate is not in session, and an appointment is necessary, the President may make appointments, but the terms of those appointments only last to the end of the Senate's next session. If the Senate is in a pro-forma session, the President may not make any appointments. With Congress only in session when there is work to be done, and the Founders believing that would likely only be once a year, the ability of the President to make appointments when Congress is not in session was a valuable, and necessary, tool. In today's political environment, it seems like Congress is always in session, so recess appointments are not as common.

In early January of 2012, President Barack Obama used a recess appointment to name Richard Cordray the new Director of the Consumer Financial Protection Bureau (CFPB). The CFPB is a powerful bureaucracy created by the 2010 Dodd-Frank financial overhaul legislation. However, even though most of the members of Congress were on vacation, the United States Senate was still in session. President Obama's definition of recess, it turned out, was broader than the

Constitution's definition. In reality, the U.S. Senate was in pro-forma session. John Berlau, Director of CEI's Center for Investors and Entrepreneurs, called the nomination of former Ohio Attorney General Richard Cordray "very troubling," criticizing both Obama's controversial use of a recess appointment, and the selection of Cordray itself. Berlau later asked, "What's next, appointing nominees when the Senate takes a bathroom break?"

Article I, Section 5 also allows each House of Congress to determine its own rules, keep a journal to record proceedings and votes, and that neither house may **adjourn** without the permission of the other. Section 5 also establishes that if a member of a house does not follow the established rules, the house may punish its members for disorderly behavior, and by a two thirds vote may actually expel a member from Congress.

The establishment of rules, holding a hearing in regards to the breaking of those rules, and punishing a member for his behavior, as set forth by Article I, Section 5, was used when Charles Rangel broke the rules of the House of Representatives. He faced a panel for his actions, and was punished by **censure** in December of 2010. He later sued, spending about a third of his 2014 campaign cash on legal bills in a failed bid to overturn his fall from congressional grace. On December 11, 2013, a federal judge in Washington dismissed the lawsuit, filed by Rangel in the previous April, to get the censure overturned.

The mandate to keep a journal to record proceedings and votes was included in this section because the Founders wanted government to be transparent, accessible, and accountable to the people. Deals behind closed doors were not supposed to be a part of our political system.

Chapter 7

Congressional Compensation, Privileges, Restrictions

When President George Washington took office, he refused to accept the constitutionally allowed compensation for holding the office. He viewed his office as being a privilege, and an opportunity to once again serve the country he loved. During the Constitutional Convention, Benjamin Franklin considered proposing that elected government officials not be paid for their service. By the end of the debate, it was decided that government representatives should receive fixed stipends by which they may be compensated for the devotion of their time to public service. It was also determined, however, that the compensation should not be so high that it would become the motive for seeking office.

Article I, Section 6 of the Constitution addresses compensation, and the rules regarding such. Section 6 also establishes that members of Congress may not be detained while traveling to and from Congress, and that they cannot hold any other office in government while in Congress.

Protection from arrest while traveling to and from Congress was not only a privilege based on those enjoyed by their counterparts in the British Parliament, but also a protection from political enemies who may wish to keep certain members of Congress from voting.

This section also indicates that no member of Congress shall be appointed to a later office if while in Congress the office was created, or a raise in pay was enacted for that office.

To explain this clause, let's visit a recent violation of it during the Obama administration.

After Barack Obama won the 2008 Presidential Election, he announced that Hillary Clinton would be his new Secretary of State. The position of Secretary of State received a pay raise while Hillary Clinton was a member of the United States Senate. Since Article I, Section 6 states that *"No Senator or Representative shall, during the Time for which he was elected, be appointed to any civil Office under the Authority of the United States, which shall be been created, or the Emoluments whereof shall have been encreased during such time."* Since Clinton was a Senator at the time the position of Secretary of State was given a raise, technically she was not eligible for the position to which she was appointed. To resolve this problem, and still allow Mrs. Clinton to accept the position, the Democrats applied the **Saxbe Fix**, meaning they undid the raise, and Hillary Clinton received the compensation that was in place before the vote she participated in while in the Senate. The Saxbe Fix, or a Salary rollback, is an unconstitutional action. The clause in the Constitution is clear: *"No Senator or Representative shall, during the Time for which he was elected, be appointed to any civil Office under the Authority of the United States, which shall have been created, or the Emoluments whereof shall have been encreased during such time."*

The Saxbe Fix, or the rollback of the salary, does not change the fact that the emoluments increased during the time Hillary Clinton was in the U.S. Senate.

As a tool, the Saxbe fix was nothing new. The salary rollback in the case of a violation of Article I, Section 6, a mechanism by which the President of the United States can avoid restrictions by the United States Constitution which prohibits the President from appointing a current or former member of Congress to a position that was created, or to an office position for which the pay and/or benefits were increased, during the term for which that member was elected until the term has expired, was first used in 1909. The "Saxbe" name was applied to the political maneuver later in history. The Saxbe Fix is named for William Saxbe, a Senator appointed Attorney General by President Richard Nixon in 1973.

Chapter 8

Making Law

As covered when we studied Article I, Section 1, all legislative powers belong to the Legislative Branch. According to Article I, Section 7, Clause 2, all bills must be approved by both the House of Representatives and the U.S. Senate before they can be presented to the President for signature. Article I, Section 7, Clause 1 indicates that all bills for raising revenue shall originate in the House of Representatives.

The structure for making law was established by the Founding Fathers in the way that it was in order to ensure all parts of the system had a voice in the approval, or disapproval, of the law. The people vote their approval, or disapproval, of a bill through their representatives in the House of Representatives. The States did the same through their voice in the United States Senate. The federal government's voice through the executive branch serves as the final approval. If the executive does not approve of the proposed law, a decision during the early decades of this country that was primarily based on the President's opinion regarding the constitutionality of the bill, and was not normally based on whether or not he ideologically agreed with the bill, he can *veto* it. However, the whole process does not stop there. The President does not always represent the final say on a bill. If he rejects the bill, and if Congress feels strongly enough about the bill, and has enough votes, they can override a presidential veto with two-thirds vote in each House, which in turn allows the legislature to make the bill a law without the signature, and therefore approval, of the President.

The President may choose to use the **pocket veto**, where he can hold the measure passed by Congress for ten days to review it. If the president has not signed the bill after 10 days, it becomes law without his signature. If Congress adjourns during the 10-day period, the bill does not become law.

In 1913, the 17th Amendment changed the process in which United States Senators are chosen. Originally, the State Legislatures appointed the U.S. Senators, making the U.S. Senate a voice of the States in a similar manner as the House of Representatives. The Senators, prior to the 17th Amendment, voted in line with the interests of their State legislatures, and more specifically with the intent of protecting their State's sovereignty, in mind. With the House of Representatives acting as the voice of the people, and the Senate acting as the voice of the States, the dynamics of making law was quite different from what it is today.

The process of making a law as originally intended ensured that the people, the States, and the federal government, all each had the opportunity to approve or disapprove the piece of legislation. If either the people, or the States, did not like the bill, its journey to become a law stopped. If the federal government, via the President, felt the bill was unconstitutional, or that its passage was not in the best interest of the nation, he could veto the bill. The veto by the President in turn could be overturned with a two thirds vote from each house of Congress, a function prior to 1913 that required the people, and the States to work together to accomplish. The reason for this system was for the purpose of checks and balances, and to keep the States involved in monitoring the federal government through advise and consent authorities. This gave the people through the House of Representatives, and the States through the U.S. Senate, the ability to check each other, and the ability of them together to check the executive and judicial branches of the federal government. The people and the States together, if in agreement, served as a united check against the federal government, or more specifically in the case of making law, the executive branch.

The States hold **original authority** regarding all authorities. Some of those authorities were given to the federal government so that it may function as originally intended. In today's political environment, in regards to the process of making law, the members of the United States House of Representatives and U.S. Senate are both voted into office by **direct election** of the people, and have both become the voice of the people.

Under British rule, during the time of the Revolutionary War, original authority had shifted back to the monarchy, as per Royal Prerogative; but in the United States, original authority belonged to the people through their States.

Article I, Section 7, Clause 1 establishes that all bills for raising revenue originate in the House of Representatives. The Constitution grants to the voice of the people the power to fund, or defund, any function of government affected by legislative action. The power of the purse-strings gives the House of Representatives the ultimate check against the other parts of government, and ultimately gives the House of Representatives a significant amount of power. Should the House of Representatives, for example, disapprove of a military action being carried out by the Commander in Chief, the action can be stopped by the House of Representatives simply defunding the military operation by not including funding for that action in a budget proposal. Refusal to accept the proposal by the Senate, or the Executive, places at risk the funding for other parts of government as well. The Senate, though unable to originate bills raising revenue, may propose amendments to be added to such a bill that originated in the House of Representatives, but no bill raising revenue may originate in the Senate. Upon approval by the Senate, if the Senate made changes, the bill is still required to go back to the House of Representatives for approval. The approval by both houses of Congress must be for an identical bill.

If the President approves the bill, and signs it after it has been approved with a majority vote in each of the two houses of Congress, the bill becomes law. If the President does not approve of the bill, he may refuse to sign it, or veto the bill, and return it with a written explanation of his disapproval.

All votes in the two houses of Congress shall be determined by yeas and nays, which will be entered into the respective house's journal. The journal entry will include the names and votes of the members voting for, or against, the bill. This requirement was included to ensure the voters could monitor the voting records of their representatives, and that the State legislatures could monitor the voting records of their Senators.

If the President refuses to sign the bill presented to him, but does not return the bill with his written objection within ten days (excluding Sundays) the bill becomes law as if the President signed it. The exception to this clause is if Congress does anything to prevent the bill's return, such as through their adjournment. In that case, the bill remains to be only a bill, and only becomes law should any of the afore mentioned processes be met.

Chapter 9

Enumerated Powers

The powers granted to the federal government in relation to legislative powers are listed in Article I, Section 8. These authorities are also known as **Express Powers**.

Implied Powers is a concept invented by Alexander Hamilton while he served as Treasury Secretary in 1791. He wrote in a report titled, "Opinion on the Constitutionality of the Bank of the United States" that "there are implied, as well as express powers, in the Constitution, and that the former are as effectually delegated as the latter. Implied powers are to be considered as delegated to the federal government equally with the express ones."

Hamilton, in his report, went on to argue that a nationalized bank was one of these implied powers. Hamilton's argument stated that his power to create a nationalized bank was implied as "necessary and proper" for the federal government to carry out its enumerated powers, such as borrowing money, regulating currency, and providing for the general welfare of the country.

Thomas Jefferson disagreed, arguing that the express powers delegated to the federal government by Article I, Section 8 of the Constitution were expressly stated because they were the only powers granted to the federal government by the sovereign States when they ratified the Constitution. New authorities could only be granted by the amendment process, which includes the requirement of ratification by three-quarters of the States. George Washington still signed the "bank bill" into law, though he proclaimed it was "with hesitation," to establish the First Bank of the United States on February 25, 1791.

The Concept of Implied Powers remained in place, thanks to Hamilton's persistence, and the statists of history have used Implied Powers to rewrite the Constitution through regulatory actions, and liberal **judicial activism** ever since.

From the emergence of Implied Powers came the theory that the Constitution is a living document that can be modified at will through interpretation and the use of Implied Law. Hamilton's concept of Implied Powers laid the groundwork for generations of lawyers and judges using the courts, rather than the amendment process, to alter the Constitution, and render the limiting principals powerless. The concept of Implied Powers is one of the concepts that have fed the false idea that the courts "interpret" the Constitution.

Alexander Hamilton also argued that there were **resulting powers** as well, which are powers that exist as a result of any action the government takes. These "resulting powers" are considered to be *de facto* constitutional by virtue of the fact that the action by the federal government occurred in the first place.

With the use of unconstitutional concepts like Implied Powers and resulting powers, Hamilton believed the central government had unlimited powers to act as any member of the federal government deemed necessary.

General Welfare Clause

"If Congress can do whatever in their discretion can be done by money, and will promote the General Welfare, the Government is no longer a limited one, possessing enumerated powers, but an indefinite one, subject to particular exceptions." --James Madison

The General Welfare Clause is one of the most misunderstood clauses in the U.S. Constitution - and it was not even supposed to be a clause in the legal sense.

Article I, Section 8, Clause 1 includes "General Welfare" not as an authority to the federal government, but as a description of the Republic should the laws of the land be made in accordance with the authorities granted by the Constitution.

If we go back to the Preamble, we read that one of the reasons the Founding Fathers created this new government with the writing of the Constitution was to "insure domestic Tranquility." One must ask, "Why was there a need for domestic tranquility?"

The States were much like siblings. The States bickered over just about everything. They argued over commerce, borders, legal jurisdictions, currency, weights and measures, communication, religion, and a number of other issues. Yet, despite their disagreements, when it came to the American Revolution, they united against a common enemy. After the war, the quarrels resumed. The fighting between the States became such a problem that many worried it would tear apart the union. One of the many reasons for the need of a new government, as provided by the U.S. Constitution, was so that the central government would have enough authority to act as a mediator between the States.

Acting as a referee to mediate matters that caused disputes between the States would help the federal government provide for the General Welfare of the republic.

Another reason for the writing of the new constitution was to give the federal government enough power to defend the union from invasion and domestic insurrection. Under the Articles of Confederation, the central government was unable to provide for the common defense because the government had neither the authority nor the financial means to field a military. With the ability to field a fighting force, the federal government would be able to protect the States from foreign invasion, while also keeping internal conflict at bay as well.

By providing for the common defense, the federal government would also be ensuring the General Welfare of the Republic.

In other words, if the federal government was doing what it was supposed to do, as a mediator between the States, and as a protector of the States by providing for the common defense, the States would enjoy a general welfare of the Republic. The Founding Fathers wanted to make sure that squabbles, internal conflict, or foreign intrusion did not place the welfare of the union in jeopardy.

General Welfare is a description of the Republic should the federal government follow its constitutional authorities, and perform its function as originally intended. General Welfare was not intended to be an authority for unconstitutional actions.

The General Welfare of the Republic was the goal, which would be achieved if the federal government abided by the limiting principles of the U.S. Constitution.

Taxes and Debt

Article I, Section 8 grants Congress the power to lay and collect Taxes, **Duties**, **Imposts**, and **Excises**.

The authority to tax was for the express purpose of protecting, preserving, and promoting the union. The federal government could tax the States only if the taxes were uniform throughout the United States. The federal government could not originally tax the individual citizens directly.

The stated purposes for giving the Congress the power to tax are to "provide for the common Defence and general Welfare of the United States."

The need for the central government to be able to defend the union militarily was one of the initial reasons some of the Founding Fathers planned the Constitutional Convention at the Annapolis Convention in 1786. **Shays' Rebellion** proved to the men of that era that the United States government under the Articles of Confederation was too weak to defend the union against not only foreign enemies, but internal insurrections.

Some of the members of the Constitutional Convention were concerned that a military may be used by the federal government against the States, but the reality of the world they lived in was that the union would not survive without the ability to defend itself. It was argued that the independent **militias** needed to be joined under a single federal army, and for the protection of the trade routes a United States Navy also needed to be established. In order to afford to have a military, however, the federal government would need to be authorized to have the power to tax.

The second clause of Article I, Section 8 grants the authority to the U.S. Congress to borrow money on the credit of the United States. If the federal government ever found the necessity to enter into military operations on the battlefield, to help pay for the expensive endeavor of warfare, the federal government would need to be able to borrow money for the war effort. Therefore, the States through the new Constitution granted to the federal government the authority to create a national debt. The founders did not recognize any reason other than for war that the

United States would need to borrow money. Alexander Hamilton, however, suggested that a continuous national debt was necessary to hold together the union, for if the States all felt they were responsible for the repayment of the deficit, they would be less likely to break away from the union.

Commerce Clause

Article I, Section 8, Clause 3 grants to the Congress the authority *to regulate commerce with foreign nations, and among the several states, and with the Indian tribes.*

The States were often at odds regarding a number of issues. Interstate commerce was among their disagreements. The States implemented **Protectionist Tariffs**, designed to protect domestic industries against competition from other States. As sovereign entities, the States continually tried to gain the upper hand on each other in regard to commerce across State lines. Recognizing that the squabbles between the States were actually hindering the movement of commerce across State lines, the federal government in this clause was given the authority to do what was necessary to enable the flow of commerce to be more regular.

When you turn on a faucet full blast you are regulating the flow, just as you are regulating the flow when you restrict it by turning the faucet off. Likewise, the federal government was expected to act as a mechanism that ensured the flow of commerce between the States was more regular.

The 1828 Webster Dictionary defines **regulated** in its second definition: "To put in good order." Some historians state that the word "regulate" in the 18th Century meant "To make regular." The word "restrict" was not used in the 1828 definition until the third and final definition of the word, or as the "least used" definition. In today's dictionary "restrict" appears in the first definition of regulate.

In modern politics, the Commerce Clause has been interpreted to mean the opposite of its original intent. The Commerce Clause in today's political atmosphere is used as a means to restrict and heavily control commerce between the States. If one was to adopt the progressive definition of the Commerce Clause, one could then surmise that the Founders wrote this clause because commerce was flowing too easily, and needed to be controlled by the federal government. Such a notion is not only untrue, but is not consistent with the context of the times. The

Founders believed in limiting the powers of the Federal Government, so why would they allow the Federal Government the kind of unlimited powers over interstate commerce as suggested by today's progressives?

The federal government's role according to the Commerce Clause was to act as a referee, or mediator, whenever the flow of commerce was hindered by disagreements or conflicts between the States, while with foreign nations and the Indian Tribes the federal government was expected to take a more active role.

Naturalization

Article I, Section 8, Clause 4 gives the Congress the authority *to establish an uniform rule of Naturalization.* This is the clause that is often used as evidence that the federal government has authorities over immigration issues. Though Congress does maintain certain powers regarding the immigration issue, this clause does not grant those authorities. The "Naturalization Clause" establishes all naturalization rules must be identical in all States, and the Congress of the United States has the authority to establish those rules.

Based on the Naturalization Clause, one State cannot decide to have rules for the naturalization of an immigrant that are different than what the federal government has established. This is an example of an **exclusive jurisdiction**. Only the federal government has the authority to establish naturalization rules.

Naturalization is not immigration. Naturalization is the process through which someone becomes a citizen after they have immigrated to the United States. Immigration is a **concurrent issue**, with authorities held by both federal government and the States, as will be discussed when we discuss Article I, Section 9.

Bankruptcies

In Article I, Section 8, Clause 4 the federal government is also given the authority *to establish uniform rules on the subject of bankruptcies throughout the United States.*

Prior to the ratification of the U.S. Constitution, each State had its own rules on **bankruptcy**. Citizens would simply cross State lines to start over financially. The clause bringing bankruptcy under federal jurisdiction was for the purpose to stop the abuses, and to establish uniform rules nationwide, thus establishing the development of a commercial republic. Federal laws regarding bankruptcy were also seen as an opportunity to temper pro-debtor State legislation, which was common under the Articles of Confederation.

States tended to establish laws that protected State interests, redistributing money from out-of-State creditors to their own rural agricultural interests. Under a system where the States independently maintained their own bankruptcy laws, it was often unclear if debtors could collect a debt from a debtor in another State. These laws created a conflict in regards to the reliability of contracts, and created a number of obstructions for creditors trying to collect their judgments after a court ruling when debtors fled to other States to avoid paying their debt.

Consistent bankruptcy laws were also necessary to ensure a healthy flow of interstate commerce. James Madison wrote in Federalist Number 42, *"The power of establishing uniform laws of bankruptcy is so intimately connected with the regulation of commerce, and will prevent so many frauds where the parties or their property may lie or be removed into different States that the expediency of it [i.e., Congress's power to regulate bankruptcy] seems not likely to be drawn into question."*

Congressional authority to deal with bankruptcy and insolvency was viewed as a necessary authority in order to hold together the union in terms of economic unity, and to put in good order some of the aspects of debt that played a part in encouraging **Shays' Rebellion**.

Under British law, only merchants and traders could declare bankruptcy. In the English system a bankruptcy would then allow the merchants or traders to have their debts discharged upon the satisfaction of certain requirements. The average citizen, however, did not have the opportunity to claim bankruptcy, and instead was resolved to seek refuge under insolvency laws. Insolvency laws released a debtor from imprisonment, but did not discharge the debtor from his indebtedness.

As the delegates in the Constitutional Convention of 1787 toiled over whether or not to grant to the federal government the power to regulate bankruptcies through legislation, it was suggested that the bankruptcy laws also be extend to non-merchants. The proponents of such an idea argued the traditional distinction between merchants and non-merchants, in regards to bankruptcy, had vanished during the mid-eighteenth century. As far as many of the delegates were concerned, the terms "bankruptcy" and "insolvency" were interchangeable, so the United States Congress should be granted the power to regulate (put in good order) all insolvent debtors.

Subsequent court decisions did not recognize the States as having **concurrent powers** regarding the issue of bankruptcy.

The clause authorizes the federal government to pass legislation to ensure the bankruptcy laws are uniform throughout the States, but congressional powers do not extend to the general regulation of debtor-creditor law, and is limited to the adjustment of relations between a debtor and its creditors and does not extend to assisting third parties that may be affected by the bankruptcy.

Non-bankruptcy law that governs debtor-creditor relations remains to be in the purview of the States. Therefore, treatment of debtors and creditors in each State may be different from State to State based on the State laws addressing the issue. Once the debtor declares bankruptcy, the issue falls under the federal authority to establish uniform laws on the subject of bankruptcy, and based on that authority, it is forbidden for certain bankruptcy laws to affect only particular debtors.

Money, Weights, and Measures

Article I, Section 8, Clause 5 establishes the duty of coining money belongs to Congress. Note that the Constitution calls for coining money, rather than printing federal reserve notes (**bills of credit**). The coins produced by Congress were expected to be made of metals that reflected the worth of the coins. In other words, the gold in a coin, if taken to a goldsmith, should be worth the same as the value of the coin. Later, the banks realized they could loan on the gold in their vaults backing the currency, leaving less gold as a reserve. They did this by issuing receipts, or bills of credit. When this happened, if there was a bank run, where everyone brought their receipts in to cash it in for gold all at once, the bank would be left in a situation where they did not have enough gold to cover all of the notes.

Under the Articles of Confederation the United States government had no power to regulate the value of foreign coin, an omission, which would destroy any uniformity in the value of the current coin, since the respective States might, by different regulations, create a different value in each. As a result, the States were prohibited in Article I, Section 10 from coining their own money, thus taking away their ability to manipulate the value of currency as a means of affecting the economies of the other States.

The authority to coin money was granted specifically to Congress so that no outside interest could manipulate the value of American money. This included private banks. Nonetheless, we have seen three nationalized banks run by private bankers in the United States issuing the currency. The third is the currently existing Federal Reserve Bank.

Coining money was also specifically established because during the Revolutionary War the government under the Articles of Confederation, unable to tax in order to fund the war, and depending completely upon borrowed money, paid the militiamen with United States Government issued bills of credit. The paper money was backed by no value, therefore the **fiat money** was worthless, leaving the veterans incapable of paying their debt. Frustrated that their debt had continued to accumulate during the war, and their pay for their service during the Revolutionary War was worthless paper, the militiamen blamed the government for their inability to pay their debt, and began blocking courthouse steps to stop legal actions against them. The insurrection became known as **Shays' Rebellion**. Based on their knowledge of the events that led to Shays' Rebellion in 1786, the delegates at the Federal Convention of 1787 recognized the issuance of paper currency as being a threat to the nation's economy. Therefore, the delegates in the Federal Convention disallowed the issuance of paper money by calling for Congress to only have the authority to "coin money" in the Constitution.

Thomas Jefferson was against the concept of national banks issuing the currency. Alexander Hamilton created the "Bank of the United States" in 1791 for the purpose of acting as a depository of government funds, issuing paper currency backed by gold and silver, and creating a system of **mercantilism** in America. The bank's **charter** lapsed in 1811. The Second Bank of the United States was formed in 1817, and lasted until President Andrew Jackson vetoed the renewal of its charter in 1836. The bank existed for 5 more years as an ordinary bank before going bankrupt in 1841. In a letter to John Taylor in 1816, Thomas Jefferson wrote, *"I sincerely believe, with you, that banking establishments are more dangerous than standing armies; and that the principle of spending money to be paid by posterity, under the name of funding, is but swindling futurity on a large scale."*

Article I, Section 8, Clause 5 also establishes that Congress shall have the power to fix the Standard of Weights and Measures. Fixing a standard of weights and measures was important for the reason of uniformity, and the ease of commerce. This clause suggests that before the Constitutional Convention the States were able to independently fix their own weights and measures, which not only added confusion to commerce, but enabled the States to use unsavory trading tactics against each other.

Article 1, Section 8, Clause 6 establishes the U.S. Congress will provide for the punishment of counterfeiting the securities and current coin of the United States. This power would naturally flow, as an incident, from the antecedent powers to borrow money, and regulate the coinage. Indeed, without the ability to provide for the punishment of counterfeiting, the powers of coining money, or creating securities, would be without any adequate sanction. The word **securities**, in this clause, means: a contract that can be assigned a value so that it may be traded, like a "bond."

Post Offices and Roadways

In Article I, Section 8, Clause 7 the Congress is granted the *authority to establish post offices and post roads.*

As with the other clauses in Article I, Section 8, this clause is designed to promote the Union. In the case of establishing the postal service, the Constitution ensures that communication throughout the union remains intact. The clause gives the federal government the authority to establish post offices, but nowhere in the Constitution does the federal government have the authority to partially privatize the post office as we have seen in the modern era.

Article I, Section 8, Clause 7 gives the federal government the authority to "establish" post roads, but not create or maintain them. The Constitution does not give the federal government any other authority over roadways. In fact, this is the only reference to roadways to the federal government in the entire Constitution. This clause makes the federal highway and Interstate highway system, as well as the other workings of the federal transportation department, unconstitutional. It was up to the States to create and maintain their roadways. If the States desired to remain connected, and receive their mail, they would keep up their roads.

In 1817, Congress proposed a bill that would provide federal funding for boatways and roadways, claiming it was for the "general welfare" of the nation. President James Madison vetoed the bill, claiming it to be unconstitutional, because the federal government was not given the authority to fund transportation routes.

Our modern political system allows the federal government to regulate private companies that perform functions similar to the postal service, such as Federal Express, or UPS. The authority cited by those that support regulation against private parcel services is Alexander Hamilton's imaginary constitutional authority of "Implied Powers." Since there are no express powers granted to the federal government allowing for regulation against a private business conducting business similar to the functions performed by the postal service, the federal regulations against these private entities are unconstitutional.

Patents and Copyrights

Article I, Section 8, Clause 8 authorizes Congress *to promote the progress of science and useful arts, by securing for limited times to authors and inventors the exclusive right to their respective writings and discoveries.*

This clause is the basis for the creation of the U.S. Patent Office, and Copyright Office. Patent and copyright protections already existed in the British Empire, and for the protection of American inventions and writings, the Founding Fathers saw the need to establish such a power under the federal government as well, expecting that by being under federal authority, the rules would be uniform.

Federal Inferior Courts

Article I, Section 8, Clause 9 authorizes Congress *to constitute tribunals inferior to the Supreme Court.* Article III also begins with a reference to this authority: ". . . *and such inferior Courts as the Congress may from time to time ordain and establish.*" This means that the legislative branch is tasked with the duty of establishing the lower federal court system. However, by enabling Congress to establish new courts whenever necessary, this has given some administrations an opportunity to abuse this power in the hopes of stacking the courts, when a big government President is joined by a Congress of which both Houses share the President's **ideology** or political ambitions.

John Adams was the first example of this abuse, when he appointed many **midnight judges** in order to help retain Federalist power in the courts as Jefferson's Republicans gained the White House, and the majority in Congress. Some may argue that Adams' decision to expand the court was not as sinister as Thomas Jefferson made it out to be, for John Adams had been requesting an expansion of the judiciary for years.

President Franklin D. Roosevelt also sought to "pack" the courts with justices favorable to his social policies. His animosity toward the Supreme Court emerged when his New Deal of social and economic reform via government intrusion was struck down as unconstitutional by justices who had been largely appointed by rival Republicans.

The high court invalidated the Railroad Retirement Act of 1934, a law that had established pensions for railway workers, and the National Industrial Recovery Act of 1933. Roosevelt's anger against the justices for their rulings led him to hold contempt for the conservative-minded court of "Nine Old Men." In January 1936, the court ruled the Agricultural Adjustment Act of 1933 unconstitutional, as well.

In 1937, Roosevelt disclosed to his aides a bill he was going to propose that was designed to reorganize the federal judiciary. The measure called for all federal judges to retire by age 70. If they failed to do so, the president could appoint another judge to serve in tandem with each one older than 70. If the bill passed, it would enable Roosevelt to appoint six more Supreme Court justices immediately, increasing the size of the court to 15 members. The Democrat dominated Congress, he believed, would undoubtedly approve the appointment of judges friendly to Roosevelt and his New Deal agenda.

The proposal never got off the ground, as Roosevelt's explanation regarding why the proposal was necessary fell flat.

Both the federal government, and the States, have court systems. The shared power by both the federal government and the State governments to establish a judiciary is a concurrent power.

With the ability to establish the inferior courts also comes the authority to eliminate them. Congress, in addition to the authority to establish federal inferior courts, can also shut them down. During the 2012

Republican primaries, presidential candidate Newt Gingrich stated that Congress should use the federal marshal to bring unconstitutional judges to face members of Congress and answer for their actions. He was accurate in his assertion that Congress has the authority to perform such a task.

Trade Routes and Offenses Against The Law of Nations

Article I Section 8, Clause 10 authorizes Congress to define and punish piracies and felonies committed on the high seas, and offenses against the Law of Nations.

One of the factors in having this clause included in the Constitution was the problem the new nation was having with piracy in the Caribbean, caused by the sailing vessels attached to the Muslim States of the Barbary Coast. Though the United States was careful to create a system of justice that included due process for the citizens of the nation, the Constitution gave the federal government the power to punish offenses by foreign forces on the high seas without having to worry about **habeas corpus**, while still providing a separate courtroom setting for the offenders. In Federalist 42, James Madison carefully explains that this provision *"extends no further than to the establishment of courts for the trial of these offenses,"* such as military courts or tribunals, or international courts established for the purpose of addressing international war crimes.

This clause is the only place where the Law of Nations is mentioned. Some historians claim that the capitalization of the "Law of Nations" in this clause suggests that the founders were specifically referring to Vatell's volumes of which the founders often used for definitions and the clarification of concepts like **Natural Born Citizen**.

War, Army, and Navy

Article I, Section 8, Clause 11 gives Congress the power to *declare War, grant Letters of Marque and Reprisal, and make Rules concerning Captures on Land and Water.*

During the debates, according to Madison's *Notes on the Federal Convention*, the delegates debated over whether or not to give the legislative branch the power to make war. After intense debate, it was decided to grant the Commander in Chief the authority to wage war, and Congress the power to declare war. A declaration of war is a formal declaration that warns those not involved to stay out of the conflict. If those entities become involved, they become open targets. The President, as per the debates, may wage war without prior approval by Congress, or without a declaration of war being issued. In the Articles of Confederation, the powers of waging war, and declaring war, were listed separately, but in that document, both powers were granted to the Congress.

Though, under the Constitution, the President has the authority to wage war, his war powers are checked by Congress. The House of Representatives, in possession of the power of the purse strings, may refuse to fund any military conflict. This keeps the President from abusing his position as Commander in Chief by giving Congress a way to limit executive wartime authorities. If the President continues to act upon his war powers in a manner not approved by Congress, and does so despite the lack of funding for the military operations, Congress also has the authority to impeach the President in order to stop the Executive's objectionable actions.

A Letter of Marque and Reprisal was a government license authorizing a private vessel to attack and capture enemy vessels, and bring them before admiralty courts for condemnation and sale. Cruising for prizes with a Letter of Marque was considered an honorable calling combining **patriotism** and profit, in contrast to unlicensed piracy which was universally reviled. These mercenaries were also known as **privateers**.

Congress was also given the power to make rules regarding captures on land and water. This is the clause used when President George W. Bush, with the blessings of Congress, decided to hold prisoners captured during the war on terrorism at Guantanamo Bay, Cuba, and to use military tribunals as the vessel of their trials.

Article I, Section 8, Clauses 12 authorizes Congress:

To raise and support Armies, but no Appropriation of Money to that Use shall be for a longer Term than two Years;

Article I, Section 8, Clauses 13 authorizes Congress:

To provide and maintain a Navy;

Remember that one of the primary reasons for deciding to hold the Constitutional Convention in the first place was to defend the union with a uniformed military. Note that the fear of an army being used by a centralized government, and a potentially tyrannical government for that matter, as had been the case with the British Empire, influenced the writings of this document, and encouraged the Founders to limit the existence and funding of an army to two years at a time. A navy, however, was deemed as much more important, particularly because of the need to protect trade routes, and America's immediate waterways and inlets. Therefore, the authority to provide and maintain a navy was granted in perpetuity. The United States Marine Corps, from the beginning, has always fallen under the umbrella of the United States Navy.

Article I, Section 8, Clauses 14 authorizes Congress:

To make Rules for the Government and Regulation of the land and naval Forces;

The rules for the governance of the armed forces do not fall under the purview of the Constitution. It is up to Congress to provide the governing rules. Any claim that rules regarding the military are unconstitutional is a bad argument. According to Article I, Section 8, Clause 14, it is up to Congress to set the rules, regardless of the Constitution. Military training in order for the armed forces to be well disciplined may not benefit from the same social rules of the civilian world. Therefore, the basis of governance over the armed forces is not the Constitution, but instead the Uniform Code of Military Justice. However, it is the military's duty to protect and preserve the U.S. Constitution, and in a manner of tradition, constitutional principles have an unofficial influence on military politics.

Article I, Section 8, Clauses 15 authorizes Congress:

To provide for calling forth the Militia to execute the Laws of the Union, suppress Insurrections and repel Invasions;

Congress also has the authority to call forth the **Militia** to execute the laws of the Union (Constitutional federal laws), suppress insurrections (inserted in response to Shays' Rebellion), and repel invasions (one may consider the illegal entry into the United States an invasion, therefore this clause gives the federal government the authority to use the militia to guard the national borders). Currently, in this country, we have an **organized militia** (National Guard, State Militias), and an **unorganized militia** (you and I). U.S. Code Title 10 still defines these militias as such.

In Article 1, Section 10, the States are also given the authority to call the militia into action to protect the State from invasion, *"or in such imminent Danger as will not admit of delay."*

The National Guard, since it is considered a part of the organized militia, and sharing the distinction with the State Militias, is normally funded by, and called into action by the governor's office of a State. When Congress calls the National Guard, or State Militia, into action, the burden of funding then comes from the federal government.

Article II, Section 2 of the Constitution states that *"The President shall be Commander in Chief of the Army and Navy of the United States, and of the Militia of the several States, when called into the actual Service of the United States."* When the governor calls the organized militia into service, the President is not Commander in Chief over those forces, because when the governor calls the militia into service, the units are not in "the actual service of the United States."

Article I, Section 8, Clauses 16 authorizes Congress:

To provide for organizing, arming, and disciplining, the Militia, and for governing such Part of them as may be employed in the Service of the United States, reserving to the States respectively, the Appointment of the Officers, and the Authority of training the Militia according to the discipline prescribed by Congress.

The 2nd Amendment provides a clue behind the original intent of this clause. The 2nd Amendment reads, *"A well regulated Militia, being necessary to the security of a free State, the right of the people to keep and bear Arms, shall not be infringed."*

A well regulated militia must be defined by determining the definition of the word **regulated**. As previously discussed, regulated does not mean "control and restrict" as is the assumed definition in today's modern political vernacular. The word regulated, as per the definition and context of the time period, means "to put in good order." The need to ensure the militia is in good order is a reasonable necessity, since during the Revolutionary War, the militia was not in good order. The militiamen did not wear the same uniforms, and in many cases were without shirts, socks, or shoes. The muskets were different sizes, eliminating any ability to share ammunition, and the militias were not well trained.

A well regulated militia, being a militia that is in good order, would then be a militia that is well-trained, following uniform rules of conduct and discipline, uniformed, armed with equipment that is in good order and interchangeable if necessary, and properly organized.

Returning to Article I, Section 8, Clauses 16, the language of the clause becomes clearer:

The Congress shall have Power *To provide for organizing, arming, and disciplining, the Militia, and for governing such Part of them as may be employed in the Service of the United States, reserving to the States respectively, the Appointment of the Officers, and the Authority of training the Militia according to the discipline prescribed by Congress.*

Congress was the voice of the people, and the States. The executive branch and the judicial branch were not. Therefore, it is logical for the Congress to have the authority to ensure that the militia is "well regulated," or "in good order." At the end of the clause the States retain the authorities regarding the appointment of the officers, and the authority of training the Militia. The training, however, must follow the rules for discipline prescribed by Congress.

Federal Properties

Article I, Section 8, Clause 17 calls for the Congress *to exercise exclusive Legislation in all Cases whatsoever, over such District (not exceeding ten Miles square) as may, by Cession of particular States, and the acceptance of Congress, become the Seat of the Government of the United States, and to exercise like Authority over all Places purchased by the Consent of the Legislature of the State in which the Same shall be, for the Erection of Forts, Magazines, Arsenals, dock-Yards, and other needful Buildings.*

The first part of this clause was for the creation of Washington, D.C., giving the United States Congress exclusive legislative powers over the District of Columbia and other federal properties. The clause instructs that the land for the seat of government must be ceded by "particular States," in this case being land from the States of Virginia and Maryland. Because the land was by "Cession of particular States," the land no longer belonged to the States, but became exclusively federal property.

The second part of this clause addresses other lands controlled by the federal government. The clause explains that Congress will have the same authorities over federal lands as Congress is granted to have over Washington, D.C. However, the procurement of the land is different than with establishing the seat of government.

The clause reads: *"...and to exercise like Authority over all Places purchased by the Consent of the Legislature of the State in which the Same shall be, for the Erection of Forts, Magazines, Arsenals, dock-Yards, and other needful Buildings."*

Aside from Washington, D.C., according to this clause, the federal government cannot own property unless it is purchased, that the purchase was by the consent of the legislature of the State in which the land exists, and that the land is being used by the federal government for the purpose of "the erection of forts, magazines, arsenals, dock-yards, and other needful buildings."

In maps from the era immediately following the ratification of the United States Constitution, territories to the west of the original States are not listed as federal properties, but as possessions of the States. The State lines seem to extend westward as far as they can go, with no designation that the territories west of the original thirteen States belong to the federal government. This is why the Louisiana Purchase became a constitutional crisis. The federal government purchased the land from France, taking ownership of the land, designating the territories as not being a part of any of the existing States. Thomas Jefferson recognized he was treading on unconstitutional authority, so to ensure the States were involved, and to give the purchase an illusion of constitutionality, the terms of the purchase were agreed upon by treaty, which required ratification by the voice of the States in the United States Senate.

Since Article I, Section 8, Clause 17 requires that land under federal authority must be purchased with the consent of the State legislature for the purpose of needful buildings, that means that National Parks are unconstitutional, and all other federal lands seized for environmental conservation reasons are unconstitutional, as well. **Mineral Rights** are also supposed to be retained by the States.

In April of 2014, when the Bureau of Land Management seized the cattle of a rancher by the name of Cliven Bundy in Nevada, claiming that his animals were illegally grazing on federal land that Bundy refused to pay a fee for its use, the rancher's argument was that the lands his cattle were grazing on were State lands, not federal lands, so he refused to pay the fees the federal government was demanding. The federal government owns most of the land west of the Mississippi River, and a good portion of it was never purchased, the land was never handed over to the federal government through the blessings of a State legislature, and almost all of the land is not being utilized for the purpose of needful federal buildings. Therefore, Cliven Bundy was correct in his assertion. The rancher stood by his conviction, and as the standoff became a national story, people from around the country traveled to the area, standing with Mr. Bundy, until finally the federal agents backed down, and departed from the area.

Necessary and Proper Clause

Article I, Section 8, Clause 18 is known as the Necessary and Proper clause, or Elastic Clause. *"To make all Laws which shall be necessary and proper for carrying into Execution the foregoing Powers, and all other Powers vested by this Constitution in the Government of the United States, or in any Department or Officer thereof."*

The emphasis on carrying into execution the "foregoing powers" (authorities herein granted) establishes that the clause does not allow the federal government to enact laws simply because they believe the laws to be necessary and proper for any reason. Congress may only make laws that fall within the authorities granted by the U.S. Constitution, and laws the Congress recognizes to be "necessary and proper" in connection to those constitutionally enacted laws.

"The plain import of the clause is, that congress shall have all the incidental and instrumental powers, necessary and proper to carry into execution all the express powers. It neither enlarges any power specifically granted; nor is it a grant of any new power to congress. But it is merely a declaration for the removal of all uncertainty, that the means of carrying into execution those, otherwise granted, are included in the grant." --Joseph Story, Commentaries on the Constitution, 1833

In order to carry out some of the **reserved powers** of the Constitution sometimes certain actions by the government are necessary and proper. For example, when establishing a post office, as expressly authorized by this article and section, the federal government will have to grade the land, hire construction crews, purchase the equipment for carrying out the services of the post office, and so forth. All of these things are necessary and proper actions in order to carry out the "foregoing power" of establishing a post office.

Chapter 10

Prohibitions to the Federal Government

Slavery and Immigration

The first clause of Article I, Section 9 deals with slavery and immigration. The common misconception is that Article I, Section 9, Clause 1 is obsolete. The abolition of slavery in the United States did make a portion of the clause obsolete. The clause addresses the Atlantic slave trade, *and* the migration of people into the United States. Slavery was abolished by Amendment 13 so the part of Article I, Section 9, Clause 1 that addresses slavery is obsolete. But the part about migration is still in force.

Two key words are present in the first clause of Article I, Section 9, that divides the two issues in the clause. The word "importation" in this clause applies wholly to slaves. The word "migration" applies wholly to non-slaves.

The intention was that since the Constitution, as the contract that created our federal government, is a document that grants powers to the federal government, and that all authorities not expressly delegated, are **reserved** to the States, it was expected that immigration would remain as an issue that would be addressed by the States.

Other national governments prohibited migration as they saw fit, so the Founding Fathers determined that the new United States Government must have that same authority.

According to the clause, from the year 1808 Congress would possess the power to stop the importation of slaves, as well as the migration of people the Congress felt must be prohibited from entering this country as immigrants, through the congressional power of legislation.

The Constitution was written specifically in regards to the federal government. All powers originally belonged to the States. Some of those authorities were granted to the federal government for the purpose of protecting and preserving the union. Therefore, all authorities regarding slavery and immigration originally belonged to the States, and before 1808 the States had sole authority regarding each of those issues.

In Article I, Section 9, the federal government was given the opportunity to regulate the Atlantic Slave Trade, and immigration, but not until 1808. The reason for delaying the power to prevent abolishing the import of slaves, and the influx of migrants, was to make a compromise with the southern States so that they would still be willing to ratify the Constitution, and when it came to immigration to give the States twenty years to attract as many people as possible without Congressional regulatory consideration. At this time in history we had immense and almost immeasurable territory, peopled by not more than two and a half million inhabitants. Immigration was encouraged, especially of the kind of people that would bring a benefit to the new nation. The immigration of able, skillful, and industrious Europeans was encouraged.

Note that this clause gives the federal government the authority to prohibit certain persons from migrating into the United States, but it does not give the federal government the authority to dictate to the States which persons the States must admit inside their borders. Included in the groups of people the federal government decided to pass legislation to prohibit were those with disease, and criminal records. The immigration laws were established specifically to protect the receiving population from the potential dangers of disease and criminality that could be brought into the country.

As for the allowance to abolish the Atlantic Slave Trade, on the first day of January in 1808, the moment the clause allowed the Congress to do so, legislation went into effect making it unlawful to import new slaves into the country. The framers saw this as a first step towards eventually abolishing the sin of slavery for good, but recognized it may take a generation or two, and that the decision to abolish slavery, if they were to remain in line with the original narrative of the Constitution, would need to happen individually on a State by State basis.

Habeas Corpus

Article I, Section 9, Clause 2 states that *"The Privilege of the Writ of Habeas Corpus shall not be suspended, unless when in Cases of Rebellion or Invasion the public Safety may require it."*

Habeas corpus is a legal term that means in Latin: "you may have the body." In legal terms, Habeas corpus is a writ that releases a prisoner from unlawful detention. Habeas corpus comes from British common law, and has historically served as an important legal instrument safeguarding individual freedom against arbitrary state action that includes detention without the due process of law.

A writ of habeas corpus is a summons with the force of a court order that demands a prisoner be taken before the court, and that the custodian present proof of authority, allowing the court to determine if the custodian has lawful authority to detain the person. If the custodian does not have authority to detain the prisoner, then the prisoner must be released from custody.

Habeas corpus is designed to protect citizens against any detention that is forbidden by law. The U.S. Constitution specifically includes the habeas procedure, and instructs the Congress not to suspend such unless the detainment is the result of a "Rebellion or Invasion," adding that "the public Safety may require it."

Normally, habeas corpus proceedings accompany questions of jurisdiction and authorities of the court that sentenced a defendant. The suspension of habeas corpus has recently become an issue regarding the detainment of terrorists, but one must ask if the public safety requires the suspension of habeas corpus in the case of terrorists, as prescribed in the Constitution. Secondly, one must consider that the Constitution applies to American citizens, so the question on whether or not Article I, Section 9, Clause 2 applies to captured combatants seems to be a moot point since it is obvious that the detained are not American Citizens, and therefore are not protected by Constitutional protections. Also, remember that Congress has the sole authority to make rules regarding captures on land and water as per Article I, Section 8, Clause 11.

Bills of Attainder

A Bill of Attainder is when the legislature declares the guilt of a person or group of persons, and punishes them without due process (the benefit of a trial).

In Britain, **bills of attainder** were used as a convenient way for the King to convict subjects of crimes and confiscate their property without the bother of a trial, and without the need for a conviction or indeed any evidence at all. Such actions were seen as tyrannical because often this power was used against political enemies, and the Founding Fathers did not wish to give the new federal government those same kinds of powers. Some states, prior to the Constitution, did use attainders against British loyalists, but the practice all but disappeared after the Constitution so specifically forbade the use of attainders by the U.S. Congress, and the States.

Prohibiting the use of bills of attainder serves a number of purposes. One purpose is that by disallowing the bills of attainder the separation of powers is reinforced. By disallowing bills of attainder the Constitution forbids the legislature from performing a judicial function. Another purpose is in regard to the protection of the concept of **due process**, which was later reinforced by the Fifth Amendment to the Constitution.

The true danger of a bill of attainder is that such a legislative act inflicts punishment without a judicial trial, and takes away the life, liberty or property of the target.

Ex Post Facto law

Ex post facto is Latin for "from after the action" or "after the facts. **Ex post facto Law** is retroactive law, or a law that retroactively changes the legal consequences (or status) of actions committed or relationships that existed prior to the enactment of the law. Ex post facto law could criminalize actions that were legal when committed (such as gun control laws that make guns illegal that were legal when purchased), or in the case of amnesty laws, decriminalize certain acts or alleviate possible punishments. Generally speaking, ex post facto laws are seen as a violation of the **rule of law** as it applies in a free and democratic society. Ex post facto laws are expressly forbidden by the United States Constitution for both the federal government, and the States.

Direct Taxation

The U.S. Constitution originally forbade **direct taxation** upon the people by the federal government. Taxation of the people by the federal government could only be laid in relation to population. When the idea for the income tax came to fruition, an amendment (16th Amendment in 1913) had to be passed to allow for the direct taxation of the people without dependence upon the enumeration of the population.

Article I, Section 9, Clause 4 states that in addition to direct taxation, the federal government was forbidden from using **capitation**. Capitation is a head tax. A **Poll Tax** is a kind of head tax. In the context of the period, any tax that singles out groups both directly and indirectly regardless of possession of lands or personal property is capitation. Since Article I, Section 9 is a prohibitory section, the specific call by the Founding Fathers in that clause was that there shall be no capitation, which included no poll tax, by the federal government.

In early New England, in keeping with traditions from the homeland, capitation (caput, meaning head), or poll taxes, were common. These taxes were levied as a way to manipulate the people for the "good of the government."

Alexander Hamilton, though condemning capitation taxes in his **Federalist Papers** writings, was in favor of "head taxes" for emergency revenue reasons. He felt that since sources for revenue were so few, if the government needed to expand for any reason, the ability to lay head taxes, or direct taxation, needed to be an option. However, most of the Founding Fathers disagreed, not only because of their belief that taxation must be indirect and small, but also because of their opinion that the federal government must remain limited to the few authorities granted to it by the U.S. Constitution.

Article I, Section 9, Clause 4 forbids Congress to lay a tax upon individuals except uniformly, and in proportion to the **census** provided for in Article I, Section 2, Clause 3, where this subject is first brought up. In other words, *all* direct taxation was forbidden. What the federal government did was tax the States, based on proportion to the census, or enumeration. The States then taxed the people in order to cover the amount they paid the federal government. The method of taxation by the States was left up to each individual State. The federal government, in this way, used **indirect taxation** to tax the people.

As we have learned, the U.S. Constitution was not designed to necessarily tell the federal government what it can't do as much as it is designed to tell the federal government what few authorities it has. But the Founders felt this to be so important that in addition to not giving direct taxation to the federal government as an authority, they felt they must also spell it out that the Federal Government cannot tax in this manner in any form. This clause restricts the Congress a lot more because it is prohibitive. Article 1, Section 8 provides a list of "enumerated powers," but knowing that politicians would bend and twist meanings to gain more power, Article 1, Section 9 was designed to spell out some very specific things the Congress is prohibited from doing (such as direct taxation and capitation taxes).

Preference in Commerce

Article I, Section 9, Clause 6 states that *"No Preference shall be given by any Regulation of Commerce or Revenue to the Ports of one State over those of another: nor shall Vessels bound to, or from, one State, be obliged to enter, clear, or pay Duties in another."*

This proposal was placed before the Constitutional Convention by the delegates from Maryland, their fear being that congressional legislation might prefer Chesapeake Bay ports of Virginia to those of their State. Under the Articles of Confederation, each State was free to impose **duties** and make regulations to the disadvantage of others, and it was desired that equality in commerce be maintained in the future. This also gives us a clue to the intentions of the Commerce Clause in Article I, Section 8. The Founding Fathers did not wish to give the Federal Government control over commerce, only the ability to ensure that commerce was maintained in an equitable manner in regards to the several States.

U.S. Treasury

Article I, Section 9, Clause 7 reads: *"No Money shall be drawn from the Treasury, but in Consequence of Appropriations made by Law; and a regular Statement and Account of the Receipts and Expenditures of all public Money shall be published from time to time."*

This clause was inspired by the lessons learned in regards to merry old England. The Founding Fathers did not believe it should be in the power of the Executive alone, or of the legislature alone, to raise or spend the money at will. Article I, Section 7, Clause 1 requires that all bills for raising money must originate in the House of Representatives, which is the method referred to by this clause when it states *"No Money shall be drawn from the Treasury, but in Consequence of Appropriations made by Law."* The bill or resolution must also pass the Senate and be signed by the President, in order to be made by law. In 1842 Congress began to make appropriations by **joint resolution**; but as that also must be approved by both Houses, and signed by the President, there is no real difference. Also, in the interest of transparency to the people, the records of all monetary transactions both of receipts and expenditures must be made available for public scrutiny. The end of the clause indicates that the records shall be published "from time to time," meaning they did not have to publish the records after every transaction, but when the records were published they were required to reveal all receipts and expenditures of the public money.

Divided Allegiance

Article I, Section 9, Clause 8 reads: *"No Title of Nobility shall be granted by the United States: And no Person holding any Office of Profit or Trust under them, shall, without the Consent of the Congress, accept of any present, Emolument, Office, or Title, of any kind whatever, from any King, Prince, or foreign State."*

The Founding Fathers did not believe there should be any foreign influences in the affairs of our government, nor should any person be preferentially treated because of title or position.

This provision was taken from a provision in the first section of Article VI of the Articles of Confederation, which permitted persons holding office under a State to accept, with the consent of Congress, the objectionable gifts or distinctions; but the constitutions of at least two of the States at that time forbade them altogether. This republic, being a nation born as a result of the tyranny of a monarchy, should not grant titles of nobility, that much was easily understood. Nobility betrayed the trust and honor of the people through the use of prestige and favoritism. A government run by a ruling elite populated by people of position, prestige and preferential attitude was the kind of government that did not protect the liberties of the common people.

Thomas Jefferson, as President, accepted from Alexander I of Russia a bust of that Emperor, which he said would be "one of the most valued ornaments of the retreat I am preparing for myself at my native home." He said that he had laid it down as a law of his official conduct not to accept anything but books, pamphlets, or other things of minor value; but his "particular esteem" from the Emperor "places his image in my mind above the scope of the law." However, without the consent of Congress, who was the final determining factor, he could not have accepted that gift.

In 1810 Congress proposed an amendment, the original Thirteenth amendment (some would call it the lost 13th Amendment because some records showed it was ratified, then suddenly disappeared - as explained below), to add a heavy penalty to this clause by this wording:

"If any citizen of the United States shall accept, claim, receive or retain any title of nobility or honor, or shall, without the consent of Congress, accept and retain any present, pension, office or emolument of any kind whatever, from any emperor, king, prince or foreign power, such person shall cease to be a citizen of the United States, and shall be incapable of holding office of trust or profit under them, or either of them."

The original 13th Amendment was indeed a part of the United States Constitution, but suddenly vanished just prior to the commencement of the American Civil War, and in some states about a decade after the end of the **civil war**. The people were told that the proposed amendment lacked the necessary ratifying votes, and so it was removed. Ongoing research has shown that the proposed amendment was indeed properly ratified, the State Department WAS notified, and the amendment was on the books and records of some of the various States until about 1876. From 1810 to 1812, twelve states ratified this amendment. The War of 1812 destroyed the library of Congress and these documents were thought destroyed, but in 1994 it was discovered they still exist after a chance discovery in Maine in 1983 made historians aware of the existence of the original 13th Amendment.

Chapter 11

Prohibitions to the States

All of the clauses in the U.S. Constitution apply to the federal government unless otherwise noted. Article I, Section 10, notes otherwise. Each clause begins with the words "No State shall," making Article I, Section 10 prohibitive to the States. The delegates in the federal convention of 1787 recognized **original authority**, but also knew that if the federal government was going to operate in the manner they intended, there were a few things from which the States needed to be restricted.

Article I, Section 10, Clause 1 begins by disallowing the States to *enter into any Treaty, Alliance, or Confederation*. The goal was to keep the union intact, have all dealings with foreign governments go through the federal government, and to ensure there was no **divided loyalties** among the States. Treaties and alliances are external issues, and the federal government was being created by the Constitution to handle all of the external issues.

The disallowance of the States entering into a **confederation** was the argument used against the Confederacy of southern States during the American Civil War. President Lincoln echoed that opinion, considering the southern States seceding and joining into a confederation to be unlawful, partly due to this clause in the Constitution. However, by seceding, the States no longer fell under the jurisdiction of the Constitution. The States that participated in **secession** believed that the federal government had breached the **social contract** called the United States Constitution, and therefore as voluntary members of the union, seceded. By removing themselves from the union, the southern states removed themselves from the contractual agreement. Since they were no longer a part of the Constitution, they were no longer required to follow the provisions of the contract, making the Confederacy a legal arrangement.

Article I, Section 10 also indicates that *"No State shall...grant letters of*

Marque and Reprisal; or coin money; emit Bills of Credit; make any Thing but gold and silver Coin a Tender in Payment of Debts."

The authority to grant letters of marque and reprisal were powers granted to the federal government in Article I, Section 8. The federal government was tasked with the power to provide for the common defense, and granting letters of marque and reprisal were a part of that authority.

States were not allowed to coin money so that they would not use currency as a means to gain an unfair advantage over each other in relation to interstate commerce.

Article I, Section 10 prohibiting the States from emitting **bills of credit** means that almost every State of the modern era is acting unconstitutionally. Bills of credit take two forms. Bills of credit are receipts for currency, such as a treasury note, and bills of credit can be items of credit such as bonds. States could not issue paper money, nor could States issue instruments of debt.

The prohibition against printing their own money was established to protect the federal currency, as well as protect the economy from currency instruments other than coins. Paper currency during the American Revolution had proven to be dangerous to the economy, providing the printers of the currency the ability to manipulate the currency by controlling how much money is printed.

This clause also prohibits the States from creating instruments of debt. It is unconstitutional for a State to borrow money by issuing bonds, promissory notes, and other instruments of debt. Today, all but two States of the union are in debt. Each and every one of the existing State deficits is in violation of the U.S. Constitution.

The part of the clause that limits the States to allowing only gold and silver coin as a tender in the payment of debts reinforced the federal authority to establish uniform laws regarding bankruptcy, while reinforcing that only coin issued by Congress could be used to satisfy debt. This clause removes the opportunity to use paper instruments of debt, such as paper money, bank notes, or other loan instruments, to satisfy one's debt.

Article I, Section 10 prohibits the States from passing bills of attainder, *ex post facto* law, or passing any law that would impair the obligation of contracts. These same restrictions also apply to the federal government regarding bills of attainder, and *ex post facto* law, as per Article I, Section 9. This part of the clause reinforces Separation of Powers, and the prohibitions of potential tyrannical laws that could take away rights through the vote of a legislature, but at the State level.

Ex post facto law has specifically become a large concern in recent politics. *Ex post facto* law is retroactive law. By disallowing the passage of ex post facto law, the States (just like the federal government) cannot constitutionally pass laws retroactively. A gun legal at the time of purchase cannot be made retroactively illegal. Immigrants who entered the State illegally cannot be made retroactively legal. A tax cannot be retroactively imposed, creating a sudden large balance of tax due.

In a similar fashion as presented in Article I, Section 9 regarding the federal government, Article I, Section 10 prohibits the States from granting any title of nobility. The injunction against titles of nobility was inserted into the Constitution against both the federal and State government to prevent them from granting special privileges to some individuals for partisan reasons. This is a concept that runs in line with the framer's insistence that we function as a nation under the rule of law. Mercantilism, as used by the British Crown during the approach of the Revolutionary War, bestowed favors and tax advantages on some merchants, and the titles of nobility granted by the British enabled an entire class of people to function under the protection of special privileges, placing them above the remainder of the people, establishing a ruling class of oligarchs that ruled with impunity. The Founding Fathers intended that the United States would not practice preferential treatment for any business, or individual, and that in the United States the politicians would not be members of a ruling elite, but a representation of the people, by the people, and for the people.

States are allowed to tax imports or exports, but only with the consent of Congress. Because States are tasked with having their own inspection laws, any costs necessary for executing those inspection laws may be recouped through imposts or Duties without the consent of Congress. However, the States cannot keep any profit from inspections for themselves.

The clause reads, *"The net produce of all duties and imposts, laid by any State on imports or exports, shall be for the use of the Treasury of the*

United States." In other words, the States cannot over tax imports and exports. They are only to charge taxes necessary to cover their costs, such as "executing inspection laws." Any net produce, or what would be considered "profit" in the private sector, goes to the U.S. Treasury. All of the States inspection laws, or other laws regarding imports and exports, are also subject to revision and control by the Congress.

Having a military is also forbidden to the States in time of peace, except with the consent of Congress. However, if a State is invaded, or the State feels they are in imminent danger, they are allowed to have a military enlisted into active service, or more specifically, call up the militia. Currently, 23 States have State Defense Forces, or "State Militias." In recent years, State Defense Forces have proven vital to homeland security and emergency response efforts.

The Congress has the authority to call forth the militia in Article I, Section 8. The governor of a State has the authority to call forth the militia if the State is being invaded, or is in "*imminent danger as will not admit of delay.*" The President of the United States does not have the authority to call forth the militia.

In Article II the Constitution states that the President is the "Commander in Chief of the Army and Navy of the United States, and of the Militia of the several States, when called into the actual service of the United States." The President is only the Commander in Chief of the Militia of the several States, when the militia is "called into the actual service of the United States."

The National Guard, a part of the militia, is normally under the service of the State to which it is attached, and receives its funding from the State as well. If Congress calls the National Guard into service, then the federal government pays the bill. It is when Congress, and only when Congress, calls the National Guard into service that the President becomes Commander in Chief over the National Guard. If the State calls the National Guard into service, the governor is the Commander in Chief of the personnel called into action.

The distinction was established so that the President could use military forces against foreign enemies if a quick and decisive decision was necessary, but not against the States, or the American People. The standing army is not for domestic use to suppress insurrections, or repel invasions. That is what the militias are for, and the militia can only be put into action by Congress (representation of the people and the States), or State leadership. The President does not control the militias, nor does he determine when they go into action. His only relationship with the militias is when they are called into actual service of the United States.

In the case of securing the national border, the President is tasked with "faithfully executing the laws of the United States" as stated in Article II, Section 3, and he can do so with executive departments such as ICE, and the Border Patrol. The actual call for the militia (National Guard, State Militias, unorganized militia) to protect the border is the responsibility of Congress, and State leadership.

Chapter 12

Establishing the Executive Branch

Executive Power Established

Article II establishes the **Executive Branch**. The Founding Fathers were anxious regarding the creation of the office of the Executive because they feared that a leader with too much power had the potential of being tyrannical. Many of the framers argued during the federal convention of 1787 that there should not be one executive, but many, so that they may serve as checks against each other. George Mason suggested regional presidents, who worked together in the name of their region. The concerns regarding the potential of a president wielding too much power were well placed, if one considers their frame of reference was the authoritarian king of the British Empire.

Despite their fears, the delegates of the States in the assembly knew that the authorities of the President under the Articles of Confederation were too few, leaving the office of the President much too weak to adequately serve the union. The Founding Fathers were looking for a strong leader who also recognized the limitations on the authorities of the federal government as granted by the States through the articles of the new Constitution. The best model for the presidency was a simple choice. Article II was written with the President of the Constitutional Convention in mind. His name was George Washington.

Article II, Section 1, Clause 1 states that the powers of the executive are **vested**. This word, as we learned when we went over Article I, Section 1, carries a meaning similar to that of the word "granted." Vested means legally transferred, secured in the possession of, or assigned. The President's authorities are powers assigned to him through a legal transfer of authorities. The powers vested to the Executive Branch were granted by the States.

The Founders understood that whenever there is a "leader," there is a struggle for power. America has been no different. The office of the

President has increased its powers over the years, mostly through unconstitutional means. The Founding Fathers sought to limit the powers of the Executive. Among those limitations of powers is also a term-limit. The Executive is limited to a term of four years, as is the Vice President. A limit on the number of terms was not approved until after the ratification of the 22nd Amendment in 1951.

Election

The election of the President and Vice President is not accomplished by **direct election**. Appointed **electors** vote for the President and Vice President. The electors were originally appointed by the States during the early elections of American history. The formula for determining the number of electors is calculated by taking the number of Representatives and Senators the State is entitled in Congress, and combining those two numbers. This method of indirect election is also known as The **Electoral College**, which was designed in this manner specifically to protect the United States against the excesses of **democracy**.

After the 2000 election, where the winner of the popular vote was denied the presidency because he did not win the fight for electors, questions regarding the Electoral College arose. It was only the fourth time in history such an event occurred. To find precedents resembling the 2000 election one has to go back to the 19th century, to the elections of 1888, 1876, and 1824. Those were the only elections in American history prior to the election in 2000 where a winner in the popular vote was denied the presidency through the Electoral College system.

In modern politics there has been a number of officials promising to introduce legislation to abolish the Electoral College, claiming that it no longer serves a good purpose in today's American System. The reasoning by these individuals who oppose the Electoral College suggests that the United States should simply allow the popular vote of the American people be followed every four years when we elect our president.

A number of Americans have voiced their agreement with this opinion, arguing that the individual running for President receiving the most votes should win. An indirect election such as the Electoral College, argue these folks, is simply unfair and undemocratic. In other words, they believe the American political system should operate as a direct **democracy**.

The Founding Fathers purposely did not make this country a democracy. The United States is a **Republic**, equipped with checks and balances at all levels of government, including the voting process, and a president separate from the legislative branch. In a Parliamentary System, the **Prime Minister** not only handles the affairs of the state like a president, but is also a part of the legislature, usually the head of the majority party. As a republic, the United States is also not a democracy. Democracies place all of the powers in the hands of the voters, and historically democracies are proven to be violent failures.

John Adams was quoted to say, *"Democracy never lasts long. It soon wastes, exhausts, and murders itself. There is never a democracy that did not commit suicide."*

Thomas Jefferson said, *"The democracy will cease to exist when you take away from those who are willing to work and give to those who would not."*

The Founders are not the only historical figures to recognize that a democracy opposes liberty.

Karl Marx once said, *"Democracy is the road to socialism."*

Karl Marx, the father of **communism**, understood that the implementation of a democracy is a necessary step in the process of destroying our **Constitutional Republic**. Once the people are fooled to believe that they can receive gifts from the treasury rather than achieve for their livelihood through their individual aspirations, they will continually vote in the people who ensure the entitlements continue to flow. Eventually, this mindset becomes the majority. This group of government dependents then changes over time from an involved and informed electorate to a populace who lacks the understanding of the principles of liberty and can easily be manipulated into believing that sacrificing individual liberty in exchange for social justice, artificial security, and gifts from the treasury is a price that we must be willing to pay. A group dependent upon the government in such a manner, then, is primed to vote into power a potential tyranny. Eliminating the Electoral College would make it easier for these members of our society to vote into office those who promise more entitlements, while eliminating the voice of the minority States, ensuring that the President would be elected by the seven largest metropolitan areas in the country.

Once the majority of the voters in a democracy becomes the recipient of benefits from the federal government, the government achieves unchecked power, and may then violate the property rights of the productive members of society in order to provide benefits to the non-productive members of society. This is best characterized in the "tax the rich," or "redistribution of wealth," scheme we are now seeing emerge as the rallying cry by statists in government. Samuel Adams called this method of a redistribution of wealth "schemes of **leveling**."

The delegates in the federal convention of 1787 were aware of the danger of **collectivism**, which is why they established our system of government, and the Electoral College, in the manner they did. A true democracy becomes **mob rule**, and the principles of liberty become a target for elimination.

"A democracy is nothing more than mob rule, where fifty-one percent of the people may take away the rights of the other forty-nine." -- Thomas Jefferson

In order to preserve our Constitutional Republic it was imperative for the vote of the people to be indirect, except when it came to voting for their representatives in the House of Representatives. The Founding Fathers divided power as much as possible, including the power of the vote.

Originally, the State legislatures appointed the electors who cast their votes in the Presidential Election. That changed in 1824 when all but six states decided the electors should to vote in line with the popular vote of the State.

Like electors, U.S. Senators were initially appointed by the State legislatures, which ensured the voice of the States was present in the federal government. That changed in 1913 with the 17th Amendment, which transferred the vote for U.S. Senators to the popular vote. The 17th Amendment took away from the States their representation in the federal government.

The Framers of the Constitution divided the voting power as they did partially because if the power to vote for President, the House, and the Senate all fell directly to the people, and if the people were fooled by some political **ideology** that wished to destroy the Republic by fundamentally transforming the American System, a tyranny could be easily voted into control of all parts of the government without any **checks and balances** present whatsoever. When a majority of voters are uninformed in such a manner, and are given the full voting power, tyranny is inevitable.

Winston Churchill understood the dangers of trusting an uninformed electorate with the capacity to govern. He was quoted as saying, *"The best argument against democracy is a five minute conversation with the average voter."*

The elimination of the Electoral College would take away the voice of the smaller States, give the election of the President to the seven largest metropolitan centers in the United States, and lead America even closer to becoming a democracy.

Democracy is a transitional governmental system that ultimately leads to tyranny, an **oligarchy** like **socialism**, **fascism**, or a totalitarian system. This was true in the days of the French Revolution no less than it is today.

While democracy lasts it becomes more bloody than either aristocracy or monarchy...Democracy never lasts long. It soon wastes, exhausts, and murders itself. There is never a democracy that did not commit suicide. -- John Adams

Democracy is two wolves and a sheep voting on what to have for dinner -- James Bovard

My friend, Tim "Loki" Kerlin, used to say, *"A Republic is two wolves voting on what to have for dinner, and a well-armed sheep contesting the vote."*

Our country is not a democracy. Our nation was founded as a constitutionally limited republic. The indirect election of the President through the Electoral College reflects that truth, and the Electoral College is one of the last vestiges of the system of checks and balances as they apply to the voters.

A limited government is the essence of liberty.

Article II, Section 1, Clause 4 indicates that the Congress may determine the time and day the Electors are chosen, and give their votes. The day they vote for President and Vice President, according to this clause, will be the same day nationally. The rules for the popular election, if you will remember from Article I, are to be established by the State legislatures.

Eligibility

Article II, Section 1, Clause 5 states the eligibility for President includes the requirement that the individual must be a **natural born Citizen**.

Notice that the Constitution says a natural born citizen, "or" a citizen of the United States at the time of the adoption of the Constitution. This was to ensure that anyone alive at the time of the adoption of the Constitution who was a citizen was eligible, and anyone born after the adoption of the Constitution had to be a natural born citizen to be eligible. The word "or" gives us a clue that there is a difference between "natural born citizen," and "citizen."

Some people will use the Fourteenth Amendment as an argument regarding the definition of natural born citizen. The Fourteenth Amendment says, *"All persons born or naturalized in the United States and subject to the jurisdiction thereof, are citizens of the United States and of the State wherein they reside."*

The Fourteenth Amendment only addresses "citizenship," not the concept of being a natural born citizen. Therefore, it does not apply when discussing the concept of natural born citizenship. The clause in the 14th Amendment was written as it was to protect the citizenship of the children of the emancipated slaves. The word **jurisdiction** was placed in that clause to mean "full allegiance." There was a fear during that time, as there had been during the founding of this nation, of **divided allegiance**, or **divided loyalties**.

Natural Born Citizen is not defined in the Constitution primarily because the definition was common knowledge. People understood what the term "Natural Born Citizen" meant.

In today's societal environment we have a number of terms that are understood without needing to be defined. One of those terms is "fast food." Without requiring a definition provided, most people know what the definition of "fast food" is. That does not mean the term will be readily understood by some historian of the future. He may ask himself, when he comes across that term in our literature, "Why is it their food was fast? Did it run quickly away from them?" To understand what "fast food" meant to us, he may have to refer to a number of writings before he finally comes across the definition, be it a story that reveals the definition through the context of the tale, or a dictionary, or literary tool.

One of the sources the Founding Fathers used when it came to establishing the definition of "Natural Born Citizen" was **Vatell's Law of Nations**.

Vatell's Law of Nations is mentioned once in the Constitution in Article I, Section 8, Clause 10, and it is capitalized - which suggests the mention of the Law of Nations to be a proper noun, or a significant entry that required emphasis, thus supporting the argument that it is a direct reference to Vatell's writings.

In 2010, it was discovered that George Washington failed to return a couple library books to the New York City Public Library. One of those books was Vatell's Law of Nations. Washington checked the book out in 1789, shortly after the Constitutional Convention, probably because of the heavy influence the definitions in Vatell's Law of Nations played on the writing of the U.S. Constitution, coupled with his need to recognize internationally accepted political philosophies and definitions during the dawn of his new presidency.

Benjamin Franklin owned three copies of the Law of Nations - two for the convention, and one for his personal use. He received those copies from the editor, Dumas, in 1775.

Vatell's Law of Nations Section 212 indicates that to be a Natural Born Citizen both parents must be citizens at the time of the birth of the child. As with the Fourteenth Amendment that would emerge nearly a hundred years later, there was a fear of divided allegiance.

In line with Vatell's Law of Nations, the Immigration and Naturalization Act of 1790 confirmed the definition of natural born citizen not requiring the child to be necessarily born on American soil, but requiring that both parents be American citizens at the time of the child's birth. The section in the Naturalization Act of 1790 referring to natural born citizenship reads, *"And the children of citizens of the United States that may be born beyond sea, or out of the limits of the United States, shall be considered as natural born citizens: Provided, That the right of citizenship shall not descend to persons whose fathers have never been resident in the United*

States."

Note that where it says "and the children of *citizens*," the final word is in the plural. The plurality of "citizens" means both parents must be citizens at the time of the birth of the child in order for the child to be a "Natural Born Citizen." The final part of that clause places an emphasis on the American residency of the *father*.

The only court case ever to address the issue of natural born citizenship, *Minor v. Happersett* in 1875, confirmed the United States Supreme Court's opinion regarding the definition of natural born citizen, and the court's opinion supported Vatell's definition.

"The Constitution does not in words say who shall be natural-born citizens. Resort must be had elsewhere to ascertain that. At common law, with the nomenclature of which the framers of the Constitution were familiar, it was never doubted that all children born in a country of parents who were its citizens became themselves, upon their birth, citizens also. These were natives or natural-born citizens, as distinguished from aliens or foreigners."

Article II also establishes that in order to be eligible for the presidency the candidate must be at least the age of 35. This requirement, reasoned the Founders, would ensure that the immaturities of youth had passed away. Along with a relatively mature age, the Constitution indicates that the President must also have been a resident of the United States for the last fourteen years. This, once again, was a guard against divided loyalties.

The Vice President must also meet all eligibility requirements. In the 18th century the Vice President was the second place winner in the election, and therefore had to be eligible because he was originally running for President. Now, the Vice President is elected as a part of the presidential ticket. However, to ensure it was clear that the Vice President also had to be eligible for the presidency, especially since he was next in line for the presidency should the Office of President be vacated, the 12th Amendment ends with a sentence that demands the Vice President is eligible for the presidency.

In Case of Death

Article II, Section 1, Clause 6 was changed by the Twelfth Amendment.

This clause established the rules in case of the death of the President while in office. The clause gave the Office of the President to the Vice President in the case of death. The ambiguity of the clause, however, created confusion. In the case of President William Henry Harrison who died after only 30 days in office, it created a constitutional crisis. The officials of that time did not know what to do. When old Tippecanoe died, he was succeeded by his Vice-President John Tyler, but since no President had died in office before, no one was quite sure how Presidential succession worked. The Constitution stipulated that the Vice-President should become the new President, but it was not clear if the Vice-President should be considered a "real" President, or if he only "acted" as President. The Tyler administration made it clear that Vice-Presidents who became President after the death of the elected President should be treated as legitimate Presidents.

The Twelfth Amendment later addressed the problem with more specified rules. Succession was resolved once and for all with the ratification of the 25th Amendment in 1967.

Compensation

Article II, Section 1, Clause 7 allows for the President to be compensated for his service as President of the United States. This salary is not to be increased or diminished while the President serves. The President, according to this clause, is also not allowed to receive any other governmental salary from the federal government during his term as President. In George Washington's first Inaugural Address, he announced that he would accept no salary as President.

Oath or Affirmation

In the final Clause of Article II, Section 1, the "Oath or **Affirmation**" for the Office of President was established.

The reason for the clause indicating oath "or" affirmation was because an oath is to God, and an Affirmation is not. The Founders understood that not all Americans believe in God, therefore an option needed to be available for non-believers. Affirmation was also included as an option because there were some Christians who believed swearing to God to be a sin. Offering the opportunity to "affirm" gave these Christians an opportunity to take the affirmation of office without compromising their religious beliefs.

Note that the President is expected, according to the text of the oath or affirmation, to preserve, protect, and defend the Constitution of the United States. Failure to do so is considered to be **maladministration**. The President was expected to be strong, but responsible, and for his decisions to be based on the rule of law as presented by the Constitution of the United States. Maladministration was a term suggested by George Mason during the federal convention of 1787 as a ground for impeachment. Maladministration was a term in use in six of the thirteen state constitutions as a ground for impeachment, including Mason's home state of Virginia.

James Madison objected that *"so vague a term will be equivalent to a tenure during pleasure of the Senate."* Maladministration was then withdrawn, and substituted with **high crimes** and **misdemeanors.**

Placing one's hand on a Bible during the administration of the oath of office is not articulated in this article of the Constitution, nor is it a requirement listed anywhere else in our founding documents. The placement of a hand on a Bible while reciting the oath or affirmation was something that George Washington chose to do, and it has been a tradition ever since. When he requested that he should be able to place his hand on a Bible, no Bible was in the immediate area, so one was retrieved from a Masonic Temple that was up the street.

Chapter 13

Powers of the Executive Branch

Commander in Chief

Section two of Article II establishes the President as the *Commander in Chief of the Army and Navy, and of the Militia of the several States, when called into the actual Service of the United States.*

This allows for the President to wage war, if necessary, without Congressional approval. However, if Congress does not agree with the President's actions, they can pull the funding, which would force a discontinuation of the use of the military for whatever operations the President chose them to operate. In the Articles of Confederation, the powers to wage war, and to declare war, were listed as separate authorities, although in the Articles of Confederation both powers were granted to the Congress.

There were extensive debates over **war powers**. In fact, when the founders were debating over **war powers** in regards to Article I during their assembly on August 17, 1787, they considered giving to Congress the power to "make war." A number of reasons brought up during that debate convinced the delegates to give Congress the power to declare war, instead. This decision left the power to make war with the President, as Commander in Chief.

When the Framers of the Constitution were creating the executive branch, the President they had in mind was George Washington. He was, in their eyes, the perfect President. The executive branch was fashioned around Washington's personality, and abilities. The expectations were that the presidents to follow Washington would be similar to Mr. Washington in their level of sacred honor, humility, and ability to properly apply the war powers as necessary, while refraining from becoming involved in **foreign entanglements** that did not directly affect the United States of America.

Among Washington's strengths was that he was a great general. It became apparent that the President would need to be a strong military leader. However, the consideration that an executive may take that power and abuse it was in play. Therefore, a number of checks and balances against the power of the executive branch were put into place.

Part of the reason the power to make war was given to the President, and not Congress, has much to do with the time period. One must consider that when the members of Congress were at home in their districts, it could be as far as the southernmost State of Georgia. Considering the lack of technology, members of Congress could not just get on a plane, or take a drive, to get to Washington, D.C., quickly. Even the time it may take to get the messages out to the members of Congress could take longer than the time needed to begin necessary war maneuvers.

When it came to war powers, the need was for the Commander in Chief to be quick, decisive, and take care of business as needed. However, if we have a President acting in a tyrannical manner, launching military operations when it is not necessary, aside from the ability to electorally vote the President out of office, the Congress has two ways to check his behavior.

First, Congress can pull funding. If there is no money, the troops must be brought home. Second, the Congress has the power to impeach the President if he is becoming tyrannical, or is doing things that he shouldn't (maladministration).

One concern that has arisen in today's political environment, largely as a result of the change in the dynamics of our political system by the 17th Amendment in 1913 that changed the Senate from being the voice of the States, to an assembly directly voted into office by public vote, is if both Houses of Congress are in **collusion** with the President. A White House administration with both Houses of Congress working with the President could be a recipe for disaster in regards to the rule of law, creating an opportunity for those three parts of the federal government to collude against the people, which would inevitably lead to the rise of an unchecked **oligarchy**.

In the cases of the wars in Iraq, Afghanistan, or Libya, the President had every right to launch those operations. That is not to say the decisions were correct, or in the best interest of our country, but that the President had the constitutional authority to wage war in those theaters without his actions being accompanied by a congressional declaration of war.

When it came to foreign entanglements, the Founders preferred America to stay out of such conflicts unless American interests were directly influenced. George Washington in his farewell address is actually quite clear on the subject.

Congress holding the power to declare war does not mean that the President must ask Congress for permission before waging war. In today's world it would seem to be the reasonable thing to do, and I believe it would be the proper thing to do, but as far as the Constitution is concerned, congressional approval for a military action is not necessary.

A reference used to support the concept of "no war without a declaration" is The War Powers Act of 1973. The War Powers Act was simply a piece of legislation, and did not change the authorities of the President when it came to his war powers. The War Powers Act is unconstitutional. Only amendments can change the authorities granted to the President of the United States.

The two Barbary Wars, the first two international wars the United States found herself engaged in, were waged by Thomas Jefferson and James Madison. Jefferson's engagement against the Muslim States of the Barbary Coast was fought from 1802 to 1805, after Jefferson refused to continue paying a tribute to the Barbary Pirates for safe passage through the Mediterranean Sea. Hostilities were reignited in 1815, during Madison's presidency. Both wars were undeclared, waged by Jefferson and Madison without a declaration of war from the Congress, but Congress did appropriate funding for both campaigns.

Calling forth the Militia

The President of the United States is not supposed to be all powerful, or the final decision maker in the federal government. The American System of government is full of checks and balances. Even as the Commander in Chief, if he is abusing his power as the head of military operations, Congress can defund war efforts, or impeach the President.

In Article II the Constitution states that the President is the "Commander in Chief of the Army and Navy of the United States, and of the Militia of the several States, when called into the actual service of the United States." Some have argued that means he is only Commander in Chief when "he" is called into service to do so, which is accomplished by a declaration of war. That is an erroneous opinion.

As Commander in Chief, the President may engage the Army and Navy in war operations as necessary. This power of Commander in Chief does not extend to the militias at the President's whim. The President is only the Commander in Chief of the Militia of the several States, when the **militia** is called into actual service of the United States.

The distinction was established so that the President could use military forces against foreign enemies if a quick and decisive decision was necessary, but not against the States, or the American people. The standing army is not for domestic use to suppress insurrections, or repel invasions. That is what the militias are for, and the militia can only be put into action by Congress, or State leadership. The President does not control the militias, nor does he determine when they go into action. His only relationship with the militias only emerges when they are called into actual service of the United States by the United States Congress. Then, and only then, the President serves as Commander in Chief over the militias.

Article I, Section 8 states that "*Congress shall have power to provide for calling forth the Militia to execute the laws of the Union, suppress Insurrections and repel invasions.*"

States cannot call their militia into action "*unless actually invaded, or in such imminent Danger as will not admit of delay.*" (Article I, Section 10)

Though the President is tasked with "faithfully executing the laws of the United States" as stated in Article II, Section 3, and he can do so with executive departments such as I.C.E., and the Border Patrol, the actual call for the militia (National Guard, State Militias, unorganized militia) to protect the border is the responsibility of Congress, and State leadership.

Executive Departments and Agencies

Article II, Section 2, Clause 1 indicates the President may "require the Opinion, in writing, of the principal Officer in each of the executive Departments, upon any Subject relating to the Duties of their respective offices." This part of this clause is a good indication that the Founding Fathers felt the President should consult others when making decisions, especially those familiar with the departments in question.

The existence of the different executive departments is constitutional, as long as they are established to handle constitutional duties of the federal government, and their powers are limited within constitutional allowances. Originally, there were only four executive departments (and five if you separate the War Department and Department of the Navy); the War Department, the State Department, the Department of the Treasury, and the Department of Justice. The Department of the Navy served as a separate department until 1947, but worked closely with the Department of War.

There are many departments in the executive branch that are unconstitutional, and should not have even been established. The Education Department, for example, is unconstitutional in its current form because there is no place in the Constitution that gives the federal government the authority to regulate, or be involved in, education. Therefore, as per the 10th Amendment, education is a State issue.

The Energy Department and the Environmental Protection Agency are also unconstitutional. The federal government has no authority to regulate those issues. However, if those departments did not regulate, but only kept studies and records of those issues, then the existence of those agencies may be acceptable.

The executive branch can have departments and agencies that study issues not authorized by the Constitution to fall under the federal government, but they cannot have any regulatory power because any federal laws regarding those issues are not constitutionally authorized to the United States Government. Regulations are directly connected to laws, and laws must be constitutional in the first place in order to be considered the supreme law of the land.

Despite these agencies not being legally allowed to regulate unconstitutional law, agencies like the EPA are doing just that. In fact, the EPA is regulating independently, literally legislating through regulations. In other words, the EPA, as well as other agencies, have been enacting their own regulations without the benefit of a law being on the books, revealing the danger of having unconstitutional departments and agencies.

This is not to say we should not have the various departments and agencies of the executive branch. Some of them are constitutional, and absolutely necessary.

Correction of federal unconstitutionality can be sought through concepts known as **Republic Review**, and **nullification**. By using a convention of delegates from the several States to determine the unconstitutionality of particular laws, actions, or departments of the federal government, the States can be encouraged to work together to **nullify** the unconstitutional regulations set forth by the various federal agencies. The States have the authority to take care of their own business, and if a federal agency tries to regulate an issue that falls under the State's powers, the States have the right to ignore that regulation.

A common belief is that if we do not have these various federal agencies regulating things like food, energy, and actions against the environment, people will just act in ways that are unacceptable and dangerous. The opposition to the Constitution will tell you that we need the federal government to make sure that our food is safe, energy is used properly, and corporations are not polluting our fragile environment.

Local issues are supposed to be handled at the local level, and the people, through their States, are more than capable of properly regulating these issues as necessary, but in a manner that is consistent with the local opinion of the electorate.

The Founding Fathers did not trust a large, centralized, **national government**, hence, the reason the Framers only granted to the federal government authorities regarding external issues, and the power to act as a mediator between the States in the case of disagreement.

Reprieves and Pardons

The President is also given the power to grant reprieves and pardons for offenses against the United States, except in cases of **impeachment**. This was one of the first functions President Gerald Ford took advantage of when he took office after President Richard Nixon resigned, pardoning Nixon so that no criminal cases could be brought against him. No impeachment procedure had ensued, so Ford was constitutionally allowed to grant the pardon. It has been suggested that is why Nixon resigned. If he had not resigned, and was impeached, the next President would not have had the authority to pardon him.

The President is granted the ability to make treaties and to nominate members to the executive branch, Supreme Court, and other offices not expressly provided for in the Constitution. Agreement and consent of two thirds of the Senate is necessary for any treaty, or nomination for that matter, to become effective. The **advise and consent powers** granted to the **United States Senate** was a way of disallowing the executive branch from mirroring the centralized British Model of unilateral control under the king. The authority also gave the States the allowance to approve or disapprove any action by the President by requiring that the Senate concur with two-thirds vote.

The purpose of giving advise and consent powers to the U.S. Senate refers us back to the original dynamics of the United States government. The Senators in the U.S. Senate were appointed by the State Legislatures before the appearance of the 17th Amendment in 1913. The Senate was the States' representation in the federal government. The Senators were the voice of the States. Treaties, appointments, and other executive functions, though executed by the President, requires approval by the Senate. The States, as with the granting of powers to the federal government in the first place through the articles of the Constitution, had the power to approve or disapprove the President's actions through the U.S. Senate in a manner much like parents grant permission to their children before a child can perform a particular action. After all, the Senate was the voice of the States, and it was the States that created the federal government in the first place.

This was an important check upon the executive branch by the States.

The executive branch requiring the consent of the U.S. Senate for some of its actions reminds us of the amendment process. As with treaties and appointments by the executive branch, amendments must be approved, or ratified, by the States. In the case of amendments, however, the vote is three-quarters of the States in order to ratify.

The federal government, be it through amendments, or executive actions, needs the permission of the States.

Remember, the States once held all powers. It was the States that provided the authorities to the federal government so that it may exist, and function. The States had original authority over all powers, and decided to grant a few authorities to the federal government so that it may operate in a necessary manner - specifically for the purpose of protecting, preserving, and promoting the union.

The States gave permission to the federal government to function in a manner prescribed by the Constitution.

An opponent to the originalist viewpoint of the Constitution once said to me, "You have it all wrong. The federal government tells the States what to do."

If that was the case, then why would the President need to get the consent of the U.S. Senate to make treaties, and two-thirds of the Senators present have to concur? Why would the President's nominations need to be interviewed and approved by the Senate? And with that in mind, remember that before the 17th Amendment in 1913, the Senate was the voice of the States.

The executive can do very little without the Senate's approval.

War Powers seems like an exception on the surface, but even the authority to make war has its checks by Congress.

For the most part, it is up to the people and the States through Congress to ensure the President does not act in a manner unbecoming of the office.

This check is designed to protect us from tyranny.

Imagine how different the appointment hearings of Supreme Court justices have become, now that the Senate is no longer the representation of the States, anymore. The questions are probably very different than they otherwise would be. Now, the House and the Senate are really not a whole lot different. They are both voted in by the popular vote. Before 1913, the Senate was the voice of the States.

I wonder how the questions posed to the Supreme Court nominees would be different if the Senate still belonged to the States. Perhaps the questions would be more in line with protecting State sovereignty. Surely the concerns of the States would be behind much of the questioning.

The 17th Amendment changed the dynamics of our government. One of the reasons our federal government is constantly acting unconstitutionally is because it is now structured unconstitutionally. The people voting for the Senators, rather than the Senators being appointed by the State legislatures, is not in line with what was originally intended. With the voice of the States removed, the government cannot function as intended because the proper checks and balances are not in place. The 17th Amendment introduced **ideology** into the Senate, and removed one of the checks necessary to protect us against a federal government constantly seeking to become more expansive.

Recess Appointments

The final clause of Article II, Section 2 of the U.S. Constitution states: *The President shall have Power to fill up all Vacancies that may happen during the Recess of the Senate, by granting Commissions which shall expire at the End of their next Session.*

This clause refers to what is called a **recess appointment**. A recess appointment is the appointment of a senior federal official (department head, judge, etc.) by the President while the U.S. Senate is in recess. As the voice of the States in the federal government, the Senate must confirm all appointments of senior federal officers before they assume office. However, while the U.S. Senate is in recess, and during the early years of this nation that meant they could be a few days ride away, the President can make a recess appointment without Senate confirmation. However, the appointment only remains in effect until the next session. A recess appointment must be approved by the Senate by the end of the next session of Congress, or the position becomes vacant again.

Remember, the House of Representatives and the Senate were originally made up very differently from each other. The Representatives go to Washington to serve their district, and to act in accordance with the will of the people in their district, making the House of Representatives literally the voice of the people in the federal government.

The Senate was made up of Senators appointed by the State legislatures. The Senators represented the States, and they made up the State coalition of the federal government. It was through the Senate that the States had representation in the federal government, and could ensure, along with the House of Representatives, to provide a series of checks against the executive branch.

Part of the way to control power is to divide it. Then, after you divide the power, divide it again. Then, make the powers of the separate branches different from each other, that way they do not collude together against the people, or other branches of government.

One of the fears of the Founders was that the branches would collude together in an effort to take away individual freedoms.

By requiring the Senate to confirm appointments by the Executive, it kept a leash on the Executive. Even in a recess appointment, when the President could appoint without confirmation by the Senate, confirmation would still eventually be needed or else the seat became vacant again. This kept the Executive from surrounding himself with a group of cronies the States did not approve of.

He

The first word of Article II, Section 3 is "He." The word refers to the President of the United States. I have actually had some people, who oppose the Constitution, tell me that the word "He" being used is evidence that the Constitution disallows women from being President. They then argue that if a woman was to become President, because of the word "He" being used in the Constitution, anything she did in office would be unconstitutional since the Constitution does not allow women to be President of the United States.

Not necessarily.

As with other writings, such as the Holy Bible, often the word "He" may be used as a general term to represent both sexes.

In the case of the Constitution, it is conceivable, considering the mindset of the day, that the Founders did not think a woman would someday become President of the United States. I assure you, people like John Adams and Aaron Burr were exceptions to that line of thinking.

Aaron Burr was Vice President under Thomas Jefferson, and he actually was one that proposed that there be a uniform rule across the nation that enabled women to vote.

If you look through the Constitution, there is no place in the Constitution that says women cannot vote, or run for office. The reason women were not able to vote, or run for office, was because the States were given the authority over the rules of elections, and during that time the States did not allow women to vote or hold office. Much of that changed in some States and territories long before the Suffrage Movement, but it took a Constitutional amendment to make the practice uniform among all States.

Therefore, the first word of Article II, Section 3, being "He," is simply a general term. Whoever the first female President is in the future, she will be fully entitled, upon being elected, to assume the Office of the President of the United States.

State of the Union

"He shall from time to time give to the Congress Information of the State of the Union, and recommend to their Consideration such Measures as he shall judge necessary and expedient."

The **State of the Union address** is supposed to be as it is worded in the Constitution, a speech about the state of the union addressed to Congress by the President. It is not supposed to be a campaign speech, it is not supposed to be a popularity speech, nor a chance to take a stab at political opposition. The speech is simply supposed to be an opportunity for the President to give the Congress information regarding the state of the union.

The speech is also not supposed to be designed as an address to the people, either. It was expected that the electorate would be interested in hearing the speech, and that the press would report on the speech, for it is in our interest to know what the state of the union is. But, the specific reason for the State of Union address is to give Congress information of the state of the union.

There is an additional reason for the State of Union address should the President deem it necessary. According to the Constitution, he may during the speech *"recommend to their Consideration such measures as he shall judge necessary and expedient."* Of course, he can do this during the normal course of his presidency, as well. The word *"recommend to their consideration"* in this part of the clause gives us a clue to the limits on the powers of the President.

Article I, Section 1 reads: *"All legislative Powers herein granted shall be vested in a Congress of the United States, which shall consist of a Senate*

113

and House of Representatives."

This means that the authority to make law, modify law, repeal law, and strike down law - "all" legislative powers - are granted to the Congress by the States.

Article II, Section 3 says the President can "recommend" to their "consideration" such measures. He cannot act without Congress, he cannot put measures into place "with or without Congress," and at best he can "recommend" to Congress his own ideas regarding legislation that he would like to see Congress initiate. The President can only "recommend to their consideration," because he has no legislative capacity. He cannot make Congress do anything, and he cannot act legislatively without Congress.

Executive Orders

The President has the authority to issue Executive Orders. An **Executive Order** is a proclamation. Executive Orders began back when George Washington was President. His Thanksgiving Proclamation was an Executive Order. Executive Orders serve two functions. They may be used to change the processes within the Executive Branch, because the rules of the internal workings of the Executive Branch are up to the President. Or, an Executive Order may be used to issue a proclamation that is not legally binding.

No place in the Constitution does the document give the President the allowance through Executive Order to modify, repeal or make law. Executive Orders have been used often in history to modify law, but that is an unconstitutional executive action. The President does not have that kind of authority.

Since all of the **regulatory agencies** in the United States Government are a part of the executive branch, they are also bound by the same limitations. Like the President, regulatory agencies cannot act legislatively. Whenever they make a regulation that is not to directly regulate (put in good order and execute) an existing constitutional law, but to regulate an unconstitutional law, or to create a new law, it is outside the authorities granted to the executive branch by the Constitution.

On March 26, 2012, **Cap and Trade** auto emission legislation failed to pass through Congress. The Environmental Protection Agency began to auction greenhouse gas allowances anyway, effectively taxing emissions and regulating in a manner consistent with Cap and Trade should it have passed as a piece of legislation.

On December 20, 2010, when an Internet regulation bill failed to pass through Congress, the Federal Communications Commission announced it would regulate the Internet anyway. The FCC's new regulations controlled the way service providers may manage their network transmissions.

The regulatory agencies are under the **Executive Branch**, and are not a part of the **Legislative Branch**. A **Separation of Powers** exists, limiting each branch to only the authorities granted to it, and any part of the executive branch, including the regulatory agencies, do not have any **legislative authority**.

Extraordinary Occasions

"He may, on extraordinary occasions, convene both Houses, or either of them."

What is an extraordinary occasion? That would be an emergency, or during a time that matters are urgent. If the President believes a matter needs to be tended to, he can compel the Congress to be in session. In other words, it is constitutional when the President says something like, "I'm working, so Congress needs to be, too."

An extraordinary occasion can be wartime, budget discussions, or anything else the President determines to be an extraordinary occasion.

This includes when there is a "disagreement between them (the Houses)." The President may choose when the Houses will meet, as he feels is proper.

The President was expected to be a man of sacred honor, and it was believed he would use this authority wisely, and not in excess based on the whims of his ideology fancy.

In Article I, Section 5 the Constitution instructs that the Houses may not **adjourn** without the permission of the other House. But what if they refuse to allow the other House to adjourn? This is where the President comes in. If, because of disagreement, the Houses won't allow each other to adjourn, the President, if he feels it is necessary, "may adjourn them to such time as he shall think proper."

The President can compel the Houses to convene, or adjourn, as he feels necessary, as well.

He can't force them to make particular laws, per se, but he can make them be in session to get the work done, or take a break if he sees it as necessary.

As much as Congress has control over when they convene or adjourn, the President does have the authority if things are getting out of hand, or for whatever other reason he deems necessary, to override Congress' decision of when to convene or adjourn.

An appropriate example would be during wartime. The President's war powers enable him to put the military into action. If he feels there should be a declaration of war, would like to discuss his war plans with the Congress, or requires an apportionment of funding for the military effort, he can compel them to be in session. He cannot force Congress to declare war, or approve of his actions, but he can ensure they are in session so that the politics of war may be discussed.

If some of the members of Congress have a problem with the actions of the President so that they refuse to convene, he can then order Congress to convene so that he may discuss with them the issues at hand. If there are enough to qualify as a **quorum**, it is not necessary to compel the absent members to be in attendance. If Congress does not meet the requirement for a quorum, and the President believes the matter to be an extraordinary occasion, he can then compel the absent members to attend.

Receiving Ambassadors and Other Public Ministers

The President may invite important people to Washington, be they ambassadors, or other officials. Having the Chinese leader over for a dinner at the White House, or entertaining a group of diplomats, for example, is completely constitutional.

Regulatory Agencies

"He shall take Care that the Laws be faithfully executed."

This clause establishes the enforcement arm of the Executive Branch, which eventually became the **regulatory agencies**.

The clause is definitive in its instruction to the President regarding the execution of the laws of the United States by using the word "shall." The words "take Care" places an additional importance upon ensuring the laws of the United States are executed. The word "Care" in this clause is capitalized, placing emphasis on the word in a manner that we use today with *italics*. The laws must be executed with Care, and the Laws are expected to be "faithfully executed." Faithfully, without exception, without preferences, and without ideological interference.

Laws, under the federal government, are only valid laws, if they are constitutional. If the laws are not made in line with the authorities granted to the federal government by the Constitution, they are not legal laws. The executive branch shall "execute" the laws - constitutional laws.

Some people say the Executive Branch is supposed to "enforce" the laws - and in a sense that is correct. But really, the Executive Branch is supposed to execute the laws - ensure they are carried out - Laws that were put into place constitutionally.

We are the final arbiters of the Constitution, but there are other steps along the way to ensure that unconstitutional laws don't go into effect. The President represents one of those checks.

When President Obama determined DOMA was unconstitutional, and decided his agencies would not execute that law, he was acting constitutionally. The law is the law, however, and there is much discussion regarding if, considering that the President has decided the law is unconstitutional, he is compelled to ensure the law is executed. Also, if he refuses to execute constitutional law, calling it unconstitutional, it is our responsibility that he is removed, and replaced with somebody who will execute the laws appropriately.

The constitutional check in the hands of the President is not supposed to be utilized "after" a bill becomes a law, however. Unconstitutional laws are supposed to be caught before they get that far. The early President of the United States vetoed bills based on the constitutionality of the bill, and not necessarily because they disagreed with it ideologically.

In 1817, when President Madison deemed a public works bill unconstitutional, he simply refused to sign the bill into law, indicating in his written reason why he vetoed the bill that the proposed law was unconstitutional.

Congress can override a President's decision not to execute a law on the books because he deems it unconstitutional, just like they can override a **veto**. The States may also enforce the law if the President refuses. Article I, Section 8 grants to Congress the authority to "provide for calling forth the Militia *to execute the Laws of the Union.*"

The reverse is also true. If the President tries to execute law, calling it constitutional, when it is not constitutional, the States can ignore those federal laws, or **nullify** them.

Officers of the United States

"... and shall commission all the Officers of the United States. "

The "United States," as mentioned here in this final part of Article II, Section 3, does not mean The United States as a country. The United States is mentioned often in the Constitution, and whenever the "United States" is mentioned, it means one of two things. Either, it means "these States that are united," or the "federal government." Remember, to these early Americans, who considered themselves citizens of their States before they considered themselves "Americans," the United States meant "these States that are united," rather than a single, nationalistic, entity.

In this particular clause the "United States" means "federal government."

As a result of that definition, you could also say that this part of the Constitution reads: "and shall commission all the officers of the *federal government.*"

The Senate must give consent, as indicated in Article II, Section 2 and Article I, Section 3, to the appointment of these officers, therefore, giving the U.S. Senate (and therefore "the States" prior to the 17th Amendment) the power of oversight over the President's choices. This, in turn, means that *any and all* of the President's czars are unconstitutional. Officers of the United States are any office holders in the government exercising significant authority pursuant to the laws of the United States, and czars are included in that definition.

Impeachment

The President, Vice President and all civil Officers of the United States, shall be removed from Office on Impeachment for, and Conviction of, Treason, Bribery, or other high Crimes and Misdemeanors.

Impeachment is a term that means "To charge with misconduct." Removal from office does not happen unless the official is "convicted." In the case of the President and Vice President, the hearings are held by the U.S. Senate.

The reasons for impeachment may be for "Treason, Bribery, or other high Crimes and Misdemeanors."

Treason is defined in Article III, Section 3 as "levying War against them (these States that are United), or adhering to their Enemies, giving them Aid and Comfort."

Bribery is defined as meaning the exchange of money, promises, or other things, with someone in office, in order to influence that person's views or conduct.

The real confusion comes when we talk about the final part: "or other **high Crimes** and **Misdemeanors**."

When it comes to the phrase, "high crimes and misdemeanors" and the meaning of that phrase to the Founding Fathers, we must recognize the language used.

The word "high" in this context does not necessarily mean "more serious". It refers to those punishable offenses that only apply to high persons, meaning "public officials," or those who, because of their official status, are under special obligations that ordinary persons are not under.

For an official who was placed in office by the people, a crime offends the sense of justice of the people. When a public official commits these

119

crimes, they can be more serious than if the same crime is committed by a citizen, because of the trust put into the office the official holds.

One of those high crimes is **Perjury**, which is more than merely "lying under oath". Under the definitions used by the Founders, perjury also means "violation of one's oath (or affirmation)". Therefore, the President refusing to protect and defend the Constitution, could be considered perjury.

The President is bound by his oath of office in all matters until he leaves office to follow the oath of office. While he holds that office, he is always under oath, therefore his failing to uphold the oath, or lying at any time, constitutes perjury if it is not justified for national security.

An executive official is also ultimately responsible for any failures of his subordinates and for their violations of the oath he and they took, which means violations of the Constitution and the rights of persons. The President's subordinates include everyone in the executive branch, and their agents and contractors. It is not limited to those over whom he has direct supervision. He is not protected by **plausible deniability**. The President is legally responsible for everything that everyone in the executive branch is doing.

Impeachment and removal proceedings may then encompass a full range of offenses against the Constitution and against the rights of persons committed by subordinate officials and their agents which have not been adequately investigated or remedied.

The meaning of the phrase "high crimes and misdemeanors," was common knowledge during the time of the founding of this nation. The phrase imports a concept in English Common Law of the word "misdemeanors" that essentially means bad behavior.

"Misdemeanors" in the language of the Founders, then, did not necessarily refer to a criminal act as many believe, but opened up the opportunity for impeachment of the President should he be guilty of gross incompetence, gross negligence, or outright distasteful actions which clearly show "malevolence toward this country and constitution, which is unabated."

The subject of impeachment was adopted from the English concept of this idea. In England impeachment was a device to remove from office someone who abused his office or misbehaved, but who was protected by the Crown.

James Madison said during the federal convention that impeachment ought to be used to reach a bad officer sheltered by the President and to remove him "even against the will of the President; so that the declaration in the Constitution was intended as a supplementary security for the good behavior of the public officers."

At first, during the debates in the Constitutional Convention, the grounds for removal of the president were to be upon conviction "of mal-practice or neglect of duty" and subsequently this was changed to "Treason, or bribery." George Mason objected to this limitation, saying that the term did not encompass all the conduct which should be grounds for removal. So, Mason proposed adding the term **maladministration** following "bribery."

Madison objected, believing the term to be too vague, or too general. Mason then suggested "other high crimes and misdemeanors," which was adopted without further recorded debate.

Chapter 14

Judicial Branch

Among the reasons for the writing of The United States Constitution as listed in the Preamble, in addition to establishing a federal government in order to form a more perfect union for the United States of America, was to establish justice. Article III establishes the federal court system. Article I, Section 8 gives the Congress the power to "constitute tribunals inferior to the supreme Court." Given the power to establish these courts, Congress also has the authority to do away with any of these inferior courts. This power of Congress is repeated in Article III, Section 1 during the first sentence.

When reading Article III, one must keep in mind the fact that the article was specifically written to affect the federal court system, not the state courts. The authorities contained within this article, and the restrictions thereof, are to be applied to the federal courts, not the state courts. One must also bear in mind, as one reads this article, the additional limits placed on the federal courts by the 11th Amendment. No case against a state by citizens of another state, or by the citizens or subjects of a foreign state, shall be heard by a federal court.

The decision to establish a federal judiciary occurred late in the federal convention, because there were a number of delegates arguing against the creation of a federal judicial branch. They feared the federal judiciary would be used by the federal government to force the **rule of man** upon the States, rather than protect State Sovereignty by maintaining the **rule of law** as presented by the Constitution.

John Jay, the first Chief Justice of the United States Supreme Court, resigned his position in 1795, disappointed in how few powers the federal courts had, so that he could pursue a governorship in the State of New York. After his term as governor ended, John Adams, hoping to appoint a new chief justice who was a strong advocate for a strengthened federal government, approached Jay and asked him if he would be Chief Justice again. John Jay turned Adams down. He said the Court lacked "the energy, weight, and dignity which are essential to its affording due support to the national government." He also did not wish to serve under Thomas Jefferson, the victor in the 1800 Presidential Election, who was an advocate of limited government, and a judicial branch that existed as the weakest of the three branches of government.

Good Behavior

The conventional understanding of the terms of federal judges is that they receive lifetime appointments because no time restriction is placed upon them in the Constitution. The only limitation on term placed upon the judges can be found in Article III, Section 1 where the Constitution states that judges, both of the supreme and inferior courts, "shall hold their offices during good behavior." It is commonly understood that bad behavior would only include unlawful activities.

As we learned regarding **impeachment**, bad behavior does not exclusively include only illegal activities. Like all other federal officials, the judges take an oath to preserve, protect, and defend the United States Constitution, which is the Law of the Land. Bad behavior, then, may include unconstitutional actions, or failure to preserve, protect, and defend the Constitution.

Impeachment by Congress may be used if a judge acts in bad behavior. If a judge refuses to attend the hearing at the behest of the United States Senate, the federal marshal may be used to retrieve the judge, and compel them to stand before Congress to answer for their bad behavior, which may include unconstitutional rulings.

Limits

The powers of the federal courts "*shall extend to all cases, in law and equity, arising under this Constitution, the laws of the United States, and Treaties made, or which shall be made, under their authority.*"

The federal courts, in other words, may hear all cases that fall within their authority. These cases are regarding those in which the federal government has authority, be it by laws passed within the authorities granted to the federal government by the Constitution, or regarding issues related to treaties made that have been signed by the President and ratified by the U.S. Senate. The courts may not hear cases that are regarding issues not within the authorities of the federal government.

A recent example would be Proposition 8 in California. The proposition changed the State Constitution to read that marriage is between a man and a woman. Marriage is not an issue that falls under the authorities of the federal government as expressly granted by the Constitution. Therefore, the case should not have gone beyond the State Supreme Court. The federal courts hearing the case regarding Proposition 8 acted unconstitutionally, and the State of California's governor had the constitutional right to disregard all rulings by the federal courts. The action of ignoring the rulings is a type of **nullification**.

Other limitations have been placed upon the federal courts as well. The 11th Amendment changes the intent of Article III. As limited as the courts were supposed to be, the Founding Fathers realized the courts weren't limited enough, and as a result, the 11th Amendment wound up being ratified in 1795. The 11th Amendment was encouraged by a federal case called *Chisolm v. Georgia* (1793).

Chisolm v. Georgia (1793)

The problems of federal intrusion on the states via the federal court system arose in the case of *Chisholm v. Georgia* in 1793, which eventually led to the proposal, and ratification, of the 11th Amendment. A citizen of South Carolina sued Georgia for the value of clothing supplied by a merchant during the Revolutionary War. After Georgia refused to appear, claiming immunity as a sovereign state, as per the Constitution (Article III, Section 2) the federal courts took the case. The **nationalist** view of the judges deemed that in this case Georgia was not a sovereign State, therefore the Supreme Court entered a default judgment against Georgia. What ensued was a conflict between federal jurisdiction and state sovereignty that reminded the **anti-federalists** of their fears of a centralized federal government consolidating the States, and destroying their right to individual sovereignty.

Realizing the clause in Article III gave the federal courts too much power over State Sovereignty, Congress immediately proposed the 11th Amendment in order to take away federal court jurisdiction in suits commenced against a State by citizens of another State or of a foreign country. This is the first instance in which a Supreme Court decision was superseded by a constitutional amendment, and evidence the Framers recognized the **legislative branch**, and the States, as being a more powerful part of government over the federal judiciary.

Authorities

The Tenth Amendment to the Constitution of the United States of America states that, *"The powers not delegated to the United States by the Constitution, or prohibited by it to the States, are reserved to the States respectively, or to the people."* The federal courts are included in that, as being a part of the United States federal government. Federal courts can only hear cases that fall within the constitutional authorities for the federal government.

When one understands the importance of protecting State Sovereignty, and that the courts are very limited in their scope and power, Article III becomes much simpler to understand.

As stated earlier in this section, the first sentence of Article III, Section 2, reads: *The judicial Power shall extend to all Cases, in Law and Equity, arising under this Constitution, the Laws of the United States* (which are only supposed to be passed if they are within the authorities granted by the Constitution), *and Treaties made . . .*

Notice the phrase, "arising under this Constitution." If the case does not involve the federal government as one of the parties, or is not regarding an issue that falls under the authorities of the U.S. Constitution, the federal courts simply cannot take the case. In fact, by taking the case, the court is sending the message that they have authority over the issue being addressed in the case. When a federal court is not authorized to take a case, and then refuses to hear the case as a result of a lack of authority, the State Supreme Court is the highest those particular cases can go.

Judicial Review

During the forging or the United States, federal judges maintained that the federal courts should have the power of **judicial review**, or the power to determine the constitutionality of laws. In response to the judicial urgings for the powers to judge the extent of the federal government's powers, in the Kentucky and Virginia Resolutions of 1798, Thomas Jefferson and James Madison warned us that giving the federal government through its courts the power of judicial review would be a power that would continue to grow, regardless of elections, putting at risk the all important separation of powers, and other much-touted limits on power. The final arbiters of the Constitution are not the courts, argued these Founding Fathers who were believers in the limiting principles of the U.S. Constitution. The power of the federal government must be checked by State governments, and the people. The States and the People are the enforcers and protectors of the U.S. Constitution.

In today's society it is commonly accepted that one of the roles of the federal court system is to interpret the Constitution, and issue rulings determining the constitutionality of laws. The Constitution does not grant this authority. The power of judicial review was given to the courts by themselves.

During John Adams' final moments in the presidency, he appointed a whole host of "midnight judges" (appointing 16 Federalist circuit judges and 42 Federalist justices of the peace to offices created by the Judiciary Act of 1801) in the hopes of retaining Federalist control of the courts as Jefferson's Democratic-Republicans gained control of the Congress, and Jefferson himself accepted the presidency.

While Adams was still in office, most of the commissions for these newly appointed judges were delivered. However, unable to deliver all of them before Adams' term expired, some of them were left to be delivered by the incoming Secretary of State, James Madison. Jefferson ordered them not to be delivered, and without the commissions delivered, the remaining new appointees were unable to assume the offices and duties to which they had been appointed by Adams. In Jefferson's opinion, the undelivered commissions were void.

One of those judges was a man named William Marbury. He sued, and the case worked its way up to the Supreme Court. After all of the dust settled, on February 24, 1803, the Court rendered a unanimous (4-0) decision that Marbury had the right to his commission, but the court did not have the power to force Madison to deliver the commission. Chief Justice John Marshall wrote the opinion of the court, and in that opinion he wrote that the federal court system has the power of judicial review. Rather than simply applying the law to the cases, Marshall had determined, based on case law, that the courts have the authority to determine the validity of the law as well. This opinion, however, went against all of the limitations placed on the courts by the Constitution.

One of the most obvious fundamental principles of the Constitution is the limitations it places on the federal government. The Constitution is designed not to tell the federal government what it can't do, but to offer

enumerated powers to which the authorities of the federal government are limited. The powers are granted by the States, and any additional authorities must also be approved by the States. The process by which this can be accomplished is through the amendment process. It requires three-quarters of the States to ratify an amendment.

The power of judicial review, or the authority to determine if laws are constitutional, was not granted to the courts by the States in the Constitution. The courts took that power upon themselves through Justice Marshall's opinion of *Marbury v. Madison.*

The federal courts are a part of the federal government. The Constitution was designed to limit the authorities of the federal government by granting only a limited number of powers. Judicial review enables the federal government, through the courts, to determine if the laws that the federal government made are constitutional. In other words, the federal government, through judicial review, can determine for itself what its own authorities are.

The idea that the federal court system has the authority to interpret the Constitution, and can decide if a law is constitutional or not, is unconstitutional, and is simply an attempt by those that believe in big government to gain power, and work towards a more centralized big federal governmental system.

Original Jurisdiction

In Article III, Section 2, Clause 2 the Constitution reads: "*In all Cases affecting Ambassadors, other public Ministers and Consuls, and those in which a State shall be Party, the supreme Court shall have original Jurisdiction.*"

What this means is that in all cases regarding ambassadors, and other public ministers and consuls, and in all cases in which a State is a party in the case, the federal appellate courts cannot accept the case. Such cases must bypass the federal appellate system, and go straight to the Supreme Court. Since one of those stipulations is in regards to cases "*in which a State shall be a Party,*" that means that the case "*U.S. v. Arizona,*" where the federal government sued Arizona to block the State's 2010 immigration law, was unconstitutionally filed for the inferior federal courts to hear the case. The Supreme Court has **original jurisdiction**. Therefore, when the district court ruled in July of 2010 on the case, and struck down parts of the Arizona immigration law, not only did that court not have jurisdiction to hear the case in the first place, but the very act of striking down portions of the law was unconstitutional. After all, Article I, Section 1 grants the legislative branch all legislative powers, and those powers would include the ability to strike down law. The courts were not vested with any legislative powers, and therefore cannot strike down laws, or portions of laws.

Trial by Jury

Article III, Section II, Clause 3 sets up the right to a trial by jury, except in the cases of impeachment.

This clause also requires that a trial must be held in the State where the crime was committed. If the crime was not committed in any particular State, then the trial is held in such a place as set forth by the Congress.

Trial by jury is a right that is deeply embedded in the character of the American System, a guarantee mentioned in Article III, Amendment 5, Amendment 6, and Amendment 7. In other countries, crimes with penalties of fewer than two years are not normally tried by jury. Blackstone, the 18th century English scholar of law, went so far as to indicate that in English law, trial by jury was a privilege, not a right.

The American pre-trial phase regarding the choosing of jurors is even unique in American Law, where prospective jurors may be questioned not only on whether they have any personal interest in a case, but also about their general beliefs and prejudices as well. A judge can excuse anyone whose biased attitudes will interfere with his or her duties as a juror. The process in American law is designed to which weeds out biased jurors, a typically absent process in other countries, including England and Canada.

American jurors, compared to their counterparts in other countries, have so much power that they can even both decide the facts of the case and interpret the meaning of the law, regardless of what the judge told them. If the jury believes the law to be unjust, the jurors may actually nullify the law. This is known as **jury nullification**.

Jury nullification is an unspoken protocol by design. Generally, the courts disallow defense lawyers from even mentioning jury nullification as a possibility. Judges prefer jurors to follow the general protocols of the court, rather than deliver independent verdicts. In fact, the United States Supreme Court has routinely ruled that judges have no obligation to inform juries about jury nullification.

Jury nullification is permitted to exist as an option to all juries, yet this option cannot be discussed in most courtrooms.

The power of jury nullification is kept a secret because of its ability to upset the system. The judges and lawyers perch themselves above the crowd, herding juries around like compelled sheep, without the juries ever realizing they have the authority to right the wrongs inherent in our justice system. How powerful is it for a jury to be able to say, "Sure, he's guilty, but the case is dismissed because the law is unfair, or unjust."

Treason

Article III, Section 3 defines **treason**, as well as granting the power to Congress to declare the punishment. Treason is defined as, "*levying War against them [the States], or in adhering to their Enemies, giving them Aid and Comfort.*" In order to be convicted of treason, according to this clause, there must be two witnesses that directly observed the "*overt Act,*" or the accused must give confession in open court.

When the Constitution says that "*no attainder of treason shall work corruption of blood, or forfeiture except during the life of the person attained,*" it means that the punishment cannot be inherited or passed down (**corruption of blood**), nor shall the person be denied due process (attainder).

Corruption of blood also means that all inheritable qualities are destroyed, and the Founding Fathers did not believe this English practice should be an American one.

No forfeiture meant that despite treason, the properties of the person could not be forfeited to the government. The property would remain as property of the individual, or remain with family. Even in the case of treason, it was not believed the government should be able to seize assets or property.

Chapter 15

Concerning the States

Full Faith and Credit

Article IV, Section 1 begins with The **Full Faith and Credit** Clause. The clause reads, *"Full Faith and Credit shall be given in each State to the public Acts, Records, and judicial Proceedings of every other State. And the Congress may by general Laws prescribe the Manner in which such Acts, Records and Proceedings shall be proved, and the Effect thereof."*

In simple, modern day language, under the Full Faith and Credit Clause judgments rendered in one State are acknowledged in others; when a U.S. citizen resolves an issue within one of the States that resolution must be recognized by all other States.

The Founding Fathers originally intended, with the Full Faith and Credit Clause, to protect the self-government autonomy of the States, while also promoting the union of the sovereign States as well. To do this, the Founding Fathers needed to make sure that judicial rulings in one State would be respected by all States, because otherwise there would be a substantial opportunity for abuse. Doing so affirmed the autonomy of the individual States, while also ensuring that the States remained unified.

Without the Full Faith and Credit Clause, something as simple as a marriage would not be recognized outside the State where the proceeding took place. If the married couple moved to another state, it would be necessary to marry all over again, otherwise they would still be considered unmarried. However, thanks to the Full Faith and Credit Clause, the State that serves as the new home of the transplanted married couple recognizes the marriage contract agreed upon in the State of origin.

The Full Faith and Credit Clause also protects against abusive litigation.

If someone in one State sues someone and the court delivers a valid judgment in favor of the defendant, the person who filed the suit cannot file the same suit in another State against the same person. Under the Full Faith and Credit Clause, the outcome of the suit in the first State is recognized and considered to be the final judgment. Likewise, someone who is ruled against in litigation in a State cannot flee to another State to evade punishment, because the ruling in the first State's court is still valid in the new State.

As a result of the Full Faith and Credit Clause, professionals like doctors and lawyers only need to go to school once. As they move to new States, they can apply for **reciprocity** in certification so that they can practice in their new location. State privileges like drivers licenses also benefit from the Full Faith and Credit Clause, because when people move to different States, they can renew their driving licenses in the new State without having to go through drivers' education a second time, as long as the standards for licensure are similar between the two States.

Privileges and Immunities

Article IV, Section 2, Clause 1 gives the people of each State all the same privileges and immunities uniformly in each State. In other words, if a Texan moved to California, the Texan must be treated by California in no different manner than the State treats Californians. A State could not pass a law keeping Texans out of their State, but letting others in. This violates the Constitution. A State cannot play favoritism in such a manner for any reason. All persons must be treated uniformly in the eyes of the law. This is the clause the 14th Amendment's Equal Protection Clause sought to broaden, in order to ensure that the former slaves would also be afforded the same protection, privileges, and immunities.

Extradition

Article IV, Section 2, Clause 2 provides that "*A person charged in any state with treason, felony, or other crime, who shall flee from justice, and be found in another state, shall on demand of the executive authority of the state from which he fled, be delivered up, to be removed to the state having jurisdiction of the crime.*"

Fugitives that flee a State from justice to another State will be **extradited** on the demand of executive authority (governor) of the State from which the person fled from. The Constitution, in this clause, demands the extradition of fugitives who have committed "treason, **felony** or other crime," which means that it includes all acts prohibited by the laws of a State, including misdemeanors and small, or petty, offenses.

Since the word "shall" is used regarding the extradition order by the governor of the State, that means the extradition order will not be questioned. That also means the accused cannot defend himself against the charges in the extraditing State. The fugitive may only defend himself against the charges in the State receiving him.

The courts have determined that the accused may prevent extradition by offering clear evidence that he was not in the State from which he allegedly fled at the time of the crime in the case, *Hyatt v. People ex rel. Corkran* (1903).

Fugitive Slaves

Article IV, Section 2, Clause 3 is obsolete because of the abolition of slavery, as per the 13th Amendment. During the era the Constitution was written, slavery remained in place, and slaves were seen as property by the States in which slavery was legal. The Constitution, as a compromise to assure that southern States ratified the document, included Article IV, Section 2, Clause 3, as a compromise, which demanded that escaped slaves be returned to their owners in the south, even if that slave was in a northern State.

The Fugitive Slave Act of 1850 supported this clause of the Constitution, hoping to ensure under penalty of law that the slaves were in fact returned should they turn up in the north. Northern States were refusing to return escaped slaves, and the federal government refused to enforce the Fugitive Slave Act and the Constitution, creating, in the minds of the Southern States, a constitutional crisis.

Nullification is often blamed for its part in the onset of the American Civil War. Those that argue nullification was a part of bringing about the **War Between the States** will argue that the southern States were guilty of nullifying perfectly reasonable federal laws. In reality, the southern States did not nullify any federal law. It was the northern States that actively nullified federal law. They nullified The Fugitive Slave Act by ignoring the legislation, and refusing to abide by it. However, since The Fugitive Slave Act was constitutional, the nullification of the law by the northern States was unlawful, and unconstitutional. Threatened by the fact that the northern States were ignoring constitutional law, the federal government was refusing to enforce the law, and anti-slave candidate Abraham Lincoln had won the presidential election without even being on the ballot in the South, eleven southern States withdrew from the union in 1860.

New States

Article IV, Section 3, Clause 1 gives Congress the authority to admit new States. If a new State is formed within the borders of an existing State, from a portion of an existing State, or by combining two States, then the State legislatures of all States affected must also get involved. This provision came into play is when West Virginia was formed from part of Virginia during the **Civil War**. The Virginia State legislature had to approve the formation of the new State of West Virginia before the new State could claim it was a separate sovereign State.

In California, there has been a number of recommendations for breaking up the large State, from a 2014 suggestion of forming six States from the former Golden State, to thirteen counties that threatened to secede in 2010 as suggested by a local politician. If any of these plans for new States out of the existing State of California had an opportunity to follow through with their threat, the approval process would still need to go through the existing California State Legislature. The loss of taxation, and representation in Congress, would probably convince the legislature to deny losing any portion of their State to the formation of a new State.

Territories and Federal Property

Article IV, Section 3, Clause 2 gives the Federal Government "*power over the territory and property of the United States.*" Territories like Puerto Rico fall under this clause, treating the territories not as individual sovereign States, but as territories under the control of the U.S. Government. Territories still enjoy a certain amount of autonomy, but ultimately, their governance falls under the authorities granted to Congress. Washington, D.C., also falls under this clause, which means that Congress has authority over the functions of the city. In reality, Washington, D.C., was supposed to only be the seat of government, and was not supposed to contain any residences. Many of the Framers envisioned Washington, D.C., as being a thriving **commercial center**.

Border Security and Insurrection

Article IV, Section 4 reads, *"The United States shall guarantee to every State in this Union a Republican Form of Government,"* meaning that each State may have its own constitution, as well as a representative government based on the rule of law.

The second part of Article IV, Section 4 provides that the United States *"shall protect each of them [the States] against Invasion; and on Application of the Legislature, or of the Executive (when the Legislature cannot be convened) against domestic violence."*

The federal government, according to the final clause of Article IV, must protect each State from invasion, which, in line with the **Necessary and Proper** clause of Article I, Section 8, is a firm directive to the federal government to keep the national borders secure so as to protect the States from foreign invasion. If executive agencies fail to take the actions necessary to secure the border in order to protect the States from invasion, the militia can be called into service by either the Congress, or the governor of the State being invaded, in order to repel the invasion.

The federal government, in this clause, is also tasked with quelling domestic violence. This part of the clause refers to insurrection, and it is likely the writing of this clause was directly influenced by the occurrence of **Shays' Rebellion** in 1786.

Chapter 16

Amendments and Conventions

Article V is the section in the Constitution that provides the people and the States the opportunity to change the law of the land if needed by establishing the amendment process. Originally, only the States were going to be able to propose amendments. On the second to the last day of the Constitutional Convention, the Founding Fathers added as an afterthought to allow the Congress to propose amendments as well. The amendment process is the only process through which the Constitution may be altered.

Amendments, according to Article V, may be proposed by either two-thirds of both Houses of the United States Congress, or by a national convention of States. Amendments must then be ratified by approval of three-fourths of the States either through their legislatures, or through ratifying conventions.

Amendments proposed by a national convention is a process known as an **Article V. Convention**.

Current opinion regarding an Article V. Convention varies. Some people and groups have warned against such a convention, fearing a runaway convention that could be used to re-write the Constitution. The Constitution does not allow for a runaway convention. In an Article V. Convention, only amendments may be proposed.

The call for an Article V. Convention is nothing new. Forty-nine States have called for it, many of those calls beginning over a century ago. Over 700 applications have been made. The convention has never taken place because Congress will not set a time and place (the only federal duty in an Article V. Convention), for fear of the people proposing amendments, and the States ratifying them, that would limit the powers of the federal government. Centralized systems do not like it when the individual mind gets involved, and demands change.

There are three kinds of conventions. A con-con, which is a Constitutional Convention, and there was only one, held back in 1787, and there should only be one in our history. In addition to the con-con, and the Article V. Convention, is a kind of convention called **Republic Review**. A Republic Review may be used to audit the federal government, determine what is unconstitutional, and then form a plan of action to alter the federal government so that it falls in line with the principles of the United States Constitution. An Article V. Convention, or the States working together through nullification, could be the result of a Republic Review. The strategy to convene a Republic Review convention lies primarily with "We the People."

Amendments, no matter how they are proposed, require three-quarters approval from the States. This approval process is called "ratification." Ratification is the failsafe, according to Alexander Hamilton in his Federalist 85, against conventions that may be used to rewrite the Constitution. Any change to the Constitution is possible, as prescribed by Article V, as long as the amendment is capable of receiving three-quarters of the States' ratification votes.

The only exception to any amendment being possible is addressed at the end of Article V. According to the Constitution, no amendment, without the consent of the State in question, may deprive a State of equal suffrage in the Senate. This testifies to the importance, in the minds of the Framers, to the need for the United States Senate to remain unchanged, with the Senators being appointed by the State legislatures.

Since the Constitution is a document that contains **express powers** for the federal government, granted by the States, the only way to change or add authorities is through the amendment process, with State approval. When it is understood that the original authorities granted to the federal government were granted to the central government by the States, it is appropriate that it takes three-quarters of the States to ratify an amendment. When Congress proposes an amendment, it is literally a case of the federal government asking for permission of the States to have a new authority, and approval by the States requires three-quarters agreement.

Chapter 17

Debt and Supremacy

Prior Debt

Article VI begins with "*All Debts contracted and Engagements entered into, before the Adoption of this Constitution, shall be as valid against the United States under this Constitution, as under the Confederation.*"

The first clause of Article VI legally transfers all debts and engagements under the Articles of Confederation into the new government. This is not only the debts and engagements by the United States Government under the Articles of Confederation, but also includes all debts of each of the several States. After ratification of the Constitution, each and every State would be debt free, and all debt would be held by the federal government. This condition, according to the Constitution, would be the last time the States would legally be in debt. In Article I, Section 10, the Constitution forbids the States from issuing bills of credit.

Alexander Hamilton, the first Treasury Secretary, suggested that the United States should remain in perpetual debt. Maintaining a perpetual debt, he explained, would be a mechanism that could assist in holding together the union, since States would be unlikely to secede when they are responsible for a part of the national debt.

Thomas Jefferson disagreed with Hamilton. He recognized the necessity to maintain the ability to borrow, and the need for credit, but found a national debt to be a potentially dangerous proposition.

"*Though much an enemy to the system of borrowing, yet I feel strongly the necessity of preserving the power to borrow. Without this, we might be overwhelmed by another nation, merely by the force of its credit.*" -- Thomas Jefferson to the Commissioners of the Treasury, 1788.

"*I am anxious about everything which may affect our credit. My wish would be, to possess it in the highest degree, but to use it little. Were we*

139

without credit, we might be crushed by a nation of much inferior resources, but possessing higher credit." -- Thomas Jefferson to George Washington, 1788.

"*Though I am an enemy to the using our credit but under absolute necessity, yet the possessing a good credit I consider as indispensable in the present system of carrying on war. The existence of a nation having no credit is always precarious.*" -- Thomas Jefferson to James Madison, 1788.

"*I wish it were possible to obtain a single amendment to our Constitution. I would be willing to depend on that alone for the reduction of the administration of our government; I mean an additional article taking from the Federal Government the power of borrowing. I now deny their power of making paper money or anything else a legal tender. I know that to pay all proper expenses within the year would, in case of war, be hard on us. But not so hard as ten wars instead of one. For wars could be reduced in that proportion; besides that the State governments would be free to lend their credit in borrowing quotas.*" -- Thomas Jefferson to John Taylor, 1798.

"*I sincerely believe... that the principle of spending money to be paid by posterity under the name of funding is but swindling futurity on a large scale.*" -- Thomas Jefferson to John Taylor, 1816.

"*If the American people ever allow private banks to control the issue of their currency, first by inflation, then by deflation, the banks...will deprive the people of all property until their children wake-up homeless on the continent their fathers conquered.... The issuing power should be taken from the banks and restored to the people, to whom it properly belongs.*" -- Thomas Jefferson in the debate over the Re-charter of the Bank Bill (1809)

"*I believe that banking institutions are more dangerous to our liberties than standing armies.*" -- Thomas Jefferson

"*... The modern theory of the perpetuation of debt has drenched the earth with blood, and crushed its inhabitants under burdens ever accumulating.*" -- Thomas Jefferson

The Supremacy Clause

Article VI, Clause 2: *"This Constitution, and the Laws of the United States which shall be made in Pursuance thereof; and all Treaties made, or which shall be made, under the Authority of the United States, shall be the supreme Law of the Land; and the Judges in every State shall be bound thereby, any Thing in the Constitution or Laws of any State to the Contrary notwithstanding."*

Perhaps one of the most misunderstood and misapplied clauses of the U.S. Constitution, the **Supremacy Clause** has been used in line with the concept of federal supremacy. Federal supremacy is a concept our first Chief Justice, John Jay, believed in. During his stint on the Supreme Court Jay worked feverously to establish broader powers for the courts, and to transform the federal government into a national government. He quit the Supreme Court after failing, pursuing an opportunity to be governor of New York.

Chief Justice John Marshall spent his 36 years on the Supreme Court attempting to establish, and expand federal supremacy, and largely succeeded. Marshall is embraced by statists as the one to develop federal supremacy in his opinion of the *Mcculloch v. Maryland* case in 1819 where the Court invalidated a Maryland law that taxed all banks in the State, including a branch of Alexander Hamilton's creation, the national Bank of the United States. Marshall held that although none of the enumerated powers of Congress explicitly authorized the incorporation of the **national bank**, the Necessary and Proper Clause provided the basis for Congress's action. Marshall concluded that "*the government of the Union, though limited in its power, is supreme within its sphere of action.*"

During the 1930s, under Franklin Delano Roosevelt, the Court invoked the Supremacy Clause to give the federal government broader national power. The federal government cannot involuntarily be subjected to the laws of any State, they proclaimed, and is therefore supreme in all laws and actions.

The legally, and commonly, accepted definition, as a result of the courts and the persistence of, regarding the Supremacy Clause, is that all federal laws supersede all State laws.

The commonly understood definition of the Supremacy Clause is in error. To understand the true meaning of this clause, one must pay close attention to the language used.

If the federal government has a law on the books, and the law was made under the authorities granted by the States in the United States Constitution, and a State, or city, passes a law that contradicts that constitutional federal law, the federal government's law is supreme based on the Supremacy Clause. However, if the federal law is unconstitutional because it was made outside constitutional authority, it is an illegal law, and therefore is not supreme over similar State laws.

An example of the federal government acting upon the assumption that all federal law is supreme over State law is when the medical marijuana laws emerged in California in 1996 after the passage of Proposition 215. Though I do not necessarily agree with the legalization of the casual recreational use of marijuana, and believe "weed" should be heavily regulated like any other pharmaceutical drug if being used for medicinal purposes, the actual constitutional legality of the issue illustrates my point quite well.

California's law legalizing marijuana for medicinal purposes was contrary to all federal law that identified marijuana as being illegal in all applications. Using the commonly accepted authority of the federal government based on their definition of the Supremacy Clause, federal agents began raiding and shutting down medical marijuana labs in California. However, there is no place in the U.S. Constitution that gives the federal government the authority to regulate drugs, nor has there been an amendment passed to grant that authority to the federal government. From a constitutional point of view, then, the raids on medical marijuana labs in California were unconstitutional actions by the federal government.

The Supremacy Clause applies only to federal laws that are constitutionally authorized. Therefore, federal drug laws are unconstitutional. As a result, California's medical marijuana laws are constitutional because they are not contrary to any constitutionally authorized federal laws.

Language plays an important part in the Constitution, and the Supremacy Clause is no different. The clause indicates that State laws cannot be contrary to constitutionally authorized federal laws. For example, Article I, Section 8, Clause 4 states that it is the job of the U.S. Congress *to establish an uniform rule of naturalization.* The word "uniform" means that the rules for naturalization must apply to all immigrants, and to all States, in the same way. If a State was to then pass a law that granted citizenship through the naturalization process in a way not consistent with federal law, the State would be guilty of violating the Supremacy Clause.

In the case of Arizona's immigration law, S.B. 1070 in 2010, the argument by the federal government that Arizona's law is contrary to federal law was an erroneous argument. Assuming, for just a moment, that the federal government has complete authority over immigration (which is not true since immigration is one of those issues in which the federal government and the States have **concurrent powers**), Arizona's law would then need to be identical to federal law. And in most ways, the Arizona law was similar to federal immigration law. The only difference was that Arizona's law disallowed racial profiling.

The federal government's argument when the United States Department of Justice filed a lawsuit against the state of Arizona in the U.S. District Court for the District of Arizona on July 6, 2010, was that the law must be declared invalid because it interfered with the immigration regulations exclusively vested in the federal government. Therefore, a State cannot enforce immigrations laws if the federal government decides not to, nor can a State pass law regarding an issue that the federal government has sole authority over. In this way, Arizona was considered to be acting "contrary" to the federal government.

Article I, Section 9, Clause 1, and Article I, Section 10 in the final clause, provides that States hold concurrent authorities regarding immigration, and securing the border. Therefore, the federal government's argument that they held sole authority over the issue was in error.

Eric Holder, when he filed the lawsuit in the U.S. District Court also acted unconstitutionally because in Article III, Section 2, the Constitution states that all cases *"in which a State shall be Party, the supreme Court shall have original Jurisdiction."* Since the case was the *United States v. Arizona,* the case, constitutionally, could only be filed with the United States Supreme Court.

The language in Article VI, Clause 2 reveals clearly that only laws made under the authorities granted to the federal government have supremacy.

Article VI, Clause 2 reads, *"This Constitution, and the Laws of the United States which shall be made in Pursuance thereof; and all Treaties made, or which shall be made, under the Authority of the United States, shall be the supreme Law of the Land; and the Judges in every State shall be bound thereby, any Thing in the Constitution or Laws of any State to the Contrary notwithstanding."*

The clause establishes three things as being potentially the supreme law of the land. First, *"This Constitution."* Second, *"Laws of the United States which shall be made in pursuance thereof."* And Third, all *Treaties made, or which shall be made."*

"This Constitution" is the supreme law of the land. Understanding that first part of the clause is easy.

The second one has a condition attached to it. *"Laws of the United States which shall be made in pursuance thereof."*

In pursuance thereof? In pursuance of what?

Of "This Constitution."

Therefore, if a law is not made "in pursuance" of "This Constitution," then the law is an illegal law, and cannot possibly be the supreme law of the land. Unconstitutional laws are not the supreme law of the land, which reveals that not federal laws are the supreme law of the land. Illegal law made outside the authorities granted by the Constitution of the United States cannot legally be the supreme law of the land.

After "pursuance thereof" in the clause, a semicolon is used. The semicolon separates "Treaties" from the "Laws of the United States." The separation by the semicolon means that "in pursuance thereof" applies to "Laws of the United States," but not to "Treaties." This means that treaties not in line with the principles of the Constitution can be accepted as the supreme law of the land.

The concern over treaties was not great, because the Senate was the voice of the States, and the States are the final arbiters of the Constitution. If the States are willing to ratify what would be considered an unconstitutional treaty, they must be given the chance. Therefore, "in pursuance thereof" does not apply to treaties.

The importance of this part of the Supremacy Clause revealed itself during Jefferson's Louisiana Purchase in 1803. As discussed in Article I, Section 8, Clause 17, the federal government does not have the authority to buy or own land unless it is purchased from a State, by the consent of the State legislature, for the purpose of needful buildings. The details of the Louisiana Purchase did not fit Article I, Section 8, Clause 17's requirement. To get around that, President Thomas Jefferson negotiated the Louisiana Purchase with France through treaties. Since treaties were ratified by the States through the Senate, it kept the States involved in the process, and made the purchase the law of the land, even though technically it was not, constitutional.

Oath or Affirmation to Support This Constitution

Article VI, Clause 3 indicates that all elected officials are bound to support the Constitution by oath or affirmation. An **oath** is to God, and an affirmation is not a sworn oath to God. This was offered because the Founding Fathers recognized that not everyone believed in God, and that there were some religions that believed swearing to God to be a sin.

The final clause of Article VI also states that there shall be no religious test to serve. This was not the case inside the States. This was a provision only required of the federal government. At the State level, established churches, and religious tests were the norm. The Danbury Baptists in Connecticut appealed to President Jefferson because they felt they were being mistreated by the Puritans. The Baptists felt they were being treated like second class citizens in a State dominated by the Puritan Church. Jefferson replied that the federal government could not help them. It was a State issue.

Alexis de Tocqueville observed when he visited the United Sates in the 1830s that religious freedom had truly come to The States. In America, the politicians prayed, and the pastors preached politics, yet neither controlled the other. He concluded America's greatness was a result of the good in America, coining the term American **Exceptionalism**.

Chapter 18

Ratification

To ratify the Constitution, the Founding Fathers determined it should require the ratification votes of at least nine States. This meant that both northern and southern States would be needed to ratify the Constitution. The number 9 of 13 represented two-thirds of the total States at the time.

When reviewing the list of signers of the Constitution, one may notice that Rhode Island was not present, and only Alexander Hamilton signed for New York. The anti-federalists feared a federal government, afraid that the system could become centralized, and ultimately tyrannical. Such a big government system would infringe upon **States' Rights**, and the sovereignty of the States was a very important aspect of the new nation. The federal government was only supposed to protect and preserve the union, and nothing more.

The New York anti-federalists were so angry over the proceedings that they all got up and walked out, leaving Hamilton alone. Later, in the hopes of convincing the anti-federalists in New York to support the new Constitution, the 85 Federalist Papers were written by James Madison, Alexander Hamilton, and John Jay.

Chapter 19

Introduction to the Bill of Rights

The Bill of Rights does not guarantee your rights, nor was it designed to allow the federal government to protect your rights. The language used in the first ten amendments is clear. The 1st Amendment begins, "Congress shall make no law..." The 2nd Amendment ends with the words, "...shall not be infringed." The 3rd Amendment begins, "No Soldier shall..." The key phrase in the 4th Amendment is "shall not be violated." The entire Bill of Rights was designed to confirm what the first seven articles had already established. The federal government was granted only certain authorities, and for the purpose of clarity, the Bill of Rights was written to reinforce the concept that the federal government has no business infringing upon the rights of the people. The federal government is not charged with protecting those rights, or guaranteeing those rights, anywhere in the Bill of Rights. The first ten amendments were written to tell the federal government, "Hands off, do not touch, thou shalt not."

The concept that the federal government exists to guarantee our rights, or protect our rights, emerged after the ratification of the 14th Amendment. The Civil War Amendment tasked the federal government with ensuring the newly emancipated slaves were treated fairly, and that their rights were protected – even at the State level. In an effort to capitalize on that idea, the courts got involved to ensure that the former slave States behaved. The southern States, the North was convinced, could not be trusted, and often the South confirmed the lack of confidence the Union States harbored with laws designed to get around the new restrictions placed upon them.

After the American Civil War, the three amendments proposed and ratified to protect the emancipated slaves were specifically designed for the purpose of ensuring the newly freed slaves were treated equally in the eyes of the law. Statism, however, seized upon the ideas planted by Congressman John Bingham, and through the courts worked to weave an intricate tapestry that would change the culture of the United States from a union of voluntary members, to a nation of states joined in an unbreakable union. The country no longer resembled the union of sovereign states it had once been, and instead became a nation held together by the statist consequences of the ravages of war.

The federal government telling States what they can and can't do regarding our rights opens a Pandora's Box the framers of the Constitution never intended to be breached. By allowing the federal government to dictate to the States what they can and can't do regarding rights, even with the best of intentions, the precedent is established allowing federal control. A federal government that can force a State to behave in an acceptable manner can later dictate to a State to follow a federal mandate designed to reduce your access to your rights.

As President Gerald Ford once wisely said, "A government big enough to give you everything you want is a government big enough to take from you everything you have."

A significant segment of the Founding Fathers believed the **Bill of Rights** to be unnecessary. The first seven articles of the U.S. Constitution were written in such a way that the concerns of the **Anti-Federalists** had been addressed, but they still feared that the federal government would compromise the natural rights of the citizens if a Bill of Rights was not included in the Constitution.

The Constitution was written in a manner that allowed the new federal government only the authorities granted to it by the Law of the Land. Regarding **arms**, for example, the possession of guns was never an issue granted to the federal government in the first seven articles of the U.S. Constitution, therefore the federal government had no authority to restrict guns in any way, shape, or form. The Anti-Federalists, however, did not believe the federal government would abide by the limitation of authorities placed on the United States Government, and demanded that a Bill of Rights be written. Failure to provide a Bill of Rights, indicated the Anti-Federalists, would result in a failure of those States dominated by Anti-Federalists to ratify the new Constitution.

The Framers of the Constitution, understanding that without the critical approval of the Anti-Federalists, the new Constitution would never be ratified, agreed to include a Bill of Rights. James Madison was asked to gather the amendments to be proposed and potentially ratified by the States, and use them to write a Bill of Rights.

Originally, there were a large number of amendments proposed, but the final proposal that went to the States for ratification was narrowed down to twelve amendments. Only ten were ratified. Of the remaining two, one regarding apportionment remains unratified, and the other became the Twenty-Seventh Amendment in 1992.

The debates over the adoption of the Constitution found the Anti-Federalists fearful that as drafted, the Constitution created a central government that may have the opportunity to become a tyranny. These fears were based on the memory of the British violation of basic civil rights before and during the American Revolution. With past British tyranny as a frame of reference, the Anti-Federalists demanded that a "bill of rights" be written that would clarify without question the immunities of individual citizens. Though the amendments of the Bill of Rights were not proposed until 1789, several state conventions during their ratification conventions ratified the Constitution with the understanding that the amendments would be offered.

One of the fears regarding the proposal of the Bill of Rights was that by trying to protect specific rights, it might imply that any unmentioned rights would not be protected. It was believed by many that as a result, the Bill of Rights was actually unnecessary, for in the British system of **common law** natural rights were not defined, nor quantified. Adding a Bill of Rights to the Constitution may actually limit the rights of the people to those listed in the Constitution. As a result of this argument, included in the Bill of Rights is the Ninth Amendment, which indicates that rights not **enumerated** would also be protected.

Another argument against the Bill of Rights is that the ten amendments muddy the waters of the Constitution, because the first seven articles were designed to grant authorities to the federal government, and if an authority is not granted, the federal government does not have that power. The Bill of Rights tells the federal government what it cannot do. This enables those who oppose the Constitution to claim that the Constitution does not only grant express powers. By focusing on the Bill of Rights, the opposition responds to constitutional challenges with the question, "Where in the Constitution does it say the federal government can't do that?" Considering the Bill of Rights was not even necessary, this provides unnecessary ammunition to those that oppose the Constitution.

Chapter 20

Incorporation of the Bill of Rights

The Bill of Rights was originally intended to be applied only to the federal government. Even the most ardent opponent to the **originalist view of the Constitution** concedes that it is commonly understood that originally the Bill of Rights was not intended to apply to the States whatsoever. The text of the U.S. Constitution does not necessarily clearly exhibit that the Bill of Rights was only intended to apply to the federal government, but a deep study of the text of the first ten amendments, and the various writings of the Founding Fathers on the topic, reveals without a doubt that the Bill of Rights was indeed originally intended to only apply to the federal government.

Though even the most ardent opponent of the United States Constitution will admit that the Bill of Rights was originally intended to only apply to the federal government, the rule of inapplicability to the States was abandoned by statists after 1868, when it became argued that the 14th Amendment changed this rule, and served to extend most of the Bill of Rights to the States.

The section of the 14th Amendment that has been interpreted to extend the Bill of Rights to the States comes from the second sentence of Section 1 of the 14th Amendment, which reads:

"No State shall make or enforce any law which shall abridge the privileges or immunities of citizens of the United States; nor shall any State deprive any person of life, liberty, or property, without due process of law; nor deny to any person within its jurisdiction the equal protection of the laws."

Through a series of court rulings, the Supreme Court has changed the Constitution by applying parts of the Bill of Rights to the States. The process over the time period since the ratification of the 14th Amendment which works to apply the Bill of Rights to the States through court rulings and written opinions is called "The **Incorporation**

of the Bill of Rights."

The Bill of Rights was originally not meant to be a guarantee of individual freedoms at all, but a limitation of federal authority against our God given rights. In other words, the Bill of Rights was not written for the people, but for the federal government as a means of telling the federal government what it cannot do in regards to our unalienable rights.

Why not apply these amendments to the States as well?

The States already had a Bill of Rights in their own State Constitutions (and those that did not have a constitution yet, did include a Bill of Rights later). The Founding Fathers were confident that the people of the States could control their own State officials, and would be involved in their local governments. The people did not fear their local governments acting in a tyrannical manner similar to the potential of a centralized government system. Their fears were of the new and distant central government.

Originally, parts of the first amendments proposed by James Madison did in fact address the States, seeking to limit the State governments with provisions such as, "No state shall violate the equal rights of conscience, or the freedom of the press, or the trial by jury in criminal cases." The parts of the Bill of Rights that sought to be applied to the powers of the States, however, were not approved by Congress, and therefore were not a part of the proposed amendments to the States.

The Bill of Rights was understood, at its ratification, to be a bar on the actions of the federal government. Prior to the incorporation of the Bill of Rights to the States by the courts as based on their interpretation of the 14th Amendment, the Bill of Rights did not apply to the States, and was never intended to be fully applied to the States.

The argument used, despite original intent, that the Bill of Rights must also apply to the States is based more on philosophy, than historical evidence. One of the philosophical standpoints used is that if the specific rights given in the Bill of Rights are based on the more general rights to life, liberty, and property which in turn are considered to be God-given and unalienable, then State governments do not have the authority to infringe on those rights any more than can the federal government.

The argument, however, simply suggests that the Bill of Rights *ought* to apply at the State level, not that it originally did.

If the Bill of Rights originally only applied to the Federal Government, and over time has changed to be something that was applicable on the State level through court decisions, the reality is that the Constitution itself has never allowed the Bill of Rights to be applied to the States. The change was done by judicial means, meaning that the Constitution has been changed by **judicial activism**. The problem, however, is that according to the Constitution, the only way to change the Constitution is through an amendment process. Therefore, the incorporation of the Bill of Rights to the States occurred unconstitutionally.

This returns us to the argument that the 14th Amendment is the source and authority of the incorporation of the Bill of Rights to the States. The Supreme Court's first ruling regarding the scope of the 14th Amendment, and if the amendment enables the Bill of Rights to be applied to the States, was rendered in the Slaughterhouse Cases just five years after the ratification of the 14th Amendment in 1868. A five to four vote by the high court interpreted the Privileges and Immunities Clause to be the authority they needed to enforce The Bill of Rights against the States. Subsequent cases also used the 14th Amendment as an authority for incorporation. During the early twentieth century a number of court cases, using the arguments referencing the 14th Amendment, began selectively incorporating some of the specific provisions of the Bill of Rights while rejecting the incorporation of others.

The courts, through this process of incorporating The Bill of Rights to the States, have changed the Constitution through unconstitutional means, and against **original intent**. As originally intended, all provisions in the U.S. Constitution apply to the federal government, unless otherwise noted. The Bill of Rights was originally intended to apply only to the federal government, and if we are to remain in line with the original intent of the Founding Fathers, State sovereignty must remain protected by that original intent.

Congressman John A. Bingham of Ohio was the primary author of the first section of the 14th amendment, and it was his personal intention the Bill of Rights be applied to the States as well. His argument was that it was necessary in order to secure the civil rights of the newly appointed slaves. However, most of the representatives during the five months of debate on the floor of Congress argued against incorporating the Bill of Rights to the States, and so when the amendment was agreed upon for proposal, the majority of those involved intended for the 14th Amendment to not influence how the Bill of Rights was applied. In the beginning, the courts ruled that the Amendment did not extend the Bill of Rights to the States. It was after the realization that **Black Codes** were emerging in the South that the courts decided for the purpose of protecting the civil rights of the emancipated slaves, they would begin to apply parts of the Bill of Rights to the States.

Chapter 21

The First Amendment

Congress shall make no law respecting an establishment of religion, or prohibiting the free exercise thereof; or abridging the freedom of speech, or of the press; or the right of the people peaceably to assemble, and to petition the Government for a redress of grievances.

Freedom of Religion

The first part of the 1st Amendment addresses religion. The frame of reference of the Founding Fathers was Europe, and more specifically, England. In Europe, a movement to reform the Church began in 1517, influenced by Martin Luther's critiques of the Roman Catholic Church. The movement led to the **Protestant Reformation**. After the Pope denied the King of England the permission to divorce his wife, the English king created the Church of England, and established himself as head of the church, so that he may grant to himself the allowance to seek a divorce. In England the Church of England greatly influenced the centralized governmental system, and the politicians greatly influenced The Church. There was no separation between powers of the king and the church, a problem that revealed itself with the **1559 Act of Uniformity**. According to the Act of Uniformity, it was illegal to not attend Church of England services. A fine was imposed for each missed Sunday and holy day. Penalties also existed if one decided to have church services not approved by the government, which included arrest, and larger fines. The problem, the Founding Fathers reasoned, was not faith in God, but the establishment of a State Church. Therefore, to protect the governmental system from the influence of religion, while also protecting the various religious sects from a government that may give preferential treatment to an established religion, the Founders determined that the federal government must not establish a state religion (Establishment Clause).

The second part of that clause, however, was clearly designed to protect the various religious exercises by Americans from the government by

157

instructing government to not prohibit the free exercise of religion.

Freedom of religion was a big deal with those early Americans. The importance of religious freedom during that time period is common knowledge. Even the textbooks in today's public school system reveals the Pilgrims first came to the New World in search of religious freedom.

Through the passage of time secular forces in our society have worked to undermine the first clause of the 1st Amendment. Americans have been conditioned to believe in a concept known as the **Separation of Church and State**. The concept has determined the church is to have no influence, no matter how subtle, on government for any reason. Therefore, reason the secularists who support the modern concept of the separation of church and state, any mention of God in the same breath with the federal government is in direct violation of the 1st Amendment.

To understand the error of the concept of Separation of Church and State in today's society, we must go back and discover the origination of the idea. The truth demands we recognize the language used in the writings of the Founders, as well as grasp the history of the colonies - including a series of letters between the federal government and the Danbury Baptists of Connecticut, culminating in the letters to Thomas Jefferson after he became President of the United States after the Election of 1800.

Each of the colonies began as a collection of like-minded religious folk who wanted freedom for their religion (not necessarily freedom of all religions). In Jamestown, in 1610, Dales Law mandated the Jamestown colonists to attend Anglican worship. The law went so far as to have provisions against criticism of the church. Violation of Dales Law could even lead to death. The Puritan Colonies to the north had similar laws, even setting up their governments in accordance with Puritan Law. Connecticut was one of those Puritan Colonies, and in 1639 the colony enacted "The Fundamental Orders of Connecticut." The law set Connecticut up as a **theocracy**, disallowing non-Puritans from holding office. The government was the church, and the church was the government.

The practice of religious preference was not limited to Connecticut. All of the States enforced established religions, except Pennsylvania and Rhode Island.

Though Pennsylvania was largely a Quaker dominated State, William

Penn believed that religion should be free from state control, so Pennsylvania did not persecute non-Quakers. However, in Pennsylvania, in order to hold office, you still had to be a Christian.

Rhode Island, founded in 1636 as a colony, was based on the principle of true religious liberty, and took in folks who were trying to escape the religious persecution of the other colonies.

Connecticut's Puritan dominated landscape included a group of Baptists in Danbury, Connecticut who were tired of being treated like second class citizens.

Thomas Jefferson drafted the Virginia Act For Establishing Religious Freedom in Virginia, and with James Madison's assistance, finally got it enacted into law in 1786. After many letters to President Adams that resulted in no assistance, the Danbury Baptists were excited about Jefferson winning the presidential election in 1800. Finally, they would have someone in office who would help them in their fight for religious freedoms in Connecticut.

The Danbury Baptists wrote to Jefferson to congratulate him for his win, and to appeal to him for help. Thomas Jefferson responded with a letter that carries the line, "a wall of separation between church and state," which has become the source from which the infamous concept of Separation of Church and State was eventually derived.

The Founding Fathers desired that Americans be free to worship as they wished, without being compelled by government through an established religion. The key, however, is that they not only did not want the federal government compelling a person through laws regarding religion, but the government shall not "prohibit the free exercise thereof."

Thomas Jefferson, as indicated in his letter to the Danbury Baptists, and his other writings, was against the government establishing a "State Church." However, he also believed that men should be free to exercise their religion as they deem fit, and not be forced to follow a government mandate that may prohibit religion.

The Danbury Baptists were concerned over local religious freedoms, but Jefferson was clear, the federal government could not mandate anything in regards to religion. It is a State issue, and the Danbury Baptists needed to address the issue themselves through their State government.

Jefferson's reference to a wall of separation was an explanation that the federal government cannot prohibit the free exercise of religion for any reason, including on public grounds, but if a State was to prohibit the free exercise of religion, or establish a state church, it was an issue that must be resolved at the State level.

Freedom of Speech and Freedom of the Press

The point of including in the Bill of Rights the freedom of speech, and of the press, was specifically designed to protect political speech, though other speech is protected by this clause as well. The Founding Fathers believed that freedom hinged on the freedoms of political speech and the press. Benjamin Franklin wrote in the Pennsylvania Gazette, April 8, 1736, regarding the American doctrine behind freedom of speech and of the press:

"Freedom of speech is a principal pillar of a free government; when this support is taken away, the constitution of a free society is dissolved, and tyranny is erected on its ruins. Republics and limited monarchies derive their strength and vigor from a popular examination into the action of the magistrates."

James Madison in 1799 wrote, *"In every State, probably, in the Union, the press has exerted a freedom in canvassing the merits and measures of public men of every description which has not been confined to the strict limits of the common law."*

Freedom of the Right of the People To Peaceably Assemble, and to Petition the Government for a Redress of Grievances

The right to peaceably assemble means that citizens may peacefully parade and gather, and demonstrate support or opposition of public policy. This part of the 1st Amendment is closely tied to Freedom of Speech, guaranteeing one's ability to express one's views by freedom of speech and the right to peaceably assemble.

The need to protect the right to peaceably assemble was not a new concept during the Constitutional Convention. Before the Bill of Rights, the Declaration and Resolves of the First Continental Congress declared on October 14, 1774:

The inhabitants of the English colonies in North-America, by the

160

immutable laws of nature, the principals of the English constitution, and the several charters or compacts, have the following rights: They have a right peaceably to assemble, consider their grievances, and petition the king: and that all prosecutions, prohibitory proclamations, and commitments for the same are illegal.

In 1776, Pennsylvania's declaration of rights guaranteed peaceable assembly. Pennsylvania was the first State to recognize this right.

Originally, the right to assemble was considered less important than the right to petition. Now, many historians consider the two to be equally important, and to actually complement each other.

The Founding Fathers felt that the right to assemble, and petition the government for a redress of grievances, were important keys to protecting States' Rights, and the rights of the people, from the federal government. The need to assemble, to come together and share common beliefs and act upon those beliefs, is what began the drive for independence, and ultimately what led to the American Revolution. The right to assemble and petition the government for a redress of grievances, the Founding Fathers believed, was one of the primary tools available to the citizens in their drive to stop tyrannies before they could take hold.

The right to peaceable assembly provides the opportunity for all citizens to participate in America's political life and in the electoral process. A recent example of this inalienable right in action is the Tea Party Movement. The Tea Party rallies are peaceful assemblies. These rallies are protected by the Constitution when they are for a lawful purpose, are conducted in an orderly manner, and publicize some type of grievance. Many groups and organizations use assembly as a way to show support for an idea, or dispute, as characterized by the Tea Party.

Chapter 22

Keep and Bear Arms

The 2nd Amendment does not give you the right to keep and bear arms. The 2nd Amendment does not protect you against the government from taking away your guns. Your rights are given to you by God, and protecting your rights is your responsibility. Like anything else you own, if you give away your rights, or allow someone to take them, they may still belong to you as an unalienable, God-given right, but you have given up all access to them, and can no longer exercise those rights.

In the *Washington, D.C. v. Heller* case in 2008 the Supreme Court of the United States determined that the right to bear arms is an **individual right**, as opposed to a **collective right** which would only allow the bearing of arms for the purpose of participating in government approved groups, such as law enforcement agencies.

During the early years of the United States under the United States Constitution, the Anti-Federalists feared the creation of a central government because they feared the federal government would become tyrannical, and take away people's rights. Therefore, even though the Constitution in the first seven articles did not grant to the federal government any authority over gun rights, along with the rest of the rights enumerated in the Bill of Rights, those skeptical over the creation of a central government wanted an amendment that clarified the federal government had no authority to infringe on the right to keep and bear arms.

The States have **Original Authority**, meaning that all powers belonged to the States prior to the writing of the Constitution. The first seven articles of the document did not give to the federal government the authority to regulate firearms, therefore, any legislative power over gun rights is a State power. The 2nd Amendment simply confirms that. The argument then becomes about the potential tyranny of the States. If the 2nd Amendment does not apply to the States, what keeps the States from infringing on gun rights?

The State constitutions, and the people, hold the responsibility of restraining the States from infringing on the right to keep and bear arms. The Founding Fathers were not concerned with a tyranny of the States because the State governments are closer to the people, and therefore the people have fewer legal and political obstacles when acting to ensure the State governments do not infringe on individual rights.

Complacency, then, becomes our greatest enemy.

With freedom comes responsibility.

Understanding that the Framers expected their posterity to be informed problem-solvers, while recognizing that basic human nature would invite complacency and the rise of a tyrannical government, it becomes clear why the Founding Fathers put so much importance on gun rights.

In early American society the need to be armed was necessary for a number of reasons, including, but not limited to, protecting one's property, facilitating a natural right of self-defense, participating in law enforcement, enabling people to participate in an **organized militia** system, deterring a tyrannical government, repelling invasion, suppressing insurrection, and hunting.

The right to keep and bear arms is not merely about protecting your home, or hunting, though those are important, too. The whole point of the 2nd Amendment is to protect us against all enemies, foreign and domestic, which could include a potentially oppressive central government.

Noah Webster in his "An Examination of the Leading Principles of the Federal Constitution," in 1787 articulated the necessity for keeping and bearing **arms** clearly: "*Before a standing army can rule, the people must be disarmed; as they are in almost every kingdom of Europe. The supreme power in America cannot enforce unjust laws by the sword; because the whole body of the people are armed, and constitute a force superior to any band of regular troops that can be, on any pretence, raised in the United States.*"

Some will argue the 2nd Amendment does not apply to our current society because the militia is a thing of the past.

The National Guard now serves as the organized militia envisioned by the Founding Fathers, but an unorganized militia also exists.

Title 10 of the United States Code provides for both "organized" and "unorganized" civilian militias. While the **organized militia** is made up of members of the National Guard and Naval Militia, the **unorganized militia** is composed entirely of private individuals.

United States Code: Title 10 – Armed Forces, Subtitle A – General Military Law
Chapter 13 – The Militia:

Sec. 311. Militia: composition and classes

(a) The militia of the United States consists of all able-bodied males at least 17 years of age and, except as provided in section 313 of title 32, under 45 years of age who are, or who have made a declaration of intention to become, citizens of the United States and of female citizens of the United States who are members of the National Guard.

(b) The classes of the militia are -

(1) the organized militia, which consists of the National Guard and the Naval Militia; and
(2) the unorganized militia, which consists of the members of
the militia who are not members of the National Guard or the Naval Militia.

Other than age, health, gender, or citizenship, there are no additional provisions for exemption from membership in the unorganized militia. While it is doubtful that it will ever be called to duty, the United States civilian militia does legally exist. The Founding Fathers would have likely included in the definition of unorganized militia, "All able-bodied citizens capable of fighting."

McDonald v. City of Chicago (2010) challenged the City of Chicago's ban on hand guns, bringing to the surface the debate over whether or not the 2nd Amendment only applies to the federal government.

The 5-4 Decision of the *McDonald v. City of Chicago* case by the U.S. Supreme Court holds the 2nd Amendment protects the right to keep and bear arms in all cities and States. The U.S. Supreme Court concluded that originally the 2nd Amendment applied only to the federal government, but it is in the opinion of the court that the 14th Amendment incorporates the Bill of Rights, therefore applying those amendments, and more specifically the 2nd Amendment, to the States.

The decision by the Supreme Court, in this case, makes all State laws on fire arms null and void. Applying the 2nd Amendment to the States means the 2nd Amendment is supreme over any and all State laws on firearms, and according to the 2nd Amendment, "the right to keep and bear arms shall not be infringed." If "shall not be infringed" applies to both the federal government and the States governments, then all persons are allowed to possess a firearm. The words, "shall not be infringed" carries no exceptions.

The reason the 2nd Amendment is absolute in its language is because it was intended to only apply to the federal government. The federal government shall not infringe on the right to keep and bear arms in any way, but the States retain the authority to regulate guns as necessary based on the needs and allowances of the local electorate.

The U.S. Constitution applies to the federal government except where specifically noted otherwise.

In reference to *McDonald v. Chicago*, I am uneasy anytime the federal government tells a city or state what they have to do, even if on the surface it is for a good cause.

If we give the federal government the right to tell cities they have to allow gun ownership, what stops them from doing the opposite later? This case created a precedent of allowing the federal government to dictate to the States and cities what they have to do, and that kind of federal intrusion constitutes great danger to **State Sovereignty**.

Breaking down the language used in the 2nd Amendment assists in clarifying what the original intent was.

The 2nd Amendment begins, *"A well regulated Militia."* The immediate understanding of that phrase by the average American in today's culture recognizes it as meaning, "A militia under the control of the government," or "regulated by government agencies," or "managed by federal law."

All of the above definitions are wrong.

As discussed regarding the Commerce Clause in Article I, Section 8, the word "regulated" does not mean "controlled or restricted by government." The definition used by the Framers, and the one that fits best with the context of the period, and the principles of the Constitution, can be found in the 1828 Webster Dictionary. Webster defined **regulated** as: "To put in good order." Some historians state that the word "regulate" in the 18th Century meant "To make regular." The word "restrict" was not used in the 1828 definition until the third and final definition of "regulated," revealing that today's most common definition was the "least used" definition during the time of the writing of the United States Constitution.

Since "regulate" did not mean "to control and restrict," but instead meant "to put in good order," that means a well regulated militia is one that is in good order.

The need to have a militia in good order makes sense when one considers that during the Revolutionary War the militia was not in good order. The muskets were all different sizes, often the clothing of some members of the militia was tattered, and many didn't even have shoes.

To put the militia in good order, Congress was required to create standards for the militia to follow. The authority to Congress regarding this power is revealed in Article I, Section 8, Clause 16, where the Constitution says, *"The Congress shall have Power. . . To provide for organizing, arming, and disciplining, the Militia, and for governing such Part of them as may be employed in the Service of the United States, reserving to the States respectively, the Appointment of Officers, and the Authority of training the Militia according to the discipline prescribed by Congress."*

The next part of the 2nd Amendment reveals that a well regulated militia is *"necessary to the security of a free State."*

The word *State*, in that instance, means "individual, autonomous, sovereign State." In other words, a well regulated militia is necessary to the security of a free Massachusetts, a free Pennsylvania, a free Virginia, a free New York, a free Ohio, a free California, and so on.

"Necessary to the security of a free State." A militia is necessary, not just recommended, *to the security of a free State.* Security against

whom? A foreign invader? Isn't that what the standing army was supposed to be for? Why would States need militias, capable of being called up by the governor of the State, for their "security," and to ensure that security is for them to remain a *"free State?"*

Foreign enemies were a concern, but not as much of a concern as a tyrannical central government. Thomas Jefferson so distrusted a central government that he suggested there would be a bloody revolution every twenty years.

"... can history produce an instance of a rebellion so honourably conducted? I say nothing of it's motives. They were founded in ignorance, not wickedness. God forbid we should ever be 20 years without such a rebellion. The people can not be all, and always, well informed. The part which is wrong will be discontented in proportion to the importance of the facts they misconceive. If they remain quiet under such misconceptions it is a lethargy, the forerunner of death to the public liberty. We have had 13 states independant 11 years. There has been one rebellion. That comes to one rebellion in a century and a half for each state. What country ever existed a century and a half without a rebellion? And what country can preserve it's liberties if their rulers are not warned from time to time that their people preserve the spirit of resistance? Let them take arms. The remedy is to set them right as to facts, pardon and pacify them. What signify a few lives lost in a century or two? The tree of liberty must be refreshed from time to time with the blood of patriots and tyrants. It is it's natural manure." -- Thomas Jefferson to William Stephens Smith, Paris, 13 Nov. 1787

The **Declaration of Independence** also states that the people have the right to stand up against their government should it become tyrannical. In the second paragraph of the Declaration of Independence it reads:

"That to secure these rights, Governments are instituted among Men, deriving their just powers from the consent of the governed, --That whenever any Form of Government becomes destructive of these ends, it is the Right of the People to alter or to abolish it, and to institute new Government, laying its foundation on such principles and organizing its powers in such form, as to them shall seem most likely to effect their Safety and Happiness."

The right to alter or abolish a tyrannical government walks hand in hand with the right to keep and bear arms. How could it ever be logical that the right to keep and bear arms could ever be influenced or restricted by the very government that that right exists to protect the people against in the first place?

Chapter 23

Quartering

The Founding Fathers feared a centralized government with a powerful military. One of the final straws that began the road to the American Revolution was the **Quartering Act of 1765** where the colonists became required to house and feed the British troops they despised. The Quartering Act enabled the British Empire to exercise greater control over the populace. It was also known as one of the **Intolerable Acts**.

The Quartering Act served as a major reason for the writing of the 3rd Amendment, which reads: *"No Soldier shall, in time of peace be quartered in any house, without the consent of the Owner, nor in time of war, but in a manner to be prescribed by law."*

Tyrannical governmental systems use unwarranted influence through military means. To guard against the potential for the disastrous rise of misplaced power, the Framer's concerns about **standing armies** became evident in the 3rd Amendment.

To help the populace protect themselves, and be able to enforce the 3rd Amendment, in case the federal government violated the clause, the Founding Fathers also gave us the 2nd Amendment: *"A well regulated Militia, being necessary to the security of a free State, the right of the people to keep and bear Arms, shall not be infringed."*

The concept of a Militia that is not a federal army is the realization that the United States will not be one where there is a **standing army** that can be used against its citizens. Article I, Section 8, Clause 12 gives the Congress the power to raise and support armies, but limits them to no more than two years funding.

When a military arm of a tyrannical government can compel the citizenry to house the military machinery of defense, a **police state** is present and liberty is at risk. Such was the reasoning behind the 3rd Amendment.

Until the Revolutionary War, the American States had no military, and the militias were populated by the colonists. The Constitution gave the U.S. Government the authority to build a military for the defense of the union. A military establishment, in the minds of the Founders, was a potentially dangerous thing. The Founding Fathers desired to protect the union, but did not desire that the American military become an authoritarian tool of a potentially tyrannical federal government.

Chapter 24

Warrants, Searches, and Seizures

The 4th Amendment to the United States Constitution was added as part of the Bill of Rights on December 15, 1791. It was written with the purpose of protecting people from the government searching their homes and private property without properly executed **search warrants**.

"The right of the people to be secure in their persons, houses, papers, and effects, against unreasonable searches and seizures, shall not be violated, and no Warrants shall issue, but upon probable cause, supported by Oath or affirmation, and particularly describing the place to be searched, and the persons or things to be seized."

What this means is that the federal government, in order to search a person's home, business, papers, bank accounts, computer or other personal items, in most cases, must obtain a search warrant signed by the proper authority, which usually means by a judge.

The issuance of a warrant must accompany reasonable belief that a crime has been committed and that by searching the premises of a particular location, evidence will be found that will verify the crime. The government officer does not have to be correct in his assumption, he just has to have a reasonable belief that searching someone's private property will yield evidence of the crime. The task of determining whether or not the officer's assumptions are a reasonable belief falls on the judge who is considering issuing the search warrant.

The concept that citizens must be protected from unreasonable searches and seizures goes back into English history. The British Crown was known for performing searches and seizures that were unlawfully conducted. Often, these searches were conducted by the king's representatives.

The British government saw the American Colonies as a source of revenue. As a result, taxation against the American colonies was a continuous practice, in the hopes of generating as much money from the colonists as possible. The colonists resented this and engaged in substantial smuggling operations in order to get around the customs taxes imposed by the British government.

The King responded to the Colonist's smuggling activities by using **writs of assistance**, which were search warrants that were very broad and general in their scope. British agents, once obtaining these writs, could search any property they believed might contain contraband goods. They could enter someone's property with no notice and without any reason given. Tax collectors could interrogate anyone about their use of goods and require the cooperation of any citizen. Searches and seizures of private property based on very general warrants became an epidemic in colonial America.

In 1756, the Massachusetts legislature passed search and seizure laws outlawing the use of general warrants. The friction created between the Royal Governor and the people of Massachusetts grew with each passing moment.

In 1760 James Otis, a Boston lawyer, strongly objected to these arbitrary searches and seizures of private property and consequently resigned his position with the government, and then became the lawyer for a group of over 50 merchants who sued the government claiming that the **writs of assistance** were unjust.

James Otis represented these merchants for free. His speech condemning British policies, including writs of assistance and general search warrants, was so powerful and eloquent, that it was heard of throughout the colonies and catapulted him to a place of leadership in the swelling tide of disillusionment toward Great Britain.

Twenty-five year old John Adams, who would become the second president of the United States some time later, was sitting in the courtroom and heard Otis' famous speech that served as a spark that led to igniting the American Revolution.

The 4th Amendment, a part of The Bill of Rights, became law on December 15, 1791.

The 4th Amendment applies only to the federal government. State constitutions are written similarly, and States also have laws that are consistent with the intention of the 4th Amendment. The 4th Amendment provides protection from illegal search and seizure by federal government officials, but not by private citizens. So, if an employer unreasonably searched your possessions at work, the 4th Amendment would not have been violated, but local laws may have been.

In recent history The PATRIOT Act was seen as a breach of the 4th Amendment because it allowed the federal government to pursue a number of strategies in their search for terrorists that includes warrantless phone taps, access to phone logs, and monitoring of online communications such as email. The debate still goes on regarding the constitutionality of The PATRIOT Act, with both sides presenting reasonable arguments, ranging from the constitutional necessity of the law for the purpose of "providing for the common defense," to the argument that the authorities offered by the law allows the federal government to unconstitutionally intrude on the right to privacy of all Americans.

The National Defense Authorization Act (NDAA) of 2014 builds on the powers seized by the federal government through the PATRIOT Act, allowing unrestricted analysis and research of captured records pertaining to any organization or individual "now or once hostile to the United States." The definition of "hostile to the United States" is broad, and can include political opposition. Under NDAA 2014 Sec. 1061(g)(1), an overly vague definition of captured records enhances government power and guarantees indefinite surveillance.

The Internal Revenue Service is another arm of the federal government that routinely violates the 4th Amendment, doing so under the auspice of ensuring all taxes are paid.

Chapter 25

Due Process and Eminent Domain

Due Process

The majority of the Fifth Amendment provides additional reinforcement to the concept of **due process**. The language of this Amendment was designed to assure those who feared the potential tyranny of a new centralized government created by the United States Constitution that the federal government would be restrained in such a way as to ensure that the government did not perpetrate bloodshed against its citizens.

The first part of the 5th Amendment reads: *"No person shall be held to answer for a **capital crime**, or otherwise **infamous crime**, unless on a presentment or indictment of a **Grand Jury**. . ."*

The 5th Amendment attests to the Founding Father's understanding that this is a nation of property owners. As a republic of property owners, when in jeopardy of legal trouble, our rights and properties must be safeguarded. Therefore, an American Citizen in the American legal system has a right to a jury, as well as a right to the presentation of evidence. Conviction is not reached with a majority vote, either. Conviction requires a unanimous agreement among all of the members of the jury. These concepts reinforce the concept that one is innocent until proven guilty (A concept found in the Book of Deuteronomy, Chapter 19, Verse 15), and that the United States of America is a **Republic**. **Mob rule** is not allowed, for as the amendment provides, a person cannot be held until given the opportunity of due process.

Not all persons, however, are awarded this opportunity. The next part of the amendment reads: *". . . except in cases arising in the land or naval forces, or in the militia, when in actual service in time of War or public danger. . ."*

The military does not fall under the U.S. Constitution. Personnel serving in the armed forces are governed by the Uniform Code of Military

Justice (UCMJ). Instead of a civilian trial, a military service member is normally afforded a court martial. If a civilian trial is deemed appropriate by the U.S. Military, a service member can still stand trial in a civilian court, but the military has the authority to decide whether or not the member shall stand such a trial.

Having a sense of independence, individuals must be protected, then, from the tyrannical trappings of a governmental system that may try to use the judiciary against them (as the King of England had done often). The protective mechanism, or **the rule of law**, would be the U.S. Constitution and clauses like the 5th Amendment, which were designed to provide protection to the populace from unfair legal practices.

One such protection is provided in the next part of this amendment: "*. . . nor shall any person be subject for the same offence to be twice put in jeopardy of life and limb. . .*"

Protection against **Double Jeopardy** enables us not to be continuously tried for the same offense, which was a technique often used in some parts of Europe during the eighteenth century. The idea was that if a person was prosecuted enough, either they would weary of the process and break down, or the defendant would become unable to financially continue, hence unable to defend themselves.

The next part of the amendment serves as a large influence on today's **Miranda Rights**. The section reads: "*. . . nor shall be compelled in any criminal case to be a witness against himself, nor be deprived of life, liberty, or property.*"

Miranda Rights are named after the U.S. Supreme Court case, *Miranda v. Arizona* (1966). Miranda Rights are a warning given advising the accused of their right to remain silent, their right to an attorney, and the right to an appointed attorney if they are unable to afford counsel - prior to conducting a custodial interrogation. From the 5th Amendment: "*. . . nor shall be compelled in any criminal case to be a witness against himself, nor be deprived of life, liberty, or property, without due process of law.*" Miranda Rights exist to secure the 5th Amendment's privilege against self-incrimination, and to make the individual in custody aware not only of the privilege, but also of the consequences of forgoing it. The judicial opinion from the *Miranda v. Arizona* case also indicated that in order to protect the person's life, liberty or property with the due process of law, the individual must have the right to an attorney. With a lawyer present the likelihood that the police will practice coercion is reduced, and if coercion is nevertheless exercised the lawyer can testify to it in court. The presence of a lawyer can also help to guarantee that the accused gives a fully accurate statement to the police and that the statement is rightly reported by the prosecution at trial.

The words of the Founders continues to resonate today as the majority of the American people seem to firmly agree with the Founding Father's insistence that no one should be deprived of life, liberty, or property without due process of law. We can take satisfaction that most of our fellow citizens in our republic still hold these truths to be self-evident.

Eminent Domain

The provisions of the 5th Amendment are there to keep our courts honest, and the powers of the government constrained. The last phrase of the 5th Amendment, however, is considered too general by many, and it has been used in a manner by the federal government that is extremely troublesome, because it gives the government the right to take property if there is **just compensation**.

How is just compensation determined? Is it based on the market value of the property? How does the government officials involved in **eminent domain** calculate the non-intrinsic value? How do they compensate for the value on which nobody can put a price?

Just compensation was intended to be based on what the property owner deemed to be just. If the property owner did not deem the offer to be just compensation, then the government, from a constitutional viewpoint, is out of luck.

Chapter 26

Personal Legal Liberties

The 6th Amendment affords criminal defendants seven discrete personal liberties. *"In all criminal prosecutions, the accused shall enjoy the right to a speedy and public trial, by an impartial jury of the State and district wherein the crime shall have been committed, which district shall have been previously ascertained by law, and to be informed of the nature and cause of the accusation; to be confronted with the witnesses against him; to have compulsory process for obtaining witnesses in his favor, and to have the Assistance of Counsel for his defence."*

Rights afforded in *all* criminal prosecutions are set forth in this amendment. The word "all" at the beginning of this amendment establishes a special characteristic regarding this article of the Constitution. The Constitution applies only to the federal government, unless it states otherwise. The Sixth Amendment, by providing the word "all" in the regard to cases, establishes that this amendment is not only to be applied to the federal courts, but to the State, and lower, courts as well.

As for the rights afforded to the accused:

Speedy Trial

The concept of a speedy trial was an English concept of justice. A speedy trial allows for conditions that disallow the powerful from abusing the court system, forcing defendants to languish in jail for an indefinite period while awaiting their trial. Ensuring a speedy trial minimizes the time in which a defendant's life is disrupted and burdened by a criminal proceeding, and reduces the likelihood of a prolonged delay impairing the ability of the accused to prepare a defense.

Historically, when trials are postponed or drag out for long periods of time, witnesses disappear, and evidence is often lost or destroyed. Memories of the incident in question are also not as reliable as time passes.

A person's right to a speedy trial arises *after* the arrest, indictment, or otherwise formal accusation of a crime.

Public Trial

The right to a public trial was inherited by the Americans from Anglo-Saxon jurisprudence. Public criminal proceedings would operate as a natural check against malevolent prosecutions, corrupt judges, and perjurious witnesses. A trial that is out in the open also aids the fact-finding mission of the judiciary by encouraging citizens to come forward with relevant information.

The right to a public trial is not absolute. Persons who may disrupt proceedings may be banned from attending the trial because they present a substantial risk of hindering a trial. A disallowance of the media attending falls under the concept of "potential disruptions," but otherwise, under normal circumstances, both the public and media have a qualified First Amendment right to attend criminal proceedings. The right to a public trial does not require the presence of media, and because courtrooms have limited seating, judges may attempt to maintain decorum. For media, with today's technology, the media does not have to be in the courtroom to see or hear the proceedings of the case.

Right to Trial by an Impartial Jury

A part of the effort in achieving an impartial jury is the process of determining who will serve on the jury through a series of questions and observations, in an effort to eliminate biased jurors. The concept of protecting the defendant from a biased jury can be traced back to the Magna Carta in 1215. In the United States, the requirement for a trial by an impartial jury does not apply to juvenile delinquency proceedings, or to petty criminal offenses, which consist of crimes punishable by imprisonment of six months or less. In Great Britain, and Canada, a jury is not required for cases with potential penalties of two years or less, and the concept of an impartial jury is not entertained in the same way as in the United States. Canada and Britain choose jurors randomly, and then in an open court the jurors for a specific case are selected from the jury panel by ballot. A juror may be challenged once in the box for bias, but an extensive process to eliminate possible biased jurors before selection through a series of questions and observations is not normal practice.

The Sixth Amendment entitles defendants to a jury that represents "a jury of the defendant's peers," which means the jury should be a fair cross section of the community. From the jury pool, the presiding judge, the prosecution, and attorneys for the defense are allowed to ask members of the jury pool a variety of questions intended to reveal any latent biases, prejudices, or other influences that might affect their impartiality. The presence of even one biased juror is not permitted under the Sixth Amendment.

It is possible that the potential bias of a juror may be affected by sources outside the courtroom, so jurors are instructed to not consider newspaper, television, and radio coverage before or during trial, and are instructed not to discuss the trial with even family members, when evaluating the guilt or innocence of the defendant.

Jurors are not permitted to begin deliberations until all of the evidence has been offered. Deliberations do not begin until after the attorneys have made their closing arguments, and the judge has read the instructions. Premature deliberations have shown the potential, historically, to create early biases, or a juror may form a preconceived notion that they will then compare all evidence to, which they may have entertained as a result of premature deliberations.

Notice of Pending Criminal Charges

The 6th Amendment guarantees defendants the right to be informed of the nature and cause of the accusation against them. Defendants must receive notice of any criminal accusations that the government has lodged against them through an indictment, information, complaint, or other formal charge. Defendants may not be tried, convicted, or sentenced for a crime that materially varies from the crime set forth in the formal charge.

The requirement by the 6th Amendment to inform a defendant of the nature and cause of the accusation is an attempt by the Founding Fathers to create fundamental fairness that was not necessarily present in civil and criminal proceedings in England and the American colonies under English common law. Receiving notice of pending criminal charges in advance of trial permits defendants to prepare a defense in accordance with the specific nature of the accusation. In tyrannies, defendants are all too often incarcerated without being apprised of pending charges until the trial begins. Requiring notice of the nature and cause of the accusation against a defendant eliminates confusion regarding the basis of a particular verdict, which in turn decreases the chances that a defendant will be tried later for the same offense.

Confrontation of Witnesses Against Him

The 6th Amendment requires that defendants have the right to be confronted by witnesses who offer testimony or evidence against them, as well as the opportunity to subject them to cross-examination.

Today's courts have established rules that are enforced at the discretion of the judge who forbids questioning that pursues areas that are irrelevant, collateral, confusing, repetitive, or prejudicial. Defendants are also forbidden to pursue a line of questioning solely for the purpose of harassment.

Compulsory Process for Obtaining Witnesses In His Favor

The 6th Amendment recognizes a defendant's right to use the compulsory process of the judiciary to subpoena witnesses that may be favorable to the defense. Courts may not take actions to undermine the testimony of a witness who has been subpoenaed by the defense. Any law that attempts to establish particular persons as being incompetent to testify on behalf of a defendant is not allowed.

Defendants can also testify on their own behalf, a right not afforded in the American Colonies, or Great Britain, prior to the United States dissolving the political bands connecting them to the Crown. Common law presumed all defendants to be incompetent to give reliable or credible testimony on their own behalf. The vested interest in the outcome of the trial, it was believed, would taint the testimony of the defendant. The 6th Amendment does not require, a defendant to testify on his own behalf, but does not prohibit it, either.

Right to Counsel

The 6th Amendment states that criminal defendants have a Right to Counsel. A defendant's right to counsel does not become an issue until the government files formal charges. However, in the 5th Amendment a person has the right not to be compelled to be a witness against himself, allowing him to remain silent until he has counsel present.

In many instances, defendants have the inability to obtain counsel be it because of financial or other reasons. The 6th Amendment, by listing that assistance of counsel for his defense is a right, has compelled the government to institute a program where counsel can be assigned to a defendant if the person is unable to afford counsel, or obtain counsel for any other reason. In the occurrence of a defendant unable to afford counsel, the trial judge appoints one on his behalf. If it turns out that the defendant has financial resources previously unknown to the court, he may be required to reimburse the government for a portion of the fees paid to the court-appointed lawyer.

Defendants are not required to have counsel. Defendants have a *right* to counsel. Defendants also have the right to decline the representation of counsel and proceed on their own behalf. Defendants who represent themselves must present a waiver of the 6th Amendment right to counsel before a court will allow them to do so. The waiver must reveal that the defendant is knowingly making the decision, and understands the potential consequences.

Chapter 27

Right of Trial by Jury in Civil Suits

"In suits at Common Law, where the value in controversy shall exceed twenty dollars, the right of trial by jury shall be preserved, and no fact tried by a jury, shall be otherwise reexamined in any court of the United States, than according to the rules of the common law."

The 7th Amendment guarantees the right to a jury trial in most civil suits heard in federal court. Remember, the Constitution, and the **Bill of Rights,** apply only to the federal government unless the document states otherwise. The 7th Amendment serves to preserve the historic line separating the province of the jury from that of the judge in civil cases by separating cases that should have a jury in federal court, from those that are smaller cases, and may not require a jury. During the time the amendment was ratified, a case requiring a jury was one where "the value in controversy" exceeded twenty dollars. The cutoff in the court system today is $75,000. Any disputes that involve amounts less than $75,000, in fact, will not even be handled in a federal court.

State courts don't have to honor this provision in the 7th Amendment, and often don't. People bringing a suit do not have to have a jury trial. Individuals can waive their right to a jury trial if they so choose.

The 7th Amendment also expressly forbids federal judges to re-examine any "fact tried by a jury" except as allowed by the common law. This means that no court, trial or appellate, may overturn a jury verdict that is reasonably supported by the evidence.

Prior to the **Declaration of Rights** in 1689, English judges served the King of England. These judges showed bias towards the King, resulting in unfair rulings. Judges in the American colonies were also biased towards the king, and when King George III got rid of trials by juries in the Colonies, the colonists viewed the decision as more kindling for the fire of independence that had been blazing in the pubs, churches and meeting halls of the Colonies. The Bill of Rights applied what the

Framers learned under the rule of Britain to the American System. In the American courts the Framers believed it was important to have a fair court system, so the right to have a trial by jury is mentioned a number of times, and is a fundamental part of the United States legal system.

Together with the due process clause of the 5th Amendment and the right to an impartial jury enumerated in the 6th Amendment, the 7th Amendment guarantees civil litigants the right to not just a jury, but to a jury who is not biased for any reason.

Chapter 28

Excessive Bail, Cruel and Unusual Punishment

The 8th Amendment reads, *"Excessive bail shall not be required, nor excessive fines imposed, nor cruel and unusual punishments inflicted."*

As a nation founded on honorable Judeo-Christian principles, the United States legal system is expected to be fair and just. This means that Americans should insist upon a due process that protects individuals from excesses and abuses by the judicial system. Such expectations include that no individual should be singled out, or treated differently, in the eyes of the courts. A fair and equitable judicial system includes no excessive bails or fines, or cruel and unusual punishment, for one person while others guilty of similar crimes do not receive similar treatment.

Today's definitions attempt to set a limit on where "excessive" or "unusual" lies. When a harsh penalty is applied for a crime, even when it is similar to the punishment received by others for the same crime, challenges are launched regarding if the penalty matches the crime. These challenges are fine, and an important part of the American judicial system seeking to adjust itself in regards to its fairness, but the debates during the Federal Convention and State ratification conventions did not focus so much on where the line between excessive and not excessive, or unusual as opposed to usual, exists as much as *are the bails, fines and punishment consistent with the bails, fines and punishment consistent with others guilty of the same.*

DOUGLAS V. GIBBS

Chapter 29

A Protection of Rights Not Enumerated

The Bill of Rights was created to appease the Anti-Federalists, but many of the Framers envisioned possible dangers in its creation. In fact, Alexander Hamilton in Federalist Paper #84 suggested that there existed the possibility of misinterpretations that may place the rights of the people in danger from an overpowering federal government. In Federalist #84 Hamilton suggested that government may create exceptions to powers not granted, and argue the power exists because it is not denied by the Bill of Rights. In other words, because the Constitution was designed to grant authorities, and those not listed are not granted, the Bill of Rights muddies the waters because those amendments tell the federal government what it can't do. Furthermore, many of the delegates in the Federal Convention of 1787 argued that the Bill of Rights is unnecessary, because prior to the creation of the Bill of Rights, the federal government was not given the authorities by the first seven articles over any of the issues listed in those first ten amendments in the first place.

Regardless, the Anti-Federalists demanded the inclusion of the Bill of Rights in the Constitution, or they would not ratify the document. Needing the support of the Anti-Federalists in order for the Constitution to be made law, the Founding Fathers that were at odds with the creation of the Bill of Rights compromised, and James Madison was given the task to write out the Bill of Rights based on proposals received from the several States.

Hundreds of proposed amendments were offered by the States. Only twelve were considered. Ten were ratified by the States during that time period. Answering concerns of the Founding Fathers that the federal government may interfere with rights not enumerated by the Bill of Rights, the 9th Amendment was included as one of those ten.

The Founders expected the people to protect their own rights through self-government. With freedom comes responsibility, therefore the people, when it came to their rights, should be governed by their conscience, not government. This concept tasked the people, with their individual judgment, to be civil, and to not encroach on one another's freedoms. If citizens were guilty of violating someone else's rights, the civil court system in each State would address the issue. Local courts were controlled by juries, and left all issues regarding rights at the local level.

The very notion of the federal government putting itself into a position of encroaching on the rights of the people was seen as tyrannical, and dangerous. After all, how could a centralized, far removed, governmental power that is unfamiliar with local customs and laws properly administer private rights issues?

The problem presented by the Bill of Rights, however, is that by listing specific rights that the government shall not infringe upon, many of the founders believed that would open up the opportunity for the federal government to "interpret" the Constitution to mean that all other rights not listed are fair game. Therefore, the wording of the 9th Amendment was carefully fashioned to enable the reader to recognize its intent.

The enumeration in the Constitution, of certain rights, shall not be construed to deny or disparage others retained by the people.

In other words, the government cannot "deny or disparage" any rights, even the ones not listed in the Bill of Rights, because our rights are given to us by God. This does not give the federal government the authority to guarantee our rights, however. To allow a central government to force lower governments to abide by the rights enumerated in the Bill of Rights is to open the door for government to later dictate to the lower governments other actions they would have to take regarding rights. Since rights, as the Declaration of Independence reveals, are "self-evident," as well as individual possessions, the authority to resolve disputes regarding rights remains at the local level.

Chapter 30

State Sovereignty

"The powers not delegated to the United States by the Constitution, nor prohibited by it to the States, are reserved to the States respectively, or to the people."

The 10th Amendment was designed to restrict federal powers from encroaching on State authorities. The article states that any powers not given to the federal government by the Constitution, and any powers not prohibited to the States, belongs to the States.

We must remember that originally all powers belonged to the States, a concept known as **Original Authority**. In order to create a central government, the States granted some of their powers to the federal government so that it may function in the manner necessary to protect, preserve, and promote the union. The States, in Article I, Section 10, are denied powers that would be in conflict with the federal powers granted. However, since the States originally maintained all powers, any authorities not granted to the federal government, nor denied to the States for the purpose of enabling the federal government to do its job, were retained by the States.

The 10th Amendment was also designed to correct the problems that arose through the creation of the Bill of Rights. By the Bill of Rights being composed in such a manner that the first ten amendments tell the federal government what it cannot do, the worry was that the argument in support of unconstitutional activity by the federal government would entail the argument, "Where in the Constitution does it say the federal government can't do that?" Such an argument by the central government may open up opportunities for the federal government to compromise **Americanism**, and fundamentally transform into a big government tyranny.

The Constitution was designed to grant authorities to the federal government so that it may function in the manner originally intended.

The powers granted to the federal government are the only authorities the federal government has. If the powers are not enumerated, the federal government does not have those authorities. The 10th Amendment was written to remind us that even though the first eight amendments tell the federal government it "shall not infringe," the rule of the Constitution is that all federal powers are enumerated in the Constitution, and if the power is not granted to the federal government, nor denied to the States, the authority remains with the States.

This article was written to support **State Sovereignty**. It is the Tenth Amendment to which one must first go when debating **State's Rights**. The amendment clearly states that all federal powers are enumerated, and the remaining unlisted powers, if not prohibited, belongs to the States.

James Madison makes a clear argument in support of the concept of State Sovereignty in Federalist #45: ". . . *each of the principal branches of the federal government will owe its existence more or less to the favor of the State governments. . . The powers delegated by the proposed Constitution to the federal government are few and defined. Those which are to remain in the State governments are numerous and indefinite. The former will be exercised principally on external objects, as war, peace, negotiation, and foreign commerce. . . The powers reserved to the several States will extend to all the objects which, in the ordinary course of affairs, concern lives, liberties, and properties of the people, and the internal order, improvement, and prosperity of the State. The operations of the federal government will be most extensive and important in times of war and danger; those of the State governments in times of peace and security. . .*"

The States serve in a manner similar to that of parents. The people, through their States are the parents of the federal government, but the petulant child is not only acting in ways never authorized, but the parents, through representation, and other means, have determined for themselves that they have no ability to rein in the out of control creation. The 10th Amendment reveals the reality that the States are sovereign, and that the federal government has only limited powers.

When breaking down the language of the Tenth Amendment, the previous articles of the Constitution become clear. It is in the Tenth Amendment that the principles of a limited government are most clearly articulated.

The concept that the Constitution was designed not to tell the federal government what it cannot do, but to tell it what it can do, is presented clearly in the first portion of this amendment. Powers not delegated to the federal government by the Constitution are not authorities granted, meaning that the federal government is limited to only the powers enumerated by the Constitution.

Some powers, despite the fact that **original authority** of all powers belongs to the States, are prohibited to the States. The authorities prohibited to the States are those that, if the States had those powers, may interfere with the federal government's task of protecting, preserving, and promoting the union. The list of powers prohibited to the States, any amendments doing the same notwithstanding, are located in Article I, Section 10.

The word **reserved** was chosen carefully for this amendment. "Reserved" is used rather than the word "granted," because the States are not granted any powers by any source. All of the powers already belonged to the States from the beginning. Any powers the States did not grant to the federal government, nor decide to prohibit to themselves through the Constitution, remain with the States. The presence of the word "reserved" reveals that fact. Reserved, in the context of this article, also means "To hold for their own use."

Chapter 31

Further Limiting the Courts

The **Judicial Branch** was added almost as an afterthought. The judiciary was originally designed to be the weakest of the three branches of government. The Anti-Federalists feared the judicial branch becoming a judicial oligarchy, and therefore the judicial branch was constructed to only apply the law to cases they hear. All opinions the judges may have of the law after reviewing the law was considered to be only opinion. Any changes to law, regardless of what the courts felt about the law, could only be made legislatively. However, soon after the Constitution and the Bill of Rights, fears of a tyrannical court arose, and so additional limits were placed on the federal courts by the 11th Amendment. No case against a State by citizens of another State, or by the citizens or subjects of a foreign state, shall be heard by a federal court.

The 11th Amendment changes the intent of Article III. As limited as the courts were supposed to be, the Founding Fathers realized the courts weren't limited enough, and as a result, the 11th Amendment wound up being ratified in 1795.

Federal judges maintained that the federal courts should have the power of **judicial review**, or the power to determine the constitutionality of laws. In response to the judicial urgings for the powers to judge the extent of the federal government's powers, in the Kentucky and Virginia Resolutions of 1798, Thomas Jefferson and James Madison warned us that giving the federal government through its courts the power of judicial review would be a power that would continue to grow, regardless of elections, putting at risk the all important **separation of powers**, and other much-touted limits on power. The final arbiters of the Constitution are not supposed to be the courts, argued these Founding Fathers who were believers in the limiting principles of the U.S. Constitution. The power of the federal government must be checked by State governments, and the people. The States and the People are the enforcers and protectors of the U.S. Constitution.

As you may recall, John Jay, the first Chief Justice of the United States Supreme Court, resigned his position in 1795, disappointed in how few powers the federal courts had. When approached later by President John Adams to return to the United States Supreme Court as the high court's Chief Justice, Jay turned Adams down. He said the Court lacked "the energy, weight, and dignity which are essential to its affording due support to the national government." He also did not wish to serve under Thomas Jefferson, the victor in the 1800 Presidential Election, who was an advocate of limited government, and a judicial branch that existed as the weakest of the three branches of government.

While John Jay was Chief Justice, among the influences of his decision that the court was too weak to promote a strong, centralized **national government**, was the case of *Chisholm v. Georgia* in 1793, which eventually led to the proposal, and ratification, of the 11th Amendment. A citizen of South Carolina sued Georgia for the value of clothing supplied by a merchant during the Revolutionary War. After Georgia refused to appear, claiming immunity as a sovereign state, as per the Constitution (Article III, Section 2) the federal courts took the case. The nationalist view by the justices deemed that in this case Georgia was not a sovereign State; therefore, the Supreme Court entered a default judgment against Georgia. What ensued was a conflict between federal jurisdiction and state sovereignty that reminded the anti-federalists of their fears of a centralized federal government consolidating the States, and destroying their right to individual sovereignty.

Realizing that the clause in Article III gave the federal courts too much power over State Sovereignty, Congress immediately proposed the 11th Amendment in order to take away federal court jurisdiction in suits commenced against a State by citizens of another State, or of a foreign state. This is the first instance in which a Supreme Court decision was superseded by a **constitutional amendment**, and evidence that the Founders saw the legislative branch and the States as being more powerful parts of government than the judiciary.

Chapter 32

Electoral Procedures for Electing President Changed

"Electors shall meet in their respective states, and vote by ballot for President and Vice-President, one of whom, at least, shall not be an inhabitant of the same state with themselves; they shall name in their ballots the person voted for as President, and in distinct ballots the person voted for as Vice-President, and they shall make distinct lists of all persons voted for as President, and all persons voted for as Vice-President and of the number of votes for each, which lists they shall sign and certify, and transmit sealed to the seat of the government of the United States, directed to the President of the Senate. The President of the Senate shall, in the presence of the Senate and House of Representatives, open all the certificates and the votes shall then be counted. The person having the greatest Number of votes for President, shall be the President, if such number be a majority of the whole number of Electors appointed; and if no person have such majority, then from the persons having the highest numbers not exceeding three on the list of those voted for as President, the House of Representatives shall choose immediately, by ballot, the President. But in choosing the President, the votes shall be taken by states, the representation from each state having one vote; a quorum for this purpose shall consist of a member or members from two-thirds of the states, and a majority of all the states shall be necessary to a choice. And if the House of Representatives shall not choose a President whenever the right of choice shall devolve upon them, before the fourth day of March next following, then the Vice-President shall act as President, as in the case of the death or other constitutional disability of the President. The person having the greatest number of votes as Vice-President, shall be the Vice-President, if such number be a majority of the whole number of Electors appointed, and if no person have a majority, then from the two highest numbers on the list, the Senate shall choose the Vice-President; a quorum for the purpose shall consist of two-thirds of the whole number of Senators, and a majority of the whole number shall be necessary to a choice. But no person constitutionally ineligible to the office of President shall be eligible to that of Vice-President of the United States."

The 12th Amendment changes the procedure for electing the President and Vice President originally provided for in Article II, Section 1, Clause 3. The procedure has remained the same since its ratification, save for the States changing their procedures from appointing the electors by the choice of the State legislatures, thus following the instructions of the State legislatures, to the citizens voting for who the electors are expected to vote for. Though the electors are free to vote for anyone eligible to be President, in practice they usually vote for the candidates chosen by the voters in their State. 1824 is the last election in which electors were primarily appointed by their State legislature. In that election, six states followed that procedure. South Carolina was the final State to follow the practice, ceasing the appointment of their electors by the State legislature upon the approach of the American Civil War.

Each State is constitutionally allowed to choose how to appoint or elect their electors, and the methods vary from State to State. Generally, electors are nominated by their State political parties in the months prior to Election Day. In some States, the electors are nominated in primaries, the same way that other candidates are nominated. Other States nominate their electors in party conventions.

The need for the 12th Amendment became apparent after the problems that arose in the elections of 1796 and 1800. The Twelfth Amendment was proposed by the Congress on December 9, 1803, and was ratified by the requisite number of state legislatures on June 15, 1804.

Before the 12th Amendment, electors could vote for two candidates, though at least one had to be from a State different from that of the elector (as a protection against a larger State dominating the federal government). A majority of the vote needed to be received in order to win the presidency. If no candidate received a majority vote, then the House of Representatives chose the President.

In 1800, after a tie in the **Electoral College**, the House tied 36 times. That particular election was marked by a battle between the Federalists, and Jefferson's Democratic-Republicans. Even though Burr was Jefferson's running mate, Aaron Burr wound up Jefferson's adversary when the vote went to the House. The lame-duck House controlled by the Federalists threw their support behind Burr, because they did not trust Jefferson's philosophy of a **limited government**.

The term Electoral College did not appear until the early 1800s, and did not appear in legislation until 1845. The concept was designed to act in a manner similar to Congress, where a portion of the election was connected to the population-based premise that was also used by the House of Representatives, and another portion of the Electoral College would be based on the State appointment premise used by the U.S. Senate.

In *Federalist No. 39*, James Madison explained that the Constitution was designed to be a mixture of State-based and population-based government.

In *Federalist No. 10*, James Madison argued against "*an interested and overbearing majority*" and the "*mischiefs of faction*" in an electoral system. His definition of "faction" in relation to elections was "a number of citizens whether amounting to a majority or minority of the whole, who are united and actuated by some common impulse of passion, or of interest, adverse to the rights of other citizens, or to the permanent and aggregate interests of the community." In a republic it was necessary, according to Madison, to vary the distribution of powers, including those powers held by the members of the populace. Only a thorough division of power throughout the American System would protect the United States from the excesses of democracy, and countervail against factions. Madison further explained that the greater the population and expanse of the Republic, the more difficulty factions would face in organizing due to such issues as **sectionalism**.

Prior to the 12th Amendment, the choice of the Vice President went to the second place winner of the presidential election. The Vice President, unlike the President, did not require the votes of a majority of electors. If a tie arose, the Vice President was chosen by the Senate, with each Senator casting one vote. Though it was not specified in the Constitution whether the sitting Vice President could cast a tie-breaking vote for Vice President, because the sitting Vice President is President of the Senate and casts the tie-breaking vote, it is assumed that if that situation had arisen, the sitting Vice President would indeed be the deciding vote for his successor. Because the second place winner became Vice President, it was very possible for the President and the Vice President to be from different parties. In fact, that is what happened in the 1796 election. John Adams won that election as the Federalist Party candidate, and Jefferson became the Vice President as a Democratic-Republican candidate. The fear was that by the two men being of different parties, the Vice President may do what he could to impede the ability of the

President, or could even launch an effort to remove the President from office so that the Vice President could succeed to the office of the President.

The 12th Amendment eliminated the possibility of problems arising between the President and Vice President due to them being from different parties by having the President and Vice President elected as a ticket, thus lessening the Vice President's motivation for staging a coup.

The 12th Amendment also eliminated the "two votes for presidential candidates" method, changing it instead to the electors casting distinct votes for President and Vice President.

The 12th Amendment indicates that no elector may vote for both candidates of a presidential ticket if both candidates inhabit the same State as that elector, a provision consistent with the Framer's original language against **collusion**.

The 12th Amendment also clarified language to not allow those constitutionally ineligible to be President from being Vice President.

A majority of Electoral Votes is still required for one to be elected President or Vice President. As in the case before the 12th Amendment, when nobody has a majority, the House of Representatives, voting by States and with the same **quorum** requirements as under the original procedure, chooses a President. The 12th Amendment requires the House of Representatives to choose from the three highest receivers of Electoral Votes, rather than the top five as was the process under Article II, Section 1, Clause 3.

The Senate chooses the Vice President if no candidate receives a majority of Electoral Votes. The 12th Amendment requires a quorum of two-thirds for balloting.

Chapter 33

The End of Slavery

Prior to the Civil War, any federal legislation related to slavery dealt with the importation of slaves. Aspects of slavery inside State lines were considered a State issue.

Article I, Section 9, Clause 1 abolished the **Atlantic slave trade**, and the United States Government intervened militarily to ensure the law prohibiting the importation of slaves was enforced. The Framers of the Constitution believed that in order to ensure the southern States did their part in ratifying the Constitution, while remaining consistent with the concept of the federal government only having authority over external issues, and disputes between the States, they could not abolish slavery nationally through the articles presented by the Constitution. A large number of delegates at the federal convention in 1787 desired the immediate abolition of slavery, but the fear was that the southern States would not only refuse to ratify the Constitution, but that they would refuse to remain a part of the union, eventually succumbing to attacks from Florida and absorbed into the Spanish Empire.

A proposed amendment to abolish slavery during the **American Civil War** finally passed the Senate on April 8, 1864, by a vote of 38 to 6, but the House did not approve it.

When the proposed amendment was reintroduced by Representative Ashley, President Lincoln took an active role in working for its passage through the House by ensuring the amendment was added to the Republican Party platform for the upcoming Presidential elections. Lincoln's efforts, combined with the result of the **War Between the States**, ensured the House passed the bill on January 31, 1865, by a vote of 119 to 56.

The 13th Amendment was ratified into law on December 6, 1865.

Chapter 34

Citizenship, Civil Rights, and Apportionment

Citizenship Clause

The 14th Amendment to the United States Constitution failed in 1866 after the southern States rejected the proposed amendment. After a second attempt to ratify the amendment, it was adopted on July 9, 1868. The ratification of the 14th Amendment occurred after the federal government began to govern the South through a system of **military districts**. Some historians question the validity of the ratification of the 14th Amendment because it is believed by these historians that the southern States ratified the amendment under duress, and pressure applied by the northern governorships in each of the southern States during the early part of the **Reconstruction Period**.

The first clause of the 14th Amendment is known as "The Citizenship Clause." The clause was intended to ensure the children of the emancipated slaves, as well as the newly freed slaves, would be considered citizens without any room for argument. The clause reads:

"All persons born or naturalized in the United States and subject to the jurisdiction thereof, are citizens of the United States and of the State wherein they reside."

This clause has been misinterpreted to mean all persons born in the United States are automatically citizens, which is not the case. The defining term in this clause that enables the reader to recognize that citizenship needs more than just being born on American soil reads: "subject to the jurisdiction, thereof."

To understand the term **jurisdiction**, one may go to the debates on the congressional record of the 14th Amendment. In those debates, and in articles of that time period written to explain the intent of the language of the amendment, one finds that "full jurisdiction" was meant to mean "full allegiance to America." The intention was to protect the nation against persons with divided loyalties.

The writers of the 14th Amendment wished to follow the importance of "full loyalty" as portrayed by the Founding Fathers. As far as the founders were concerned, there could be no divided allegiances. They expected citizens to be fully American.

Despite the defeat of the Confederacy in the American Civil War, the emancipated slaves were not receiving the rights and privileges of American citizens as they should have been. The former slaves were present in the United States legally, and because they were here legally they were "*subject to the jurisdiction thereof*," but they were still not receiving any assurance of **equal protection under the law**.

The Civil Rights Act of 1866 was created in the hopes of correcting the problem. Some of the language in the Civil Rights Act of 1866 states, "All persons born in the United States, and not subject to any foreign power, excluding Indians not taxed, are hereby declared to be citizens of the United States. ... All persons within the jurisdiction of the United States shall have the same right in every State and Territory to make and enforce contracts, to sue, be parties, give evidence, and to the full and equal benefit of all laws and proceedings for the security of persons and property as is enjoyed by white citizens, and shall be subject to like punishment, pains, penalties, taxes, licenses, and exactions of every kind, and to no other."

The definition of "persons within the jurisdiction of the United States" in that act was all persons at the time of its passage, born in the United States, including all slaves and their offspring, but not having any allegiances to any foreign government.

Michigan Senator Jacob Howard, one of two principal authors of Section 1 of the 14th Amendment (Citizenship Clause), noted that its provision, "subject to the jurisdiction thereof," excluded American Indians who had tribal nationalities, and "persons born in the United States who are foreigners, aliens, who belong to the families of ambassadors or foreign ministers."

Senator Howard's responses to questions regarding the language he used in the Citizenship Clause were recorded in The Congressional Globe, which are the recorded transcripts of the debates over the 14th Amendment by the 139th Congress:

Mr. HOWARD: "I now move to take up House joint resolution No. 127."

The motion was agreed to; and the Senate, as in Committee of the Whole, resumed the consideration of the joint resolution (H.R. No. 127) proposing an amendment to the Constitution of the United States.

"The 1st Amendment is to section one, declaring that all persons born in the United States and Subject to the jurisdiction thereof, are citizens of the United States and of the States wherein they reside. I do not propose to say anything on that subject except that the question of citizenship has been fully discussed in this body as not to need any further elucidation, in my opinion. This amendment which I have offered is simply declaratory of what I regard as the law of the land already, that every person born within the limits of the United States, and subject to their jurisdiction, is by virtue of **natural law** and national law a citizen of the United States. This will not, of course, include persons born in the United States who are foreigners, aliens, who belong to the families of ambassadors or foreign ministers accredited to the Government of the United States, but will include every other class of persons. It settles the great question of citizenship and removes all doubt as to what persons are or are not citizens of the United States. This has long been a great desideratum in the jurisprudence and legislation of this country."

Senator Howard even went out of his way to indicate that children born on American soil of foreign citizens are not included.

Clearly, the framers of the 14th Amendment had no intention of freely giving away American citizenship to just anyone simply because they may have been born on American soil.

The second author of the Citizenship Clause, Illinois Senator Lyman Trumbull, added that "subject to the jurisdiction of the United States" meant "not owing allegiance to anybody else."

The full quote by Senator Trumbull:

"The provision is, that 'all persons born in the United States, and subject to the jurisdiction thereof, are citizens.' That means 'subject to the complete jurisdiction thereof.' What do we mean by 'complete jurisdiction thereof?' Not owing allegiance to anybody else. That is what it means."

Trumbull continues, "Can you sue a Navajo Indian in court? Are they in any sense subject to the complete jurisdiction of the United States? By no means. We make treaties with them, and therefore they are not subject to our jurisdiction. If they were, we wouldn't make treaties with them...It is only those persons who come completely within our jurisdiction, who are subject to our laws, that we think of making citizens; and there can be no objection to the proposition that such persons should be citizens."

Senator Howard concurred with what Mr. Trumbull had to say:

"I concur entirely with the honorable Senator from Illinois [Trumbull], in holding that the word 'jurisdiction,' as here employed, ought to be construed so as to imply a full and complete jurisdiction on the part of the United States, whether exercised by Congress, by the executive, or by the judicial department; that is to say, the same jurisdiction in extent and quality as applies to every citizen of the United States now."

Based on these explanations by the writers of the clause, then, it is understood that the intention was for those who are not born to American citizens to have no birthright to citizenship just because they simply were born inside the borders of this country.

The courts have interpreted the Citizenship Clause to mean other things, but we must remember that the Constitution cannot be changed by the courts. Changes to the Constitution can only be made by amendment (Article V.).

It was through the progressive actions of the Lincoln administration in the American Civil War, and the actions of the courts to incorporate the Bill of Rights to the States, that America ceased to be "**The United States Are**," and became a more nationalistic "**The United States Is**."

Privileges and Immunities Clause

The next clause, *"No State shall make or enforce any law which shall abridge the privileges or immunities of citizens of the United States,"* was expected to protect the newly emancipated slaves from local legislation that may treat them differently. This clause was a direct response to the **Black Codes**, laws passed in the States that were designed to limit the former slaves from obtaining all of the freedoms they thought they had been guaranteed.

The Due Process Clause of the 14th Amendment prohibits state and local governments from depriving persons of the proper due process of law. The right to a fair trial was to be extended to all persons, including the emancipated slaves.

Due Process Clause and Equal Protection Clause

The Due Process Clause, and the Equal Protection clause, have been the subject of debate since the language written by Congressman John Bingham, the principal author of the later part of Section 1 of the 14th Amendment, was first penned. Bingham believed the federal government should use all national tools available to ensure the southern States behaved as instructed. Bingham repeatedly stated his belief that the Fourteenth Amendment would enforce the Bill of Rights against the States, but the majority of the members of Congress present did not concur with his muddled and inconsistent argument.

Author Raoul Berger, in his book *Government by Judiciary*, discussed whether the 14th Amendment should be construed to enforce the Bill of Rights against the States. Relying on the analysis of Professor Charles Fairman in his published article, *Does the Fourteenth Amendment Incorporate the Bill of Rights?*, Berger concluded that Bingham was a "muddled" thinker whose views should be discounted. Berger agreed with Fairman that the framers of the 14th Amendment did not intend it to enforce the Bill of Rights against the States. Berger rejected even selective incorporation, arguing that the Amendment's framers did not intend that any of the first eight amendments should be made applicable to the States through the 14th Amendment

Antislavery activists largely supported Bingham's conclusion that that Bill of Rights must be applied to the States, and such application must be enforced by the federal government. Though the Bill of Rights was originally intended by the Founding Fathers not to apply to the States, and with less than a centuryt since the American Revolution and the writing of the Constitution behind them, Bingham's supporters contended that local jurisdiction over cases regarding an individual's rights could no longer be allowed because the southern States could not be trusted to be fair to the newly emancipated slaves.

Bingham's call for an incorporation of the Bill of Rights to the States established the concept that all people's rights are supposed to be protected by the federal government. The Founding Fathers did not apply the Bill of Rights to the States from the beginning because giving that kind of power to a potentially tyrannical federal government carries with it many pitfalls. As the quote by Gerald Ford goes, "A government big enough to give you everything you want is a government big enough to take from you everything you have." Nonetheless, despite the dangers of a central government dictating to the States regarding their laws regarding individual rights, because of the mistreatment of the former slaves by the Southern States, the Privileges and Immunities Clause, the Due Process Clause and the Equal Protection Clause, have been commonly interpreted to mean that the Bill of Rights is applicable to the States.

Since the **Incorporation of the Bill of Rights** did not take hold as a result of the 14th Amendment, as the statists that supported Bingham's position had desired, the federal courts stepped in and took pursuit. Pursuing a **nationalist** agenda, the courts disregarded the original intent of the Framers of the Constitution, as well as the conclusions of the Congress regarding the 14th Amendment, and began to selectively incorporate the Bill of Rights to the States, beginning with the Slaughterhouse Cases just five years after the ratification of the 14th Amendment in 1868. A five to four vote by the high court interpreted the Privileges and Immunities Clause as the authority to enforce The Bill of Rights against the States. Subsequent cases also used the 14th Amendment as an authority for incorporation.

The courts, through this process of incorporating The Bill of Rights to the States, have changed the Constitution through unconstitutional means, and against **original intent**. As originally intended, all provisions in the U.S. Constitution apply to the federal government, unless otherwise noted. The Bill of Rights was originally intended to apply only to the federal government, and if we are to remain in line with the original intent of the Founding Fathers, State sovereignty must remain protected by that original intent.

The attitude of the southern States, and their refusal to treat the former slaves fairly led to a perceived need for clarification and enforcement by the federal government, which led to the passage of the Civil Rights Act of 1866, and eventually to the Civil Rights Movement of the 1960s.

A **separate but equal** doctrine existed for more than fifty years, despite numerous attempts to ensure blacks enjoyed full rights and privileges of citizenship.

In modern politics, laws continue to test the limits of the Equal Protection Clause. While the clause was intended to make sure that everyone is treated equally under the law, politicians supporting the Affordable Care Act have handed out exemptions to members of Congress, and some individuals or corporations, allowing those that receive the exemptions to be treated differently under the law.

Apportionment

Section 2 of the 14th Amendment altered the rules for the apportioning of Representatives in the Congress to the States. The enumeration was changed to include all residents, while also calling for a reduction of a State's apportionment if it wrongfully denies any adult male's right to vote.

For fear that the former slaves would support the Republicans, southern Democrats worked feverishly to dissuade blacks from voting. Section 2 addressed this problem by offering to the southern States the opportunity to enfranchise black voters, or lose congressional representation.

Consequences of Insurrection

Section 3 of the 14th Amendment prohibits the election or appointment to any federal or state office of any person who had held any of certain offices and then engaged in insurrection, rebellion or treason. A two-thirds vote by each House of the Congress could override this limitation. The interest was to ban the service of any members of the Confederacy that refused to renounce their participation in the Confederacy.

Public Debt as a Result of the War

Section 4 of the 14th Amendment confirmed the legitimacy of all United States **public debt** appropriated by Congress. The clause also indicated that neither the United States nor any State would pay for the loss of slaves or debts that had been incurred by the Confederacy. This clause was to ensure that all States recognized the validity of the debt appropriated by Congress as a result of the war, while bonds secured by the Confederacy in order to help finance the South's part of the war "went beyond congressional power."

Political battles over the debt ceiling in 2011 and 2013 encouraged some politicians to argue that the "validity of the public debt" clause outlawed a debt ceiling, because placing a limit on federal spending interferes with the duty of the government to pay interest on outstanding bonds and to make payments owed to pensioners (such as Social Security). The clause in the 14th Amendment addressing the validity of the public debt, however, was never intended to be a general clause to be used by future administrations, but a specific clause only addressing the debt accrued as a result of the American Civil War.

Enforcement

The final clause of the 14th Amendment authorizes Congress to "enforce, by appropriate legislation, the provisions of this article." Federal intrusion upon the States, however, has been a long-time fear by those that support the concept of **State Sovereignty**. The question regarding enforcement was addressed in the *Civil Rights Cases* of 1883, where the opinion of the Supreme Court interpreted Section 5 of the 14th Amendment to mean that "the legislation which Congress is authorized to adopt in this behalf is not general legislation upon the rights of the citizen, but corrective legislation".

In a more recent case, *City of Boerne v. Flores,* 1997, the Supreme Court ruled that Congress's enforcement power according to the last clause of the 14th Amendment is limited to only enacting legislation as a response to a "congruence and proportionality" between the injury to a person's 14th Amendment rights and the means Congress adopted to prevent or remedy that injury.

Court interpretation of the Constitution can be a dangerous practice, and we must remember that any interpretation of the Constitution offered by the courts in a ruling are merely opinions. The final authority regarding the definitions of Constitutional law resides with the people, through their States. Any allowance of the courts to fully define the Constitution at the whims of the judges opens up the opportunity for the courts to change definitions for ideological purposes, resulting in a judicial oligarchy, rather than a **constitutional republic** driven by the consent of the governed, and the self-evident standards of **Natural Law**.

Chapter 35

Voting Rights

The 15th Amendment was designed to protect the voting rights of all citizens, regardless of race, color, or if the voter had previously been a slave or indentured servant. As stated in the amendment, this article applies to both the federal government, and the States.

As the third reconstruction amendment, the 15th Amendment faced another challenge that was unexpected. In some States the requirements were that all voters and candidates must be Christians. As originally written, the amendment would require these States to change their rules regarding the manner of elections. Realizing the ratification of the amendment may depend on the support of the States with Christianity requirements regarding elections, the amendment was revised in a conference committee to remove any reference to holding office or religion and only prohibited discrimination based on race, color or previous condition of servitude.

Democrat Party created militias, like the Ku Klux Klan, continued to try and intimidate black voters and white Republicans. The federal government promised support, assuring that black and Republican voters could both vote, and serve, in confidence. When an all-white mob in the Battle of Liberty Place attempted to take over the interracial government of New Orleans, President Ulysses S. Grant sent in federal troops to restore the elected mayor.

President Rutherford B. Hayes narrowly won the election in 1876. To appease the South after his close election, in the hopes of gaining their support and soothing angry Democrats, President Hayes agreed to withdraw the federal troops who had been occupying the South since the end of the Civil War. The hope was that the southern States were ready to handle their own affairs without a need for any interference from the North.

In the process, President Hayes also overlooked rampant fraud and electoral violence in the Deep South, despite several attempts by Republicans to pass laws protecting the rights of black voters and to punish intimidation. Without the restrictions, voting place violence against blacks and Republicans increased, including instances of murder.

By the 1890s many of the southern States had enacted voter eligibility laws that included literacy tests and poll taxes. Since the black population was normally steeped in poverty, the inability to afford the **poll tax** kept them from voting in elections.

It took nearly a century for the promise of the Fifteenth Amendment to finally take hold. The ratification of the 24th Amendment in 1964, which eliminated poll taxes, and the passage of the Voting Rights Act of 1965, served to ensure that blacks in the South were able to freely register to vote, and vote without any obstacles.

Chapter 36

Income Tax and the Federal Reserve

Income Tax

Income Tax is a direct tax. The Founding Fathers prohibited direct taxes in Article I, Section 9, Clause 4 of the United States Constitution.

The concept of an income tax emerged during the American Civil War as a means of assisting in paying for the Union war effort. In 1861, Congress drew up a bill to tax personal and corporate incomes. This first income tax measure in the United States called for a 3% tax on incomes over $800. The bill quickly passed in both the House and the Senate, but it was never put into operation.

In 1862, Abraham Lincoln signed a bill that imposed a 3% tax on incomes between $600 and $10,000 and a 5% tax on higher incomes. The bill was amended in 1864 to levy heavier taxation on higher incomes. The 1862 income tax law was repealed in 1872 and was declared to be unconstitutional, in violation of Article I, Section 9, Clause 4 of the United States Constitution.

Progressivism was on the rise in the United States around the turn of the 20th Century. Americans were concerned about the large national debt that remained with the United States as a result of the Spanish-American War, and the growing social inequality between the rich and the poor. The idea that there should be a tax that "soaks the rich" began to take root among progressives of both major parties. The Democrats took to progressivism more than the Republican Party, and the progressives of the Democrat Party were looking for a way to embarrass the conservative arm of the GOP so that they could gain some traction in the next election.

With social unrest rising among the population, a Democrat proposed the **Bailey Bill** with the express hope the Republicans would reject it. The theory was that after the Republicans rejected the bill, the Democrats could then point a finger at the Republicans, claiming for political purposes that the Republicans were in cahoots with the corrupt wealthy corporate types. A Republican rejection of the Bailey Bill, which would have imposed an income tax on the rich, would serve as proof of such an alignment between the Republicans and the wealthy. The slogan used by proponents of the Bailey Bill was "soak the rich," a direct call to tax people they considered to be **profiteers**, a class of **plutocrats** they claimed were in collusion with the Republicans.

The conservative Republicans knew what the progressives of the Democrat Party were up to, and launched a counter move. They proposed a constitutional amendment that would impose an income tax on the rich, and when the States refused to ratify the amendment, the Republicans would use that failure to ratify the amendment as proof that the people, through their State legislatures, were against the idea of a new income tax. In turn, that would defeat the Bailey Bill, for how could Congress approve an income tax against the rich through the Bailey Bill after the people and States rejected a constitutional amendment that would have done the very same thing?

The proponents of the 16th Amendment promised that if it were to be ratified (remember, it was fully expected not to be ratified) the income tax would only be imposed on the top 5% wage earners, it would be voluntary, and it would be temporary.

The progressives of the Republican Party, however, rallied behind the proposed amendment, and the Secretary of State announced the amendment was ratified on February 12, 1913.

Progressives, satisfied the 16th Amendment was ratified, hoped to use it to tax the rich. In the beginning, only 5% of the people were required to submit tax returns. Many of the rich, however, avoided the tax with charitable deductions, and other creative strategies.

During World War II Franklin Delano Roosevelt saw the income tax as a way to vastly increase revenue, and initiated a policy of withholding from "all" wages and salaries, not just the highest incomes enjoyed by the rich. Rather than the rich paying the tax at the end of the year, the tax was collected at the payroll window before it was even due to be paid by the taxpayer. This style of collection shifted the tax from its original design as a tax on the wealthy to a tax on the masses, mostly on the middle class.

In addition to violating the original intent of Article I, Section 9 prohibiting **direct taxation**, the income tax also opposes the 4th Amendment which requires that a citizen's privacy be protected. An income tax enforced by the Internal Revenue Service violates the privacy of the home, business, personal papers and personal affairs of the private citizen. Since the tax is based on income, the IRS has the task of making sure everyone pays his fair share. This task is physically impossible without prying into the private papers, private business and personal affairs of the individual citizens.

Since the ratification of the 16th Amendment, there have been questions about whether the proper number of State ratification votes were ever achieved. Despite the argument by some researchers that the 16th Amendment was never properly ratified by the requisite three-fourths of the states, and that politicians of the day were aware of the discrepancy, Secretary of State Philander Knox fraudulently declared ratification. Some may suggest that he did so under the urgings of wealthy bankers like J.P. Morgan.

Federal Reserve

The same year the 16th Amendment created the income tax, the **Federal Reserve** was also created. The Federal Reserve is not a federal agency, and is actually a privately owned corporation owned by a secret group of international bankers. The Federal Reserve holds a monopoly on the creation of money in the United States. Whenever the U.S. Government needs money it borrows the money from the Federal Reserve. The Federal Reserve gladly loans that money because doing so results in a good profit for the bankers.

The Federal Reserve is not the first central bank, but it is the longest lasting. The First Bank of the United States in 1791, created by Alexander Hamilton, became a system of control over the American economy, and was, as described by Jefferson and Madison, "an engine for speculation, financial manipulation, and corruption."

In order to properly function, a central bank needs a collection of large sums of money from the people to pay off the interest on the money the government borrows. The creation of the income tax provided that opportunity.

The Federal Reserve Act surrendered control of the monetary system to the international banking cartel and guaranteed the eventual abandonment of the gold standard. The Federal Reserve's debt-based money guaranteed the enslavement of every American under a crushing debt burden. The Federal Reserve guaranteed the ability of the international banking cartel to confiscate wealth through artificially created boom/bust cycles.

The result is that the U.S. Government, and the bankers in charge of the Federal Reserve, can manipulate the economy simply by the amount of money they decide to pump into the system. The more currency is pumped into the system, the greater the rise of **inflation** rates. A reduction of the printing of money then results in a recovering economy. Government spending, in relation to the national debt, has a direct impact on the economic cycles we experience. The more the government borrows, the more **fiat money** is pumped into the system. The result is increased inflation, and a stalled economy. Cutting spending results in less money being borrowed, which then returns value to the dollar, and in turn reduces the level of inflation while encouraging **capitalism** to thrive.

The welfare system was created to compensate for the damage caused by the Federal Reserve and the income tax.

The 16th Amendment allows for the taxation on income from whatever source derived, which gives Congress, for the most part, **carte blanche** to tax at will, while giving the IRS the power to do all of the things the founders specifically disallowed the federal government from doing. This invasion of privacy, without due process, will continue as long as the 16th Amendment remains in force.

The income tax is in line with the Marxist philosophy of destroying a capitalist society by steeply graduating taxes on income and applying heavy levies upon the estates of people when they die.

Chapter 37

State Representation in the Senate

State's Lose Their Voice in the U.S. Senate

To comprehend the 17th Amendment, we need to go back in history to understand how our political system was originally established. The Founding Fathers included a number of **checks and balances** during the creation of the federal government in the hopes of providing enough safeguards to protect the people from an ever expansive, tyrannical, consolidated central government. The **separation of powers** between the three branches of government, and between the federal government and the States, were an integral part of these protections against tyranny. However, not all of the checks and balances put in place were obvious, nor are all of the checks and balances taught to us during our school years.

The dynamics of the federal government were set up to prevent any part of government from having access to too much power. Too much power in any one part of the system could be dangerous, and this includes too much power in the hands of the people.

The general population, just like the government, cannot be fully trusted with absolute power. To prevent the danger of too much power residing in any part of government, power needed to be divided as much as possible so as to keep it under control. Too much power in the hands of anybody has the potential of being a dangerous proposition, including in the hands of the voting public.

The United States is not a **democracy**. All of the voting power was not given directly to the people. The voting power was divided to ensure the **Republic** was protected from the **mob-rule** mentality of democracy.

The vote of the people, or the people's full and unquestioned voice in government, was, and still is, manifested in the U.S. House of Representatives. Then, as now, the representatives were voted into office directly by the people. Each Representative represents a district. The members of the United States Senate were not voted in directly by the people during the time period immediately following the ratification of the United States Constitution. U.S. Senators were voted in by an **indirect vote** of the people.

The Senators were appointed by their State legislatures. The State legislators are voted into office by the people of the State. Therefore, during the early years of this nation, the Senators attained office by an indirect vote of the people through their State legislatures.

The people are represented indirectly by the States in the U.S. Senate, and by the States appointing the Senators, the method of appointment allowed State's interests to be represented in the U.S. Congress.

Since they were appointed by the State legislatures, the Senators looked at the political atmosphere in a different manner than the members of the House of Representatives. Members of the House of Representatives are directly voted into office by the people, so their concerns are more in line with the immediate concerns of the people, no matter how whimsical those concerns may be.

The Senate functioned in a very different manner because when the Senators were appointed they were expected to abide by the wishes of the State legislatures. The Senators were expected to be representative of what was best for their States; State's Rights, State Sovereignty, protecting the States not only from a foreign enemy, but from a domestic enemy, should the federal government become the potential tyranny that the Founding Fathers, and especially the Anti-federalists, feared a central government could become.

The federal government exists because the States allow it to. The powers derived by the federal government were granted to it by the States, so in a way the States birthed the federal government, making the States the parents of the government in Washington, D.C. The federal government is not supposed to be able to do much of anything without the permission of the several States. The Senate was the representation of the States so that the States could ensure the federal government remained within its authorities.

The States having representation in the federal government through the U.S. Senate was also another way that checks and balances were applied to the system. The House of Representatives represented *the people*, and the Senate represented *the States*. Through this arrangement, it gave the people the ability to check the States, and the States the ability to check the people, and together they checked the Executive. The dynamics of our government through this arrangement were a built in check and balance.

The States could not get too far without the people approving of a senatorial proposal. The people could not get much done without The States agreeing with a proposal that originated in the House of Representatives. The executive branch could get little done without both the people and the States approving of it. However, if the President did not like what the people and the States were trying to accomplish, he could veto the bill. If the people and the States felt the legislation was important enough, they could override that veto with two-thirds of a vote in both Houses.

Looking at it in another way, a bill would be approved by both the people and the States before it went to the President to become law. This gave the Executive and both parts of the legislative branch the opportunity to approve or disapprove potential laws.

In 1913, the Seventeenth Amendment changed the originally intended dynamics of the American form of government. The amendment removed the States' representation from U.S. Government proceedings. The Seventeenth Amendment changed the appointment of the Senators from that of the State legislatures to that of the **direct vote** of the people. As a result, the protection of State Sovereignty was removed, and in its place was inserted **ideology**, and the willingness of Senators to buy the votes of individual voters through gifts from the treasury in a manner that was already emerging from the House of Representatives.

Vacancies in the Senate

The Seventeenth Amendment also provides for appointments should a seat in the U.S. Senate be left vacant for any reason. The governors of the States, should the legislatures allow such, may make temporary appointments until a special election takes place. The State legislatures may change these rules as they deem necessary, such as requiring an immediate special election instead of allowing the governor to temporarily appoint a replacement. This leaves most of the power regarding filling vacancies in the hands of the State legislatures.

Massachusetts, during the reign of Democrat governors, used the rule that if there was a vacancy in the U.S. Senate, the governor could appoint the new Senator to complete that term of office. When Mitt Romney, who was a Republican, was governor, the Democrat dominated legislature feared a Republican appointment should one of the Massachusetts Senators die, so they changed the rule to require an immediate special election, fully confident the people would put another Democrat into office should one of the seats be vacated. The Massachusetts legislature even overrode a veto by Governor Mitt Romney to accomplish their rule change.

Romney did not run for reelection in 2006, and his gubernatorial term in Massachusetts ended January 4, 2007.

The new governor of Massachusetts in 2007 was Deval Patrick, a Democrat. When Senator Edward "Ted" Kennedy passed away August 25, 2009, since the State of Massachusetts had a Democrat governor, the Democrat-led legislature hurriedly changed the rule to enable the governor to appoint the new Senator as had been allowed before Mitt Romney was governor, just in case the people could not be trusted.

The appointed Democrat Party senator held the seat until a special election in January of 2010 that pitted Republican Scott Brown against Democrat Martha Coakley. To the surprise of the entire nation, Scott Brown won the election, sending tremors through the political establishment, which included the Democrats losing a filibuster-proof majority in the U.S. Senate. Brown was defeated in 2012 by Democrat Elizabeth Warren, returning the Senate Seat back to the Democrats when she took office on January 3, 2013.

More like a Democracy

In the end, the real damage caused by the ratification of the 17th Amendment was that State representation in the Congress was removed. Senators, after the ratification of the 17th Amendment, would be voted into office by the vote of the people, making the U.S. Senate more like the House of Representatives, eliminating a very important check and balance, and making the United States more like a democracy and less like the Republic the Founders originally intended.

The people, fooled by a relenting rallying cry of "The will of the people," and a common belief that the leaders of the States could not be trusted, demanded that the federal government be changed into something more like a democracy. As the progressives desired, and planned, the American form of government moved closer to a democracy with the 17th Amendment.

Karl Marx once stated that "Democracy is the road to socialism."

Progressivism was on the rise in the United States during those early years of the 20th Century, and the statists knew that one of their main obstacles to consolidating government power into the grasp of the central authority in Washington was the independent and sovereign voice of the States. The 17th Amendment was one of the vehicles the statists used to begin the process of silencing the States, with the ultimate goal of making them irrelevant in regards to the running of the federal government.

The **statists** did not reveal their true intentions. If they had proclaimed that they desired the ratification of the 17th Amendment so that they could proceed in their quest to change the United States into a socialist system, the people would have rejected it. Instead, they used a populist argument. "It is for the will of the people. You deserve a Senate voted into office by the democratic will of the people. If you directly vote for the Senators, they will be more apt to act in line with the will of the people. After all, the States are corrupt, and they can't be trusted. You, the voting public, in the interest of democracy, deserve to be able to directly vote for the Senators yourselves."

As a result, the whole American political system has been turned on its head. The entire dynamic of our government system as it was originally intended to function has changed.

The damage to the American form of government reached deeper into the dynamics of our **Constitutional Republic** than immediately meets the eye.

The Founding Fathers made the House of Representatives and the U.S. Senate different from each other for a reason.

If a President of the United States signs a treaty, before that treaty goes into force, it must be ratified by the U.S. Senate, which back then was the voice of the States. It was the Framer's way of making sure the States could act as a protective mechanism against a President who might make treaties that were dangerous to State Sovereignty. However, now the Senate no longer represents the States, so that important safeguard is no longer in place. Senators more apt to defend an ideology, rather than the best interest of their State, are in office now. The ratification of treaties has totally changed in a way that could place State Sovereignty in jeopardy. The States no longer have a voice in that part of the governing process anymore, and as a result it has become easier for the federal government to enter into treaties that compromise State interests, or local issues over which the federal government would normally not have any authority.

Another point to examine in regards to the Senate ratification of treaties, is since the people, through their States, are the final arbiters of the Constitution, the Founders felt no worry about unconstitutional treaties being ratified. After all, the final arbiters of the Constitution, the States, were the ones in charge of the ratification of all treaties. Now, since ideology now takes precedence over States' Rights in the Senate, we are faced by a number of draconian treaties . . . and there is nothing the States can do about it.

The appointment of judges, such as Supreme Court Justices, has also been altered by the passage of the 17th Amendment. Imagine how different the hearings regarding the appointment of Supreme Court Justices would be if the Senators were appointed by the State legislatures?

Do you think it would be as easy for an **activist judge** to be appointed?

Do you think the nominees would be asked questions geared towards the Constitution, and protecting State Sovereignty?

The people were told that the States could no longer be trusted in their appointment of the Senators, and the States got lazy and didn't wish to participate in that manner anymore. As a result, the 17th Amendment was ratified, and look at the mess it has caused.

Let's return to the concept of "dividing power" for a moment. The Founding Fathers divided the voting power. By the States appointing the Senators, it divided the people's voting power.

During the early years of this nation the State legislatures also appointed the Electors for president.

The people only directly voted into office the Representatives of the U.S. House of Representatives.

This division of voting power was put into place because the Founding Fathers knew that should the people be fooled while they completely controlled the vote, a tyranny could ensure that it was voted into the three primary parts of government: the Executive, the House of Representatives, and the U.S. Senate. Once tyranny had control of those three parts of government, the judicial branch would be sure to follow, if not already in **collusion** with the other two branches.

The Founders knew that should the uninformed electorate vote in a tyranny, while caught up in some kind of cult of personality, it would spell the beginning of the end of the United States as we know it.

The Founding Fathers knew that democracy of that kind would destroy the system, so they divided the power of the vote. The voting power was divided so as to protect us from the excesses of democracy.

Looking back on 2006, 2008, and 2012 we see an example of exactly what the Founding Fathers warned us about. A single ideology, one that is hostile towards the U.S. Constitution, and hostile to the American System, fooled the people, and took control of some of the most vital parts of government. The destructive reasoning by the statists of the Progressive Era for the passage of the 17th Amendment was fulfilled.

The 17th Amendment, combined with the creation of the Federal Reserve, and the implementation of an income tax, was all a part of a scheme to change the American System into a model of socialism through the guise of democracy.

We are not a democracy, and we were never meant to be a democracy. The 17th Amendment moved us in that direction. The Founding Fathers continuously spoke out against the dangers of democracy. They knew that democracies lead to mob-rule. As much as the government couldn't be trusted with too much power, neither could the voting public.

The Constitution is filled with checks and balances. Yet, the people of that time period were fooled so easily by the statists. James Madison five times in his Federalist Papers writings wrote, "We are a Republic, by

225

which I mean. . ." and then he would explain what a republic is. He felt the need to do so because those who opposed the Constitution because they believed the political system should be one of **nationalism** argued that democracy and **republicanism** were the same.

Thomas Jefferson said, "Democracy will cease to exist when you take away from those that are willing to work and give to those who would not."

John Adams said, "While it lasts, Democracy becomes more bloody than either an aristocracy or a monarchy. Democracy never lasts long; it soon wastes, exhausts, and murders itself. There is never a democracy that did not commit suicide."

Thomas Jefferson said, "A democracy is nothing more than mob-rule, where 51% of the people may take away the rights of the other 49%."

James Bovard said, "Democracy is two wolves and a sheep voting on what to have for dinner."

A friend of mine, the late Tim "Loki" Kerlin, added that a republic is "two wolves, and a well-armed sheep contesting the vote."

Benjamin Franklin, after asked what the Founders created in the Constitutional Convention, replied, "A republic, if you can keep it."

With freedom comes responsibility. It is up to us to repeal the 17th Amendment.

Chapter 38

Prohibition

Amendment 18 was ratified January 16, 1919, bringing the prohibition of alcohol to America. The amendment was repealed by Amendment 21, December 5, 1933.

Christian churches worked to bring about **prohibition** as far back as the early 1800s, largely through the campaigning by women and young adults who had been adversely affected by husbands and fathers who were heavy alcohol consumers. Alcohol was considered to be one of the most prevalent social problems in America. The concerns over the dangers of alcohol brought about the **Temperance Movement**. The American Temperance Society was founded in 1826, with the specific goal of outlawing alcohol in the United States.

Local organizations that encouraged abstinence from alcohol existed as early as 1808. It was not until 1826 that a nationwide temperance society was created. As the American Temperance Society gained steam, national and international temperance societies sprang up. Organizations like the Washington Temperance Society did not consider temperance to be a religious issue, while other groups felt compelled by God to proclaim temperance. Considering the involvement in the movement by a diverse menu of denominations, no one religion was able to claim to have been the originator of temperance ideals.

The most effective weapon of temperance was to advocate total abstinence from alcohol through personal pledges. The societies gave out pledge cards or medals with various types of pledges written on them. Not all of the pledges, however, demanded total abstinence, as indicated by the following pledge:

"We agree to abstain from all intoxicating liquors except for medicinal purposes and religious ordinances."

Concerned that being too strict may discourage many from joining their society, some organizations gave people the option to choose the extent of their pledge. One common practice was to have those who joined a society to sign a book indicating their commitment. If the person was willing to commit to total abstinence, they would place a capital "T" by their name. The "T" stood for Total or "Total Abstinence". Hence came the term "Tee Totaler" as one who has committed himself to total abstinence.

Through the use of pressure-politics the goal of nationwide prohibition was achieved during World War I with the ratification of the Eighteenth Amendment in January of 1919.

Congress, in response to the new amendment, passed the **Volstead Act** on October 28, 1919, to enforce the law. Most large cities refused to enforce the legislation. As the federal government went after bootleggers, it became quickly apparent that the understaffed agencies were fighting a losing battle. Meanwhile, though there was a slight decline in alcohol consumption around the nation, **organized crime** increased in the larger cities. Alcohol became a high demand cash crop that the criminal element could not resist.

As Prohibition became increasingly unpopular, and the element of organized crime had reached its height, the perceived need for tax revenue during the **Great Depression** also encouraged a repeal movement. The hope for tax revenue from the legal sale of alcohol, and the need to weaken organized crime, led to the 21st Amendment, which repealed the amendment that had brought Prohibition to America. The repeal returned the legalities of alcohol to the States. Though Prohibition was over nationwide, some counties remained **dry counties**, forbidding the sale of alcoholic beverages.

In our current society there are calls for the legalization of Marijuana, and other drugs. Existing federal drug laws enforce a prohibition of drugs. There is a movement in some parts of government pushing for the legalization of certain drugs, like marijuana. If at the federal level a number of politicians decided that the legalization of drugs is good for the nation, we could very well see such legislation pass through Congress. By studying the U.S. Constitution, and taking a lesson from the 18th Amendment, it is apparent that the federal government does not have the authority to ban, or legalize, drugs in America without receiving such an authority through the Amendment Process (as we saw with the 18th Amendment in regards to Alcohol). The regulation of drugs is a

State issue, as per the Tenth Amendment. This means that all federal drug laws are unconstitutional, and laws in California legalizing marijuana for medicinal purposes, and in the States of Washington and Colorado for recreational use, are completely constitutional.

Chapter 39

Women's Voting Rights

The 19th Amendment established uniform voting rights for women nationwide. It was ratified on August 18, 1920.

Women, despite popular opinion, did vote in elections prior to the ratification of the 19th Amendment. In 1869, women in the newly created territory of Wyoming became the first women in the United States to win the right to vote. Colorado gave voting rights to women in 1892, and both Utah and Idaho gave women the right to vote in 1896.

The Constitution gives the States the right to determine their own rules for elections. The women's suffrage movement worked to bring about an amendment that would give women voting rights nationwide. The amendment was first proposed in 1878, and it took forty-one years before it was submitted to the States for ratification. It took about a year to receive enough votes for ratification.

Susan B. Anthony, already known for her crusade for the abolition of slavery, and the prohibition of alcohol, added **women's suffrage** to her plate. By 1878 she was able to induce a Senator from California to introduce a resolution in Congress calling for an amendment to the Constitution which would give women throughout the United States the right to vote.

The drive for an amendment that would grant uniform voting rights for women was nothing new. Aaron Burr, the Vice President during Thomas Jefferson's presidency, was a fervent believer in women's rights, and took personal charge of his daughter's course of study, insisting she learn Greek, Latin, and French, along with literature, philosophy and sciences. His proposals for the uniform voting rights for women, however, never gained traction.

John Adams, the second President of the United States, also supported expanding women's freedoms. As a great admirer of his wife, Abigail, he often went to her for advice. In 1776, as the Founders put into full gear their drive for American independence, Abigail offered in a letter, "I long to hear that you have declared an independency. And, by the way, in the new code of laws which I suppose it will be necessary for you to make, I desire you would remember the ladies and be more generous and favorable to them than your ancestors. Do not put such unlimited power into the hands of the husbands. Remember, all men would be tyrants if they could. If particular care and attention is not paid to the ladies, we are determined to foment a rebellion, and will not hold ourselves bound by any laws in which we have no voice or representation."

A challenge to the 19th Amendment (*Leser v. Garnett*, 1922) claimed that the amendment was unconstitutionally adopted, and that the rules for elections were implicitly delegated to the individual States because of the need to preserve State Sovereignty. However, the very fact that the change in voting rules was through amendment made the argument against the 19th Amendment a moot point.

Once the 19th Amendment was ratified, with this new power, women were able to attempt to elect those who shared their beliefs, hoping that other measures that would push forward the fight for women's rights would also emerge.

After the 19th Amendment passed, the percentage of women in the workforce increased to about 25%. Though some discrimination continued, and women rarely held decision-making positions, it was definitely a step in the right direction for the purpose of encouraging the rights of women.

During World War II, women were needed in all areas since many of the men went overseas to fight. The percentage of women in the workforce increased to 36%. The boom for women was short-lived, however. When the war ended, and the soldiers returned home, two-million women were fired within fifteen months after the end of the war to make room for the men.

Despite such setbacks, by the 1980s, the percentage of women in the workforce exceeded 50%. However, the percentage of women voting has not equaled the original push shortly after the ratification of the 19th Amendment.

Advocates for family values, though supportive of equal opportunity, often view these advancements as promotion for the break-up of the family unit. With mothers participating in the workforce, advent of women's rights has also given rise to the emergence of latch-key kids.

The greatest right for women is choice, which includes the choice not to pursue the numerous opportunities available for the purpose of following a more traditional role, should they desire to make such a choice. Women in today's society have the choice to pursue a career, be a stay-at-home mom and wife, or attempt to juggle both. For the purpose of protecting the family unit, and the traditional nature of the American society, wife and mother remains the more popular choice.

Chapter 40

Election Rules

Ratified in 1933, the 20th Amendment establishes the current rules regarding the beginning and end of the terms of elected federal offices.

The amendment moved the beginning of the Presidential, Vice Presidential and Congressional terms from March 4. Congress, under the new rules established by the 20th Amendment, convenes on the third day of January, reducing the amount of time a lame duck Congress would be in session. A **lame duck Congress**, no longer fearful of the effect their decisions may have on re-election, may be more apt to support otherwise unpopular legislation during a lame duck session.

The 20th Amendment moved the terms of the President and Vice President to begin on the 20th day of January.

Section 2 of the 20th Amendment begins, *"The Congress shall assemble at least once in every year."* The phrase is consistent with the language used in Article I, Section 4, though one wonders if the delegates debating the 20th Amendment viewed meeting one day a year as overburdensome as did the Framers of the Constitution, or if they considered themselves to be professional politicians who must be constantly legislating, as does today's legislators.

The 20th Amendment's Section 3 addresses vacancies to the presidency before the new President has the opportunity to take office. The clause assigns the presidency to the Vice President in the case of the death of the President, if the President dies before he can take office. Assigning the presidency to the Vice President was in line with Article II, Section 1, Clause 6, and the 12th Amendment assigning to the Vice President the Office of the President should the President die after he took office. In the case it turns out the President does not qualify for the office, this article grants to Congress the authority to declare who shall act as President. "Failing to qualify for office" refers to an occasion that the Electoral College fails to resolve who will be the President or Vice

President. A key point of this provision, and a critical protection against an outgoing faction attempting to retain some semblance of power, in the case that the candidates fail to qualify for office, is that the decision still devolves to Congress, but to the newly elected Congress, as opposed to the outgoing one. As established in Article II, Section 1, the decision for President would continue to rest upon the House of Representatives, and the choice of Vice President would continue to be the choice of the United States Senate.

Section 4 of the 20th Amendment addresses succession, giving Congress the authority to establish a **line of succession,** in the case of death of the President, or of the Vice President. The more astute student may recall that today's constitutional protocols calls upon the President to appoint a new Vice President, should that seat be vacated, but that provision did not become law until the ratification of the 25th Amendment in 1967.

The final two sections of the 20th Amendment address when the amendment would take effect should it be ratified, and a time limit of the proposal should the States not ratify it in a timely fashion. Section 5 states that the first two sections of the amendment, the parts of the amendment that alters the date the terms of President, Vice President, and members of Congress shall begin, "shall take effect on the 15th day of October following the ratification of this article." If ratification reached completion during an election year, that would put the new amendment into effect a couple weeks before the next election. The amendment was ratified January 23, 1933, not in time for Franklin Delano Roosevelt's victory in the 1932 Election. FDR had to wait until March of 1933 to take office.

In Section 6 of the 20th Amendment, for the first time in American History, a limitation was placed upon a proposed amendment, requiring that the amendment be ratified within seven years from the date of its submission. The same stipulation would be added at the end of the 21st and 22nd amendments, as well as a number of proposals that failed to be ratified within the allotted time period (like the Equal Rights Amendment). The 27th Amendment, ratified in 1992, reveals that without a limitation, proposed amendments remain in place and can stay on the active list indefinitely. The 27th Amendment was originally proposed as a part of the original Bill of Rights, submitted September 25, 1789.

Chapter 41

Presidential Term Limit

The 22nd Amendment was passed in 1951. It was designed to ensure no president could seek a third term. Though the Constitution did not limit the number of terms a president could serve prior to this amendment, many consider the fact that George Washington chose not to seek a third term as evidence the Founding Fathers recognized two terms should be the expected standard.

George Washington's popularity would have easily enabled him to be President for the rest of his life, and many even tried to encourage him to be king. However, Washington saw himself as no different than everyone else, and recognized the presidency as a privilege to serve. He felt that more than two terms opened the opportunity for abuse of power by an Executive, which would hinge on the idea of a monarchy.

Following George Washington, James Madison and James Monroe also adhered to the two-term principle. No Presidents afterward sought a third term, with the exceptions of Ulysses S. Grant, Theodore Roosevelt, and Franklin Delano Roosevelt. No President achieved a third term until FDR.

Franklin D. Roosevelt in 1940 became the only President to be elected to a third term. World War II has often been cited as the reason. The public was not fond of the idea of a change in Commander in Chief during such a crucial event in history. In 1944, while World War II continued to rage, Roosevelt won a fourth term. He died before he could complete it.

The 22nd Amendment was proposed and ratified during the Truman presidency.

The failure of the Founding Fathers to establish a term limit on the President in the early articles of the United States Constitution aligns with a prevailing opinion the Framers held that term limits were the

237

responsibility of the voter. Their belief hinged on a reliance on the people and the Electoral College, and that electorally a third term would be prevented, unless a third term was absolutely necessary.

Under the 22nd Amendment, the only President who would have been eligible to serve more than two terms would be Lyndon B. Johnson. LBJ was the Vice President of the United States at the time of the assassination of President John F. Kennedy, and after serving the remainder of JFK's term, Johnson had only been President for fourteen months. The 22nd Amendment provides that *"No person shall be elected to the office of the President more than twice, and no person who has held the office of President, or acted as President, for more than two years of a term to which some other person was elected President shall be elected to the office of the President more than once."*

Chapter 42

Washington, D.C., Receives Electoral Votes

The rallying cry during the American Revolution, as we have been taught, was "No taxation without representation." Yet, despite that famous call for revolution, after the United States became a nation, there were those who were taxed without representation in the United States Government. The most famous case was Washington, D.C. The movement for representation for Washington, D.C., led to the proposal, and ratification, of the 23rd Amendment.

Washington, D.C., is a ten mile by ten mile section of land donated by Maryland and Virginia to serve as the **seat of government**. The land was easy for those two States to let go of because it was undesirable. While it is popular to say that Washington, D.C., sits on swampland, it is actually a tidal plain, land that was a mix of thickly wooded slopes, bluffs and hills, crop land, and several major waterways. The location was chosen by George Washington because of its central location between the northern and southern States as a compromise between Alexander Hamilton and northern States who wanted the new federal government to assume Revolutionary War debts, and Thomas Jefferson and southern States who wanted the capital placed in a location friendly to slave-holding agricultural interests.

The District was not supposed to be a city in the sense that we see it today. The District of Columbia was not supposed to have a population, for the creation of the district was for the sole purpose of being the seat of the United States Government. The Congress was given full power over the functioning of the city, and the inhabitants were supposed to only be the temporary visitors of government officials, or employees. The Founding Fathers envisioned Washington, D.C., to be the seat of the federal government, and a vibrant **commercial center**.

As time passed, Washington, D.C., attracted residents, eager to partake in the opportunities offered in the way of government jobs. The incoming population largely consisted of Free Blacks prior to the beginning of the

American Civil War, and after the abolition of slavery in the District in 1850. After the **War Between the States**, the growth of Washington, D.C.'s population exploded.

John Adams, the second President of the United States, did not like Washington, D.C. He viewed it as hardly being a city at all, and nothing more than a clump of dirty buildings, arranged around "unpaved, muddy cesspools of winter, waiting for summer to transform them into mosquito-infested swamps."

As the population of Washington, D.C., grew during the twentieth century, it became glaringly apparent to the residents that their taxation did not accompany representation. At one point, "Taxation without representation" became such a rallying cry that Washington, D.C., license plates even held the phrase.

After the cries for representation reached a crescendo, the Twenty-Third Amendment was proposed and ratified, allowing the citizens in Washington, D.C., to vote for Electors for President and Vice President. The amendment was ratified in 1961.

Since Washington, D.C., is not a State, the District is still unable to send voting Representatives or Senators to Congress. However, Washington, D.C., does have delegates in Congress that act as observers.

The amendment restricts the district to the number of Electors of the least populous state, irrespective of its own population. That number is currently three.

Chapter 43

Poll Taxes and Open Primaries

The 24th Amendment to the U.S. Constitution ratified in 1964 made it unconstitutional for a State to use payment of taxes as a requirement to vote in national elections. Few blacks could vote in States using poll taxes as a requirement to vote because they had little money. The **poll tax** to vote in these states was $1.50. After the ratification of the 24th Amendment a number of districts continued the practice of requiring a poll tax in order to vote. A woman named Evelyn T. Butts decided to take the poll tax issue to court. In October 1965, the U.S. Supreme Court agreed to hear Evelyn T. Butts' appeal. In 1966 the Supreme Court of the United States declared poll taxes unconstitutional in accordance with the 24th Amendment.

A poll tax is a uniformed tax levied on every adult in the community, called a **capitation** tax by the Founding Fathers. Poll taxes have their roots in ancient tax systems and have been criticized as an unfair burden on the poor. Historically, in the U.S., poll taxes were enacted in the South as a prerequisite for voting, disfranchising many African-Americans and poor whites.

One argument regarding the article claims the spirit of the 24th Amendment also disallows **closed primaries** by leaving out of the process independent voters. As a result, a number of States have been passing laws enabling their States to make their election primaries open to all voters. In an **open primary** you can vote for anyone you want regardless of party affiliation during the **primary election**. Some proponents of open primaries contend closed primaries are unconstitutional - a violation of the 24th Amendment.

General discontent with the **two-party system** has emerged in American society. A party system, however, is a natural result of human nature. Every issue is divided by those who support the issue, and those that oppose it. As human beings, we tend to gravitate toward those who think like ourselves (birds of a feather flock together), and parties ultimately

241

form out of that natural tendency to organize. Once the groups form, they become organizations, appoint leadership positions, and a political party is born. Political parties are the natural result, fueled by our own human nature, of this kind of political organization.

In a party system such as ours, to allow voters to cross party-lines in the primaries can be dangerous because it opens up the potential for unethical voting techniques that are designed to injure the other party. Open primaries allow members of opposing parties to vote in their opponent's primary in the hopes of affecting the outcome, and putting the weaker candidate on the ballot so that their own party has a better chance to win. If both parties of a two party system is doing such, the result will always be the two weakest candidates facing off against each other. Open primaries nullify the whole point of the primary elections, and often result in the best candidates not being elected.

Not all States have primaries, and the rules for choosing candidates for a particular party varies from State to State - as it should. Some States have **caucuses**, which are meetings of the members of a legislative body who are members of a particular political party, to select candidates. The choosing of the delegates varies from State to State.

States are given the authority to make their own election rules, and maintain the elections in their State, according to Article I, Section 4 of the United States Constitution, and reinforced by Article II. This is why the Florida-Chad controversy in 2000 should have never resulted in the federal courts, or even the State courts, getting involved. According to the Constitution, the decision on what to do regarding the controversy in Florida in 2000 should have remained with the State Legislature.

Some supporters of open primaries contend that closed primaries are in violation of the 24th Amendment because limiting who can vote in a primary by party membership is a poll tax as per **implied law**.

By strict definition, a poll tax is a **tax**, which would be a monetary amount expected as a prerequisite for voting. Closed primaries do not impose a monetary tax, and therefore are not in violation of the 24th Amendment, based on the language of the amendment. One may suggest the 24th Amendment *implies* that no action can be taken to close any election to any person - but primaries are simply party oriented. People who couldn't vote in the primary would have been able to by joining a political party, and regardless of the ability to vote in the primaries, will be able to vote in the general election, and therefore are not being declined the opportunity to participate in the electoral process.

Chapter 44

Presidential Disability and Succession

The 25th Amendment, Section 1, reads, *"In case of the removal of the President from office or of his death or resignation, the Vice President shall become President."*

Section 1 of the 25th Amendment is clear, concise, and to the point. After nearly two centuries of questions regarding if the Vice President actually became President in the case of the removal, death or resignation of the President, or was to merely act as President if such an instance would arise, the 25th Amendment sought to clarify without question the confusion that haunted Article II, Section 1, Clause 6, and the 12th Amendment.

When President William Henry Harrison became the first U.S. President to die in office in 1841, Representative John Williams had previously suggested that the Vice President should become Acting President upon the death of the President. Vice President John Tyler concurred, asserting that he would need to succeed to the office of President, as opposed to only obtaining its powers and duties. Though Tyler took the oath of President (precedent for full succession was established, becoming known as the "Tyler Precedent"), nothing was done to amend the Constitution regarding the procedure.

When President Wilson suffered a stroke in 1919, no one officially assumed the Presidential powers and duties, and the office of President essentially remained unmanned during the remainder of Wilson's second term.

It was clear that a set of guidelines needed to be established.

In 1963, a proposal enabling Congress to enact legislation establishing a line of succession by Senator Kenneth Keating of New York based upon a recommendation by the American Bar Association in 1960 surfaced, but it never gained enough support.

On January 6, 1965, Senator Birch Bayh proposed in the Senate, and Representative Emanuel Celler proposed in the House of Representatives, what would become the 25th Amendment. Their proposal provided a way to not only fill a vacancy in the Office of the President by the Vice President, but also how to fill the Office of the Vice President before the next presidential election.

The line of succession the 25th Amendment establishes is as follows:

If the President is removed from office, dies, or resigns, the Vice President immediately becomes President. Prior to the 25th Amendment there was no provision for Vice Presidential vacancies. Under Section Two of the 25th Amendment the President nominates a successor who becomes Vice President if confirmed by a majority vote of both Houses of Congress, which occurred when President Richard Nixon appointed Gerald Ford to be his Vice President, after Spiro Agnew resigned as Vice President of the United States.

In Section 3 of the amendment, if the President provides a written declaration to the President Pro Tempore of the Senate and the Speaker of the House of Representatives that *"he is unable to discharge the powers and duties of his office, and until he transmits to them a written declaration to the contrary, such powers and duties shall be discharged by the Vice President as Acting President."*

Section 4, which has never been invoked, enables the Vice President, together with a majority of either the leading officers of the Executive Department, or of *"such other body as Congress may by law provide"*, to declare the President disabled by submitting a written declaration to the President Pro Tempore and the Speaker of the House of Representatives. If the President is unable to discharge his duties as indicated, the Vice President would become Acting President.

If the President's incapacitation prevents him from discharging the duties of his office and he himself does not provide a written declaration, the President may resume exercising the Presidential duties by sending a written declaration to the President Pro Tempore and the Speaker of the House. If the Vice President and the officers of the Cabinet believe the President's condition is preventing him from discharging the duties of President, they may within four days of the President's declaration submit another declaration that the President is incapacitated. If not in session, the Congress must, in this instance, assemble within 48 hours. Within 21 days of assembling or of receiving the second declaration by the Vice President and the Cabinet, a two-thirds vote of each House of Congress is required to affirm the President as unfit. If such actions are satisfied the Vice President would continue to be Acting President. However, if the Congress votes in favor of the President, or if the Congress makes no decision within the 21 days allotted, then the President would resume discharging all of the powers and duties of his office.

Chapter 45

Voting Age

The 26th Amendment establishes the voting age at the age of 18, rather than 21 as it was previously. The amendment was proposed in 1971, in an attempt to respond to student activism against the Vietnam War. Originally, President Nixon had signed a law making the voting age 18, but a number of States challenged the law, and under pressure the amendment was proposed and ratified.

The slogan, "Old enough to fight, old enough to vote," which surfaced as far back as World War II, had finally become a worn-out enough slogan that the majority began to support it. Arguments of various viewpoints regarding the wisdom of this amendment continue to this day, but one thing is clear, the original argument of "Old enough to fight, old enough to vote," was a ruse.

The Democrat Party was in trouble, and desperate for votes. President Nixon was wildly popular. The 1972 election was coming, and the Democrats needed to find a way to gain more votes, and to gain them fast.

The college-aged population was protesting against the war. The younger generation, molded by left-leaning public school teachers, and leftist college professors, were ripe for the picking, but most of them were too young to vote. The Democrats knew that if the protesting students could vote, they would vote for the Democrat candidate for president, and give the Democrats a fighting chance to gain seats in Congress. The push for the 26th Amendment, though in part about "old enough to fight, old enough to vote," was in reality an attempt to gain more votes for the Democrats. However, despite the ratification of the amendment in time for the election allowing people as low as the age of eighteen to vote, Richard Nixon still won the election in 1972 by a landslide.

Chapter 46

Congressional Salaries

The 27th Amendment prohibits any law that increases or decreases the salary of members of the Congress from taking effect until the start of the next set of terms of office for Representatives. Ratified in 1992, the proposal remained in waiting for 203 years after its initial submission in 1789.

The reason for ratification was anger over a Congressional pay raise. Wyoming became the last State to ratify the amendment. Four States (California, Rhode Island, Hawaii, and Washington) ratified the amendment after the required number of States was met.

A battle over whether or not cost of living increases are affected by this amendment continues to this day. Currently, cost of living increases take effect immediately, without a vote.

APPENDIX I

Changed or obsolete passages are in [brackets]

The Constitution of the United States, 1787

Preamble

We the People of the United States, in Order to form a more perfect Union, establish Justice, insure domestic Tranquility, provide for the common defence, promote the general Welfare, and secure the Blessings of Liberty to ourselves and our Posterity, do ordain and establish this Constitution for the United States of America.

Article I

Section 1

All legislative Powers herein granted shall be vested in a Congress of the United States, which shall consist of a Senate and House of Representatives.

Section 2

The House of Representatives shall be composed of Members chosen every second Year by the People of the several States, and the Electors in each State shall have the Qualifications requisite for Electors of the most numerous Branch of the State Legislature.

No Person shall be a Representative who shall not have attained to the Age of twenty five Years, and been seven Years a Citizen of the United States, and who shall not, when elected, be an Inhabitant of that State in which he shall be chosen.

[Representatives and direct Taxes shall be apportioned among the several States which may be included within this Union, according to their respective Numbers, which shall be determined by adding to the whole Number of free Persons, including those bound to Service for a Term of Years, and excluding Indians not taxed, three fifths of all other Persons.] *(Changed by section 2 of the Fourteenth Amendment)* The actual Enumeration shall be made within three Years after the first Meeting of the Congress of the United States, and within every subsequent Term of ten Years, in such Manner as they shall by Law direct. The Number of Representatives shall not exceed one for every thirty Thousand, but each State shall have at Least one Representative; and until such enumeration shall be made, the State of New Hampshire shall be entitled to chuse three, Massachusetts eight, Rhode-Island and Providence Plantations one, Connecticut five, New-York six, New Jersey four, Pennsylvania eight, Delaware one, Maryland six, Virginia ten, North Carolina five, South Carolina five, and Georgia three.

When vacancies happen in the Representation from any State, the Executive Authority thereof shall issue Writs of Election to fill such Vacancies.

The House of Representatives shall chuse their Speaker and other Officers; and shall have the sole Power of Impeachment.

Section 3

The Senate of the United States shall be composed of two Senators from each State, [chosen by the Legislature thereof] *(Changed by the Seventeenth Amendment)* for six Years; and each Senator shall have one Vote.

Immediately after they shall be assembled in Consequence of the first Election, they shall be divided as equally as may be into three Classes. The Seats of the Senators of the first Class shall be vacated at the Expiration of the second Year, of the second Class at the Expiration of the fourth Year, and of the third Class at the Expiration of the sixth Year, so that one third may be chosen every second Year; [and if Vacancies happen by Resignation, or otherwise, during the Recess of the Legislature of any State, the Executive thereof may make temporary Appointments until the next Meeting of the Legislature, which shall then fill such Vacancies.] *(Changed by the Seventeenth Amendment)*

No Person shall be a Senator who shall not have attained to the Age of thirty Years, and been nine Years a Citizen of the United States, and who shall not, when elected, be an Inhabitant of that State for which he shall be chosen.

The Vice President of the United States shall be President of the Senate, but shall have no Vote, unless they be equally divided.

The Senate shall chuse their other Officers, and also a President pro tempore, in the Absence of the Vice President, or when he shall exercise the Office of President of the United States.

The Senate shall have the sole Power to try all Impeachments. When sitting for that Purpose, they shall be on Oath or Affirmation. When the President of the United States is tried, the Chief Justice shall preside: And no Person shall be convicted without the Concurrence of two thirds of the Members present.

Judgment in Cases of Impeachment shall not extend further than to removal from Office, and disqualification to hold and enjoy any Office of honor, Trust or Profit under the United States: but the Party convicted shall nevertheless be liable and subject to Indictment, Trial, Judgment and Punishment, according to Law.

Section 4

The Times, Places and Manner of holding Elections for Senators and Representatives, shall be prescribed in each State by the Legislature thereof; but the Congress may at any time by Law make or alter such Regulations, except as to the Places of chusing Senators.

The Congress shall assemble at least once in every Year, and such Meeting shall be [on the first Monday in December,] *(Changed by*

Section 2 of the Twentieth Amendment) unless they shall by Law appoint a different Day.

Section 5

Each House shall be the Judge of the Elections, Returns and Qualifications of its own Members, and a Majority of each shall constitute a Quorum to do Business; but a smaller Number may adjourn from day to day, and may be authorized to compel the Attendance of absent Members, in such Manner, and under such Penalties as each House may provide.

Each House may determine the Rules of its Proceedings, punish its Members for disorderly Behaviour, and, with the Concurrence of two thirds, expel a Member.

Each House shall keep a Journal of its Proceedings, and from time to time publish the same, excepting such Parts as may in their Judgment require Secrecy; and the Yeas and Nays of the Members of either House on any question shall, at the Desire of one fifth of those Present, be entered on the Journal.

Neither House, during the Session of Congress, shall, without the Consent of the other, adjourn for more than three days, nor to any other Place than that in which the two Houses shall be sitting.

Section 6

The Senators and Representatives shall receive a Compensation for their Services, to be ascertained by Law, and paid out of the Treasury of the United States. They shall in all Cases, except Treason, Felony and Breach of the Peace, be privileged from Arrest during their Attendance at the Session of their respective Houses, and in going to and returning from the same; and for any Speech or Debate in either House, they shall not be questioned in any other Place.

No Senator or Representative shall, during the Time for which he was elected, be appointed to any civil Office under the Authority of the United States, which shall have been created, or the Emoluments whereof shall have been encreased during such time; and no Person holding any Office under the United States, shall be a Member of either House during his Continuance in Office.

Section 7

All Bills for raising Revenue shall originate in the House of Representatives; but the Senate may propose or concur with Amendments as on other Bills.

Every Bill which shall have passed the House of Representatives and the Senate, shall, before it become a Law, be presented to the President of the United States: If he approve he shall sign it, but if not he shall return it, with his Objections to that House in which it shall have originated, who shall enter the Objections at large on their Journal, and proceed to reconsider it. If after such Reconsideration two thirds of that House shall agree to pass the Bill, it shall be sent, together with the Objections, to the other House, by which it shall likewise be reconsidered, and if approved by two thirds of that House, it shall become a Law. But in all such Cases the Votes of both Houses shall be determined by yeas and Nays, and the Names of the Persons voting for and against the Bill shall be entered on the Journal of each House respectively. If any Bill shall not be returned by the President within ten Days (Sundays excepted) after it shall have been presented to him, the Same shall be a Law, in like Manner as if he had signed it, unless the Congress by their Adjournment prevent its Return, in which Case it shall not be a Law.

Every Order, Resolution, or Vote to which the Concurrence of the Senate and House of Representatives may be necessary (except on a question of Adjournment) shall be presented to the President of the United States; and before the Same shall take Effect, shall be approved by him, or being disapproved by him, shall be repassed by two thirds of the Senate and House of Representatives, according to the Rules and Limitations prescribed in the Case of a Bill.

Section 8

The Congress shall have Power To lay and collect Taxes, Duties, Imposts and Excises, to pay the Debts and provide for the common Defence and general Welfare of the United States; but all Duties, Imposts and Excises shall be uniform throughout the United States;

To borrow Money on the credit of the United States;

To regulate Commerce with foreign Nations, and among the several States, and with the Indian Tribes;

To establish an uniform Rule of Naturalization, and uniform Laws on the subject of Bankruptcies throughout the United States;

To coin Money, regulate the Value thereof, and of foreign Coin, and fix the Standard of Weights and Measures;

To provide for the Punishment of counterfeiting the Securities and current Coin of the United States;

To establish Post Offices and post Roads;

To promote the Progress of Science and useful Arts, by securing for limited Times to Authors and Inventors the exclusive Right to their respective Writings and Discoveries;

To constitute Tribunals inferior to the supreme Court;

To define and punish Piracies and Felonies committed on the high Seas, and Offences against the Law of Nations;

To declare War, grant Letters of Marque and Reprisal, and make Rules concerning Captures on Land and Water;

To raise and support Armies, but no Appropriation of Money to that Use shall be for a longer Term than two Years;

To provide and maintain a Navy;

To make Rules for the Government and Regulation of the land and naval Forces;

To provide for calling forth the Militia to execute the Laws of the Union, suppress Insurrections and repel Invasions;

To provide for organizing, arming, and disciplining, the Militia, and for governing such Part of them as may be employed in the Service of the United States, reserving to the States respectively, the Appointment of the Officers, and the Authority of training the Militia according to the discipline prescribed by Congress;

To exercise exclusive Legislation in all Cases whatsoever, over such District (not exceeding ten Miles square) as may, by Cession of particular States, and the Acceptance of Congress, become the Seat of the Government of the United States, and to exercise like Authority over all Places purchased by the Consent of the Legislature of the State in which the Same shall be, for the Erection of Forts, Magazines, Arsenals, dock-Yards, and other needful Buildings;--And

To make all Laws which shall be necessary and proper for carrying into Execution the foregoing Powers, and all other Powers vested by this Constitution in the Government of the United States, or in any Department or Officer thereof.

Section 9

The Migration or Importation of such Persons as any of the States now existing shall think proper to admit, shall not be prohibited by the Congress prior to the Year one thousand eight hundred and eight, but a Tax or duty may be imposed on such Importation, not exceeding ten dollars for each Person.

The Privilege of the Writ of Habeas Corpus shall not be suspended, unless when in Cases of Rebellion or Invasion the public Safety may require it.

No Bill of Attainder or ex post facto Law shall be passed.

No Capitation, or other direct, Tax shall be laid, unless in Proportion to the Census or enumeration herein before directed to be taken.

No Tax or Duty shall be laid on Articles exported from any State.

No Preference shall be given by any Regulation of Commerce or Revenue to the Ports of one State over those of another; nor shall Vessels bound to, or from, one State, be obliged to enter, clear, or pay Duties in another.

No Money shall be drawn from the Treasury, but in Consequence of Appropriations made by Law; and a regular Statement and Account of the Receipts and Expenditures of all public Money shall be published from time to time.

No Title of Nobility shall be granted by the United States: And no Person holding any Office of Profit or Trust under them, shall, without the Consent of the Congress, accept of any present, Emolument, Office, or Title, of any kind whatever, from any King, Prince, or foreign State.

Section 10

No State shall enter into any Treaty, Alliance, or Confederation; grant Letters of Marque and Reprisal; coin Money; emit Bills of Credit; make any Thing but gold and silver Coin a Tender in Payment of Debts; pass any Bill of Attainder, ex post facto Law, or Law impairing the Obligation of Contracts, or grant any Title of Nobility.

No State shall, without the Consent of the Congress, lay any Imposts or Duties on Imports or Exports, except what may be absolutely necessary for executing it's inspection Laws: and the net Produce of all Duties and Imposts, laid by any State on Imports or Exports, shall be for the Use of the Treasury of the United States; and all such Laws shall be subject to the Revision and Controul of the Congress.

No State shall, without the Consent of Congress, lay any Duty of Tonnage, keep Troops, or Ships of War in time of Peace, enter into any Agreement or Compact with another State, or with a foreign Power, or engage in War, unless actually invaded, or in such imminent Danger as will not admit of delay.

Article II

Section 1

The executive Power shall be vested in a President of the United States of America. He shall hold his Office during the Term of four Years, and, together with the Vice President, chosen for the same Term, be elected, as follows:

Each State shall appoint, in such Manner as the Legislature thereof may direct, a Number of Electors, equal to the whole Number of Senators and Representatives to which the State may be entitled in the Congress: but no Senator or Representative, or Person holding an Office of Trust or Profit under the United States, shall be appointed an Elector.

[The Electors shall meet in their respective States, and vote by Ballot for two Persons, of whom one at least shall not be an Inhabitant of the same State with themselves. And they shall make a List of all the Persons voted for, and of the Number of Votes for each; which List they shall sign and certify, and transmit sealed to the Seat of the Government of the United States, directed to the President of the Senate. The President of the Senate shall, in the Presence of the Senate and House of Representatives, open all the Certificates, and the Votes shall then be counted. The Person having the greatest Number of Votes shall be the President, if such Number be a Majority of the whole Number of Electors appointed; and if there be more than one who have such Majority, and have an equal Number of Votes, then the House of Representatives shall immediately chuse by Ballot one of them for President; and if no Person have a Majority, then from the five highest on the List the said House shall in like Manner chuse the President. But in chusing the President, the Votes shall be taken by States, the Representation from each State having one Vote; A quorum for this purpose shall consist of a Member or Members from two thirds of the States, and a Majority of all the States shall be necessary to a Choice. In every Case, after the Choice of the President, the Person having the greatest Number of Votes of the Electors shall be the Vice President. But if there should remain two or more who have equal Votes, the Senate shall chuse from them by Ballot the Vice President.] *(Changed by the Twelfth Amendment)*

The Congress may determine the Time of chusing the Electors, and the Day on which they shall give their Votes; which Day shall be the same throughout the United States.

No Person except a natural born Citizen, or a Citizen of the United States, at the time of the Adoption of this Constitution, shall be eligible to the Office of President; neither shall any Person be eligible to that Office who shall not have attained to the Age of thirty five Years, and been fourteen Years a Resident within the United States.

[In Case of the Removal of the President from Office, or of his Death, Resignation, or Inability to discharge the Powers and Duties of the said Office, the Same shall devolve on the Vice President, and the Congress may by Law provide for the Case of Removal, Death, Resignation or Inability, both of the President and Vice President, declaring what Officer shall then act as President, and such Officer shall act accordingly, until the Disability be removed, or a President shall be elected.] *(Changed by the Twenty-Fifth Amendment)*

The President shall, at stated Times, receive for his Services, a Compensation, which shall neither be increased nor diminished during the Period for which he shall have been elected, and he shall not receive within that Period any other Emolument from the United States, or any of them.

Before he enter on the Execution of his Office, he shall take the following Oath or Affirmation:--"I do solemnly swear (or affirm) that I will faithfully execute the Office of President of the United States, and will to the best of my Ability, preserve, protect and defend the Constitution of the United States."

Section 2

The President shall be Commander in Chief of the Army and Navy of the United States, and of the Militia of the several States, when called into the actual Service of the United States; he may require the Opinion, in writing, of the principal Officer in each of the executive Departments, upon any Subject relating to the Duties of their respective Offices, and he shall have Power to grant Reprieves and Pardons for Offences against the United States, except in Cases of Impeachment.

He shall have Power, by and with the Advice and Consent of the Senate, to make Treaties, provided two thirds of the Senators present concur; and he shall nominate, and by and with the Advice and Consent of the Senate, shall appoint Ambassadors, other public Ministers and Consuls, Judges of the supreme Court, and all other Officers of the United States, whose Appointments are not herein otherwise provided for, and which shall be established by Law: but the Congress may by Law vest the Appointment of such inferior Officers, as they think proper, in the President alone, in the Courts of Law, or in the Heads of Departments.

The President shall have Power to fill up all Vacancies that may happen during the Recess of the Senate, by granting Commissions which shall expire at the End of their next Session.

Section 3

He shall from time to time give to the Congress Information of the State of the Union, and recommend to their Consideration such Measures as he shall judge necessary and expedient; he may, on extraordinary Occasions, convene both Houses, or either of them, and in Case of Disagreement between them, with Respect to the

Time of Adjournment, he may adjourn them to such Time as he shall think proper; he shall receive Ambassadors and other public Ministers; he shall take Care that the Laws be faithfully executed, and shall Commission all the Officers of the United States.

Section 4

The President, Vice President and all civil Officers of the United States, shall be removed from Office on Impeachment for, and Conviction of, Treason, **Bribery**, or other high Crimes and Misdemeanors.

Article III

Section 1

The judicial Power of the United States shall be vested in one supreme Court, and in such inferior Courts as the Congress may from time to time ordain and establish. The Judges, both of the supreme and inferior Courts, shall hold their Offices during good Behaviour, and shall, at stated Times, receive for their Services a Compensation, which shall not be diminished during their Continuance in Office.

Section 2

The judicial Power shall extend to all Cases, in Law and Equity, arising under this Constitution, the Laws of the United States, and Treaties made, or which shall be made, under their Authority;--to all Cases affecting Ambassadors, other public Ministers and Consuls;--to all Cases of admiralty and maritime Jurisdiction;--to Controversies to which the United States shall be a Party;--to Controversies between two or more States;-- [between a State and Citizens of another State,] *(Changed by the Eleventh Amendment)* --between Citizens of different States,--between Citizens of the same State claiming Lands under Grants of different States, [and between a State, or the Citizens thereof, and foreign States, Citizens or Subjects.] *(Changed by the Eleventh Amendment)*

In all Cases affecting Ambassadors, other public Ministers and Consuls, and those in which a State shall be Party, the supreme Court shall have original Jurisdiction. In all the other Cases before mentioned, the supreme Court shall have appellate Jurisdiction, both as to Law and Fact, with such Exceptions, and under such Regulations as the Congress shall make.

The Trial of all Crimes, except in Cases of Impeachment, shall be by Jury; and such Trial shall be held in the State where the said Crimes shall have been committed; but when not committed within any State, the Trial shall be at such Place or Places as the Congress may by Law have directed.

Section 3

Treason against the United States, shall consist only in levying War against them, or in adhering to their Enemies, giving them Aid and Comfort. No Person shall be convicted of Treason unless on the Testimony of two Witnesses to the same overt Act, or on Confession in open Court.

The Congress shall have Power to declare the Punishment of Treason, but no Attainder of Treason shall work Corruption of Blood, or Forfeiture except during the Life of the Person attainted.

Article IV

Section 1

Full Faith and Credit shall be given in each State to the public Acts, Records, and judicial Proceedings of every other State. And the Congress may by general Laws prescribe the Manner in which such Acts, Records and Proceedings shall be proved, and the Effect thereof.

Section 2

The Citizens of each State shall be entitled to all Privileges and Immunities of Citizens in the several States.

A Person charged in any State with Treason, Felony, or other Crime, who shall flee from Justice, and be found in another State, shall on Demand of the executive Authority of the State from which he fled, be delivered up, to be removed to the State having Jurisdiction of the Crime.

[No Person held to Service or Labour in one State, under the Laws thereof, escaping into another, shall, in Consequence of any Law or Regulation therein, be discharged from such Service or Labour, but shall be delivered up on Claim of the Party to whom such Service or Labour may be due.] *(Changed by the Thirteenth Amendment)*

Section 3

New States may be admitted by the Congress into this Union; but no new State shall be formed or erected within the Jurisdiction of any other State; nor any State be formed by the Junction of two or more States, or Parts of States, without the Consent of the Legislatures of the States concerned as well as of the Congress.

The Congress shall have Power to dispose of and make all needful Rules and Regulations respecting the Territory or other Property belonging to the United States; and nothing in this Constitution shall be so construed as to Prejudice any Claims of the United States, or of any particular State.

Section 4

The United States shall guarantee to every State in this Union a Republican Form of Government, and shall protect each of them against Invasion; and on Application of the Legislature, or of the Executive (when the Legislature cannot be convened), against domestic Violence.

Article V

The Congress, whenever two thirds of both Houses shall deem it necessary, shall propose Amendments to this Constitution, or, on the Application of the Legislatures of two thirds of the several States, shall call a Convention for proposing Amendments, which, in either Case, shall be valid to all Intents and Purposes, as Part of this Constitution, when ratified by the Legislatures of three fourths of the several States, or by Conventions in three fourths thereof, as the one or the other Mode of Ratification may be proposed by the Congress; Provided that no Amendment which may be made prior to the Year One thousand eight hundred and eight shall in any Manner affect the first and fourth Clauses in the Ninth Section of the first Article; and that no State, without its Consent, shall be deprived of its equal Suffrage in the Senate.

Article VI

All Debts contracted and Engagements entered into, before the Adoption of this Constitution, shall be as valid against the United States under this Constitution, as under the Confederation.

This Constitution, and the Laws of the United States which shall be made in Pursuance thereof; and all Treaties made, or which shall be made, under the Authority of the United States, shall be the supreme Law of the Land; and the Judges in every State shall be bound thereby, any Thing in the Constitution or Laws of any State to the Contrary notwithstanding.

The Senators and Representatives before mentioned, and the Members of the several State Legislatures, and all executive and judicial Officers, both of the United States and of the several States, shall be bound by Oath or Affirmation, to support this Constitution; but no religious Test shall ever be required as a Qualification to any Office or public Trust under the United States.

Article VII

The Ratification of the Conventions of nine States, shall be sufficient for the Establishment of this Constitution between the States so ratifying the Same.

done in Convention by the Unanimous Consent of the States present the Seventeenth Day of September in the Year of our Lord one thousand seven hundred and Eighty seven and of the Independance of the United States of America the Twelfth In witness whereof We have hereunto subscribed our Names,

G°. Washington
Presidt and deputy from Virginia

Delaware
Geo: Read
Gunning Bedford jun
John Dickinson
Richard Bassett
Jaco: Broom

Maryland
James McHenry
Dan of St Thos. Jenifer
Danl. Carroll

Virginia
John Blair
James Madison Jr.

North Carolina
Wm. Blount
Richd. Dobbs Spaight
Hu Williamson

South Carolina
J. Rutledge
Charles Cotesworth Pinckney
Charles Pinckney
Pierce Butler

Georgia
William Few
Abr Baldwin

New Hampshire
John Langdon
Nicholas Gilman

Massachusetts
Nathaniel Gorham
Rufus King

Connecticut
Wm. Saml. Johnson
Roger Sherman

New York
Alexander Hamilton

New Jersey
Wil: Livingston
David Brearley
Wm. Paterson
Jona: Dayton

Pennsylvania
B Franklin
Thomas Mifflin
Robt. Morris
Geo. Clymer
Thos. FitzSimons
Jared Ingersoll
James Wilson
Gouv Morris

Bill of Rights – Amendments 1-10, Ratified December 15, 1791

Amendment I

Congress shall make no law respecting an establishment of religion, or prohibiting the free exercise thereof; or abridging the freedom of speech, or of the press; or the right of the people peaceably to assemble, and to petition the Government for a redress of grievances.

Amendment II

A well regulated Militia, being necessary to the security of a free State, the right of the people to keep and bear Arms, shall not be infringed.

Amendment III

No Soldier shall, in time of peace be quartered in any house, without the consent of the Owner, nor in time of war, but in a manner to be prescribed by law.

Amendment IV

The right of the people to be secure in their persons, houses, papers, and effects, against unreasonable searches and seizures, shall not be violated, and no Warrants shall issue, but upon probable cause, supported by Oath or affirmation, and particularly describing the place to be searched, and the persons or things to be seized.

Amendment V

No person shall be held to answer for a capital, or otherwise infamous crime, unless on a presentment or indictment of a Grand Jury, except in cases arising in the land or naval forces, or in the Militia, when in actual service in time of War or public danger; nor shall any person be subject for the same offence to be twice put in jeopardy of life or limb; nor shall be compelled in any criminal case to be a witness against himself, nor be deprived of life, liberty, or property, without due process of law; nor shall private property be taken for public use, without just compensation.

Amendment VI

In all criminal prosecutions, the accused shall enjoy the right to a speedy and public trial, by an impartial jury of the State and district wherein the crime shall have been committed, which district shall have been previously ascertained by law, and to be informed of the nature and cause of the accusation; to be confronted with the witnesses against him; to have compulsory process for obtaining witnesses in his favor, and to have the Assistance of Counsel for his defence.

Amendment VII

In Suits at common law, where the value in controversy shall exceed twenty dollars, the right of trial by jury shall be preserved, and no fact tried by a jury, shall be otherwise re-examined in any Court of the United States, than according to the rules of the common law.

Amendment VIII

Excessive bail shall not be required, nor excessive fines imposed, nor cruel and unusual punishments inflicted.

Amendment IX

The enumeration in the Constitution, of certain rights, shall not be construed to deny or disparage others retained by the people.

Amendment X

The powers not delegated to the United States by the Constitution, nor prohibited by it to the States, are reserved to the States respectively, or to the people.

Amendments 11-27

Amendment XI

Passed by Congress March 4, 1794. Ratified February 7, 1795.

The Judicial power of the United States shall not be construed to extend to any suit in law or equity, commenced or prosecuted against one of the United States by Citizens of another State, or by Citizens or Subjects of any Foreign State.

Amendment XII

Passed by Congress December 9, 1803. Ratified June 15, 1804.

The Electors shall meet in their respective states and vote by ballot for President and Vice-President, one of whom, at least, shall not be an inhabitant of the same state with themselves; they shall name in their ballots the person voted for as President, and in distinct ballots the person voted for as Vice-President, and they shall make distinct lists of all persons voted for as President, and of all persons voted for as Vice-President, and of the number of votes for each, which lists they shall sign and certify, and transmit sealed to the seat of the government of the United States, directed to the President of the Senate; -- the President of the Senate shall, in the presence of the Senate and House of Representatives, open all the certificates and the votes shall then be counted; -- The person having the greatest number of votes for President, shall be the President, if such number be a majority of the whole number of Electors appointed; and if no person have such majority, then from the persons having the highest numbers not exceeding three on the list of those voted for as President, the House of Representatives shall choose immediately, by ballot, the President. But in choosing the President, the votes shall be taken by states, the representation from each state having one vote; a quorum for this purpose shall consist of a member or members from two-thirds of the states, and a majority of all the states shall be necessary to a choice. [And if the House of Representatives shall not choose a President whenever the right of choice shall devolve upon them, before the fourth day of March next following, then the Vice-President shall act as President, as in case of the death or other constitutional disability of the President. −] *(Superseded by section 3 of the Twentieth Amendment)* The person having the greatest number of votes as Vice-President, shall be the Vice-President, if such number be a majority of the whole number of Electors appointed, and if no person have a majority, then from the two highest numbers on the list, the Senate shall choose the Vice-President; a quorum for the purpose shall consist of two-thirds of the whole number of Senators, and a majority of the whole number shall be necessary to a choice. But no person constitutionally ineligible to the office of President shall be eligible to that of Vice-President of the United States.

Amendment XIII

Passed by Congress January 31, 1865. Ratified December 6, 1865.

Section 1.
Neither slavery nor involuntary servitude, except as a punishment for crime whereof the party shall have been duly convicted, shall exist within the United States, or any place subject to their jurisdiction.

Section 2.
Congress shall have power to enforce this article by appropriate legislation.

Amendment XIV

Passed by Congress June 13, 1866. Ratified July 9, 1868.

Section 1.
All persons born or naturalized in the United States, and subject to the jurisdiction thereof, are citizens of the United States and of the State wherein they reside. No State shall make or enforce any law which shall abridge the privileges or immunities of citizens of the United States; nor shall any State deprive any person of life,

liberty, or property, without due process of law; nor deny to any person within its jurisdiction the equal protection of the laws.

Section 2.
Representatives shall be apportioned among the several States according to their respective numbers, counting the whole number of persons in each State, excluding Indians not taxed. But when the right to vote at any election for the choice of electors for President and Vice-President of the United States, Representatives in Congress, the Executive and Judicial officers of a State, or the members of the Legislature thereof, is denied to any of the male inhabitants of such State, [being twenty-one years of age,] *(Changed by section 1 of the 26th amendment)* and citizens of the United States, or in any way abridged, except for participation in rebellion, or other crime, the basis of representation therein shall be reduced in the proportion which the number of such male citizens shall bear to the whole number of male citizens twenty-one years of age in such State.

Section 3.
No person shall be a Senator or Representative in Congress, or elector of President and Vice-President, or hold any office, civil or military, under the United States, or under any State, who, having previously taken an oath, as a member of Congress, or as an officer of the United States, or as a member of any State legislature, or as an executive or judicial officer of any State, to support the Constitution of the United States, shall have engaged in insurrection or rebellion against the same, or given aid or comfort to the enemies thereof. But Congress may by a vote of two-thirds of each House, remove such disability.

Section 4.
The validity of the public debt of the United States, authorized by law, including debts incurred for payment of pensions and bounties for services in suppressing insurrection or rebellion, shall not be questioned. But neither the United States nor any State shall assume or pay any debt or obligation incurred in aid of insurrection or rebellion against the United States, or any claim for the loss or emancipation of any slave; but all such debts, obligations and

claims shall be held illegal and void.

Section 5.
The Congress shall have the power to enforce, by appropriate legislation, the provisions of this article.

Amendment XV

Passed by Congress February 26, 1869. Ratified February 3, 1870.

Section 1.
The right of citizens of the United States to vote shall not be denied or abridged by the United States or by any State on account of race, color, or previous condition of servitude--

Section 2.
The Congress shall have the power to enforce this article by appropriate legislation.

Amendment XVI

Passed by Congress July 2, 1909. Ratified February 3, 1913.

The Congress shall have power to lay and collect taxes on incomes, from whatever source derived, without apportionment among the several States, and without regard to any census or enumeration.

Amendment XVII

Passed by Congress May 13, 1912. Ratified April 8, 1913.

The Senate of the United States shall be composed of two Senators from each State, elected by the people thereof, for six years; and each Senator shall have one vote. The electors in each State shall have the qualifications requisite for electors of the most numerous branch of the State legislatures.

When vacancies happen in the representation of any State in the

Senate, the executive authority of such State shall issue writs of election to fill such vacancies: Provided, That the legislature of any State may empower the executive thereof to make temporary appointments until the people fill the vacancies by election as the legislature may direct.

This amendment shall not be so construed as to affect the election or term of any Senator chosen before it becomes valid as part of the Constitution.

Amendment XVIII

Passed by Congress December 18, 1917. Ratified January 16, 1919.

[Section 1.
After one year from the ratification of this article the manufacture, sale, or transportation of intoxicating liquors within, the importation thereof into, or the exportation thereof from the United States and all territory subject to the jurisdiction thereof for beverage purposes is hereby prohibited.

Section 2.
The Congress and the several States shall have concurrent power to enforce this article by appropriate legislation.

Section 3.
This article shall be inoperative unless it shall have been ratified as an amendment to the Constitution by the legislatures of the several States, as provided in the Constitution, within seven years from the date of the submission hereof to the States by the Congress.]
(Repealed by amendment 21)

Amendment XIX

Passed by Congress June 4, 1919. Ratified August 18, 1920.

The right of citizens of the United States to vote shall not be denied or abridged by the United States or by any State on account of sex.

Congress shall have power to enforce this article by appropriate legislation.

Amendment XX

Passed by Congress March 2, 1932. Ratified January 23, 1933.

Section 1.
The terms of the President and the Vice President shall end at noon on the 20th day of January, and the terms of Senators and Representatives at noon on the 3rd day of January, of the years in which such terms would have ended if this article had not been ratified; and the terms of their successors shall then begin.

Section 2.
The Congress shall assemble at least once in every year, and such meeting shall begin at noon on the 3d day of January, unless they shall by law appoint a different day.

Section 3.
If, at the time fixed for the beginning of the term of the President, the President elect shall have died, the Vice President elect shall become President. If a President shall not have been chosen before the time fixed for the beginning of his term, or if the President elect shall have failed to qualify, then the Vice President elect shall act as President until a President shall have qualified; and the Congress may by law provide for the case wherein neither a President elect nor a Vice President shall have qualified, declaring who shall then act as President, or the manner in which one who is to act shall be selected, and such person shall act accordingly until a President or Vice President shall have qualified.

Section 4.
The Congress may by law provide for the case of the death of any of the persons from whom the House of Representatives may choose a President whenever the right of choice shall have devolved upon them, and for the case of the death of any of the

persons from whom the Senate may choose a Vice President whenever the right of choice shall have devolved upon them.

Section 5.
Sections 1 and 2 shall take effect on the 15th day of October following the ratification of this article.

Section 6.
This article shall be inoperative unless it shall have been ratified as an amendment to the Constitution by the legislatures of three-fourths of the several States within seven years from the date of its submission.

Amendment XXI

Passed by Congress February 20, 1933. Ratified December 5, 1933.

Section 1.
The eighteenth article of amendment to the Constitution of the United States is hereby repealed.

Section 2.
The transportation or importation into any State, Territory, or Possession of the United States for delivery or use therein of intoxicating liquors, in violation of the laws thereof, is hereby prohibited.

Section 3.
This article shall be inoperative unless it shall have been ratified as an amendment to the Constitution by conventions in the several States, as provided in the Constitution, within seven years from the date of the submission hereof to the States by the Congress.

Amendment XXII

Passed by Congress March 21, 1947. Ratified February 27, 1951.

Section 1.

No person shall be elected to the office of the President more than twice, and no person who has held the office of President, or acted as President, for more than two years of a term to which some other person was elected President shall be elected to the office of President more than once. But this Article shall not apply to any person holding the office of President when this Article was proposed by Congress, and shall not prevent any person who may be holding the office of President, or acting as President, during the term within which this Article becomes operative from holding the office of President or acting as President during the remainder of such term.

Section 2.
This article shall be inoperative unless it shall have been ratified as an amendment to the Constitution by the legislatures of three-fourths of the several States within seven years from the date of its submission to the States by the Congress.

Amendment XXIII

Passed by Congress June 16, 1960. Ratified March 29, 1961.

Section 1.
The District constituting the seat of Government of the United States shall appoint in such manner as Congress may direct:

A number of electors of President and Vice President equal to the whole number of Senators and Representatives in Congress to which the District would be entitled if it were a State, but in no event more than the least populous State; they shall be in addition to those appointed by the States, but they shall be considered, for the purposes of the election of President and Vice President, to be electors appointed by a State; and they shall meet in the District and perform such duties as provided by the twelfth article of amendment.

Section 2.
The Congress shall have power to enforce this article by appropriate legislation.

Amendment XXIV

Passed by Congress August 27, 1962. Ratified January 23, 1964.

Section 1.
The right of citizens of the United States to vote in any primary or other election for President or Vice President, for electors for President or Vice President, or for Senator or Representative in Congress, shall not be denied or abridged by the United States or any State by reason of failure to pay poll tax or other tax.

Section 2.
The Congress shall have power to enforce this article by appropriate legislation.

Amendment XXV

Passed by Congress July 6, 1965. Ratified February 10, 1967.

Section 1.
In case of the removal of the President from office or of his death or resignation, the Vice President shall become President.

Section 2.
Whenever there is a vacancy in the office of the Vice President, the President shall nominate a Vice President who shall take office upon confirmation by a majority vote of both Houses of Congress.

Section 3.
Whenever the President transmits to the President pro tempore of the Senate and the Speaker of the House of Representatives his written declaration that he is unable to discharge the powers and duties of his office, and until he transmits to them a written declaration to the contrary, such powers and duties shall be discharged by the Vice President as Acting President.

Section 4.
Whenever the Vice President and a majority of either the principal officers of the executive departments or of such other body as

Congress may by law provide, transmit to the President pro tempore of the Senate and the Speaker of the House of Representatives their written declaration that the President is unable to discharge the powers and duties of his office, the Vice President shall immediately assume the powers and duties of the office as Acting President.

Thereafter, when the President transmits to the President pro tempore of the Senate and the Speaker of the House of Representatives his written declaration that no inability exists, he shall resume the powers and duties of his office unless the Vice President and a majority of either the principal officers of the executive department or of such other body as Congress may by law provide, transmit within four days to the President pro tempore of the Senate and the Speaker of the House of Representatives their written declaration that the President is unable to discharge the powers and duties of his office. Thereupon Congress shall decide the issue, assembling within forty-eight hours for that purpose if not in session. If the Congress, within twenty-one days after receipt of the latter written declaration, or, if Congress is not in session, within twenty-one days after Congress is required to assemble, determines by two-thirds vote of both Houses that the President is unable to discharge the powers and duties of his office, the Vice President shall continue to discharge the same as Acting President; otherwise, the President shall resume the powers and duties of his office.

Amendment XXVI

Passed by Congress March 23, 1971. Ratified July 1, 1971.

Section 1.
The right of citizens of the United States, who are eighteen years of age or older, to vote shall not be denied or abridged by the United States or by any State on account of age.

Section 2.
The Congress shall have power to enforce this article by appropriate legislation.

Amendment XXVII

Originally proposed Sept. 25, 1789. Ratified May 7, 1992.

No law, varying the compensation for the services of the Senators and Representatives, shall take effect, until an election of representatives shall have intervened.

Note: Congress submitted the text of the Twenty-Seventh Amendment to the States as part of the proposed Bill of Rights on September 25, 1789. The Amendment was not ratified together with the first Ten Amendments, which became effective on December 15, 1791. The Twenty-Seventh Amendment was ratified on May 7, 1992, by the vote of Michigan.

APPENDIX II

The Declaration of Independence

IN CONGRESS, July 4, 1776.

The unanimous Declaration of the thirteen united States of America,

When in the Course of human events, it becomes necessary for one people to dissolve the political bands which have connected them with another, and to assume among the powers of the earth, the separate and equal station to which the Laws of Nature and of Nature's God entitle them, a decent respect to the opinions of mankind requires that they should declare the causes which impel them to the separation.

We hold these truths to be self-evident, that all men are created equal, that they are endowed by their Creator with certain unalienable Rights, that among these are Life, Liberty and the pursuit of Happiness.--That to secure these rights, Governments are instituted among Men, deriving their just powers from the consent of the governed, --That whenever any Form of Government becomes destructive of these ends, it is the Right of the People to alter or to abolish it, and to institute new Government, laying its foundation on such principles and organizing its powers in such form, as to them shall seem most likely to effect their Safety and Happiness. Prudence, indeed, will dictate that Governments long established should not be changed for light and transient causes; and accordingly all experience hath shewn, that mankind are more disposed to suffer, while evils are sufferable, than to right themselves by abolishing the forms to which they are accustomed. But when a long train of abuses and usurpations, pursuing invariably the same Object evinces a design to reduce them under absolute Despotism, it is their right, it is their duty, to throw off such Government, and to provide new Guards for their future security.--Such has been the patient sufferance of these Colonies; and such is now the necessity which constrains them to alter their former Systems of Government. The history of the present King of Great Britain is a history of repeated injuries and usurpations, all having in direct object the establishment of an absolute Tyranny over these States. To prove this, let Facts be submitted to a candid world.

He has refused his Assent to Laws, the most wholesome and necessary for the public good.

He has forbidden his Governors to pass Laws of immediate and pressing importance, unless suspended in their operation till his Assent should be obtained; and when so suspended, he has utterly neglected to attend to them.

He has refused to pass other Laws for the accommodation of large districts of people, unless those people would relinquish the right of Representation in the Legislature, a right inestimable to them and formidable to tyrants only.

He has called together legislative bodies at places unusual, uncomfortable, and distant from the depository of their public Records, for the sole purpose of fatiguing them into compliance with his measures.

He has dissolved Representative Houses repeatedly, for opposing with manly firmness his invasions on the rights of the people.

He has refused for a long time, after such dissolutions, to cause others to be elected; whereby the Legislative powers, incapable of Annihilation, have returned to the People at large for their exercise; the State remaining in the mean time exposed to all the dangers of invasion from without, and convulsions within.

He has endeavoured to prevent the population of these States; for that purpose obstructing the Laws for Naturalization of Foreigners; refusing to pass others to encourage their migrations hither, and raising the conditions of new Appropriations of Lands.

He has obstructed the Administration of Justice, by refusing his Assent to Laws for establishing Judiciary powers.

He has made Judges dependent on his Will alone, for the tenure of their offices, and the amount and payment of their salaries.

He has erected a multitude of New Offices, and sent hither swarms of Officers to harrass our people, and eat out their substance.

He has kept among us, in times of peace, Standing Armies without the Consent of our legislatures.

He has affected to render the Military independent of and superior to the Civil power.

He has combined with others to subject us to a jurisdiction foreign to our constitution, and unacknowledged by our laws; giving his Assent to their Acts of pretended Legislation:

For Quartering large bodies of armed troops among us:

For protecting them, by a mock Trial, from punishment for any Murders which they should commit on the Inhabitants of these States:

For cutting off our Trade with all parts of the world:

For imposing Taxes on us without our Consent:

For depriving us in many cases, of the benefits of Trial by Jury:

For transporting us beyond Seas to be tried for pretended offences

For abolishing the free System of English Laws in a neighbouring Province, establishing therein an Arbitrary government, and enlarging its Boundaries so as to render it at once an example and fit instrument for introducing the same absolute rule into these Colonies:

For taking away our Charters, abolishing our most valuable Laws, and altering fundamentally the Forms of our Governments:

For suspending our own Legislatures, and declaring themselves invested with power to legislate for us in all cases whatsoever.

He has abdicated Government here, by declaring us out of his Protection and waging War against us.

He has plundered our seas, ravaged our Coasts, burnt our towns, and destroyed the lives of our people.

He is at this time transporting large Armies of foreign Mercenaries to compleat the works of death, desolation and tyranny, already begun with circumstances of Cruelty & perfidy scarcely paralleled in the most barbarous ages, and totally unworthy the Head of a civilized nation.

He has constrained our fellow Citizens taken Captive on the high Seas to bear Arms against their Country, to become the executioners of their friends and Brethren, or to fall themselves by their Hands.

He has excited domestic insurrections amongst us, and has endeavoured to bring on the inhabitants of our frontiers, the merciless Indian Savages, whose known rule of warfare, is an undistinguished destruction of all ages, sexes and conditions.

In every stage of these Oppressions We have Petitioned for Redress in the most humble terms: Our repeated Petitions have been answered only by repeated injury. A Prince whose character is thus marked by every act which may define a Tyrant, is unfit to be the ruler of a free people.

Nor have We been wanting in attentions to our Brittish brethren. We have warned them from time to time of attempts by their legislature to extend an unwarrantable jurisdiction over us. We have reminded them of the circumstances of our emigration and settlement here. We have appealed to their native justice and magnanimity, and we have conjured them by the ties of our common kindred to disavow these usurpations, which, would inevitably interrupt our connections and correspondence. They too have been deaf to the voice of justice and of consanguinity. We must, therefore, acquiesce in the necessity, which denounces our Separation, and hold them, as we hold the rest of mankind, Enemies in War, in Peace Friends.

We, therefore, the Representatives of the united States of America, in General Congress, Assembled, appealing to the Supreme Judge of the world for the rectitude of our intentions, do, in the Name, and by Authority of the good People of these Colonies, solemnly publish and declare, That these United Colonies are, and of Right ought to be Free and Independent States; that they are Absolved from all Allegiance to the British Crown, and that all political connection between them and the State of Great Britain, is and ought to be totally dissolved; and that as Free and Independent States, they have full Power to levy War, conclude Peace, contract Alliances, establish Commerce, and to do all other Acts and Things which Independent States may of right do. And for the support of this Declaration, with a firm reliance on the protection of divine Providence, we mutually pledge to each other our Lives, our Fortunes and our sacred Honor.

The 56 signatures on the Declaration appear in the positions indicated:

Column 1
Georgia:
  Button Gwinnett
  Lyman Hall
  George Walton

Column 2
North Carolina:
  William Hooper
  Joseph Hewes
  John Penn
South Carolina:
  Edward Rutledge
  Thomas Heyward, Jr.
  Thomas Lynch, Jr.
  Arthur Middleton

Column 3
Massachusetts:
John Hancock
Maryland:
Samuel Chase
William Paca
Thomas Stone
Charles Carroll of Carrollton
Virginia:
George Wythe
Richard Henry Lee
Thomas Jefferson
Benjamin Harrison
Thomas Nelson, Jr.

Francis Lightfoot Lee
Carter Braxton

Column 4
Pennsylvania:
  Robert Morris
  Benjamin Rush
  Benjamin Franklin
  John Morton
  George Clymer
  James Smith
  George Taylor
  James Wilson
  George Ross
Delaware:
  Caesar Rodney
  George Read
  Thomas McKean

Column 5
New York:
  William Floyd
  Philip Livingston
  Francis Lewis
  Lewis Morris
New Jersey:
  Richard Stockton
  John Witherspoon
  Francis Hopkinson
  John Hart
  Abraham Clark

Column 6
New Hampshire:
  Josiah Bartlett
  William Whipple
Massachusetts:
  Samuel Adams

John Adams
Robert Treat Paine
Elbridge Gerry

Rhode Island:
Stephen Hopkins
William Ellery
Connecticut:
Roger Sherman
Samuel Huntington
William Williams
Oliver Wolcott
New Hampshire:
Matthew Thornton

BIBLIOGRAPHY

Introduction

Brian P. Trotter, William S. Norton, *The Miracle of America, Birth of a Nation*; Washington: National Center for Constitutional Studies (2010)

Kelly Knauer and the Editors of TIME, *The Making of America: Life, Liberty and the Pursuit of a Nation*; New York: TIME Inc. (2005)

Chapter 1

Akhil Reed Amar, *America's Constitution: A Biography*; New York: Random House (2005)

Alexis de Tocqueville, *Democracy in America*; New York: Penguin Group (1984) Originally published 1835, 1840.

Articles of Confederation, March 1, 1781; *http://avalon.law.yale.edu/18th_century/artconf.asp*

J.H. Elliott, *Empires of the Atlantic World: Britain and Spain in America, 1491-1830*; New Haven, Connecticut: Yale University Press (2006).

James Madison, "Federalist No. 41: General View of the Powers Conferred by The Constitution," *http://www.constitution.org/fed/federa41.htm*

John L. Hancock, *Liberty Inherited: The Untold Story of America's Exceptionalism*; California: Liberty Lane Media (2011)

John Taylor, *New Views of the Constitution of the United States*; Washington City: By Way and Gideon (1823)

Jonathan Locke Hart, *Representing the New World: The English and French Uses of the Example of Spain*; New York, Palgrave (2001).

Karlyn Bowman, "Understanding American Exceptionalism," The American, April 28, 2008, http://www.american.com/archive/2008/april-04-08/understanding-american-exceptionalism

Kelly Knauer (ed.), *The Making of America: Life, Liberty and the Pursuit of a Nation*; New York, Time Books (2005).

Lance Banning, *The Sacred Fire of Liberty: James Madison and the Founding of the Federal Republic*; New York: Cornell University Press (1995).

Larry Schweikart and Michael Allen, *A Patriot's History of the United States*; New York: Sentinel (2004).

Madison's Notes on the Constitutional Convention, Avalon Project, Yale University:
http://avalon.law.yale.edu/subject_menus/debcont.asp

Peter H. Schuck and James Q. Wilson, *Understanding America: The Anatomy of an Exceptional Nation*; New York: Public Affairs (2008).

Philip B. Kurland and Ralph Lerner, *The Founder's Constitution – Volume One –Major Themes*; Indianapolis: Liberty Fund (1987).

Philip B. Kurland and Ralph Lerner, *The Founder's Constitution – Volume Two - Preamble through Article I, Section 8, Clause 4*; Indianapolis: Liberty Fund (1987).

Prof. Paul Eidelberg The Jewish Torah Roots of the American Constitution, Destination Yisra'el: *http://destination-yisrael.biblesearchers.com/destination-yisrael/2010/07/the-jewish-torah-roots-of-the-american-constitution-by-prof-paul-eidelberg.html*

The Laws of the Twelve Tables, Constitution.org:
http://www.constitution.org/sps/sps01_1.htm

The Magna Carta, Constitution.org:
http://www.constitution.org/eng/magnacar.htm

Thomas J. DiLorenzo, *Hamilton's Curse*; New York: Three Rivers Press (2008).

W. Cleon Skousen, *The 5000 Year Leap: The 28 Great Ideas That Changed The World*, Washington: National Center for Constitutional Studies (1981)

W. Cleon Skousen, *The Making of America: The Substance and Meaning of the Constitution*, Washington: National Center for Constitutional Studies (1985)

Chapter 2

James Madison, "Federalist No. 41: General View of the Powers Conferred by The Constitution,"
http://www.constitution.org/fed/federa41.htm

John Taylor, *New Views of the Constitution of the United States*; Washington City: By Way and Gideon (1823)

Larry Schweikart and Michael Allen, *A Patriot's History of the United States*; New York: Sentinel (2004).

Madison's Notes on the Constitutional Convention, Avalon Project, Yale University: *http://avalon.law.yale.edu/subject_menus/debcont.asp*

Philip B. Kurland and Ralph Lerner, *The Founder's Constitution – Volume Two - Preamble through Article I, Section 8, Clause 4*; Indianapolis: Liberty Fund (1987).

Thomas J. DiLorenzo, *Hamilton's Curse*; New York: Three Rivers Press (2008).

Understanding Madison's Notes on Nullification, Tenth Amendment Center: *http://tenthamendmentcenter.com/2014/01/21/understanding-madisons-notes-on-nullification/*

W. Cleon Skousen, *The 5000 Year Leap: The 28 Great Ideas That Changed The World*, Washington: National Center for Constitutional Studies (1981)

W. Cleon Skousen, *The Making of America: The Substance and Meaning of the Constitution*, Washington: National Center for Constitutional Studies (1985)

Chapter 3

Eric Foner, *Reconstruction: America's Unfinished Revolution, 1863-1877*; New York: Harper Perennial Modern Classics (2002)

Joseph Andrews, *A Guide for Learning and Teaching The Declaration of Independence and The U.S. Constitution - Learning from the Original Texts Using Classical Learning Methods of the Founders*; San Marcos: The Center for Teaching the Constitution (2010)

Madison's Notes on the Constitutional Convention, Avalon Project, Yale University: *http://avalon.law.yale.edu/subject_menus/debcont.asp*

Philip B. Kurland and Ralph Lerner, *The Founder's Constitution – Volume Two - Preamble through Article I, Section 8, Clause 4*; Indianapolis: Liberty Fund (1987)

Chapter 4

Joseph Andrews, *A Guide for Learning and Teaching The Declaration of Independence and The U.S. Constitution - Learning from the Original Texts Using Classical Learning Methods of the*

Founders; San Marcos: The Center for Teaching the Constitution (2010)

Madison's Notes on the Constitutional Convention, Avalon Project, Yale University:
  http://avalon.law.yale.edu/subject_menus/debcont.asp

Philip B. Kurland and Ralph Lerner, *The Founder's Constitution – Volume Two - Preamble through Article I, Section 8, Clause 4*; Indianapolis: Liberty Fund (1987)

The Ten Most Important Things to Know About the U.S. Senate, CongressLink:
  http://www.congresslink.org/print_expert_tenthingssenate.htm

Chapter 5

Madison's Notes on the Constitutional Convention, Avalon Project, Yale University:
  http://avalon.law.yale.edu/subject_menus/debcont.asp

Philip B. Kurland and Ralph Lerner, *The Founder's Constitution – Volume Two - Preamble through Article I, Section 8, Clause 4*; Indianapolis: Liberty Fund (1987)

Chapter 6

Edwin Mora, "Top Democrat Dodges Question on Constitutionality of Obama Appointments, Says Pro Forma Sessions Are 'Games Being Played'," CNSnews.com (January 6, 2012):
  http://cnsnews.com/news/article/top-democrat-dodges-question-constitutionality-obama-appointments-says-pro-forma

Madison's Notes on the Constitutional Convention, Avalon Project, Yale University:
  http://avalon.law.yale.edu/subject_menus/debcont.asp

Nicole Ciandella, "Obama's Recess Appointment of Cordray Eschews Constitutional Process," Competitive Enterprise Institute (January 4, 2012): *http://cei.org/news-releases/obamas-recess-appointment-cordray-eschews-constitutional-process*

Philip B. Kurland and Ralph Lerner, *The Founder's Constitution – Volume Two - Preamble through Article I, Section 8, Clause 4*; Indianapolis: Liberty Fund (1987)

Chapter 7

Madison's Notes on the Constitutional Convention, Avalon Project, Yale

University:
  http://avalon.law.yale.edu/subject_menus/debcont.asp
Philip B. Kurland and Ralph Lerner, *The Founder's Constitution –*
  Volume Two - Preamble through Article I, Section 8, Clause 4;
  Indianapolis: Liberty Fund (1987)
William B. Saxbe, *I've Seen the Elephant: An Autobiography*; Kent State
  University Press (2000).

Chapter 8

How a Bill Becomes a Law, the Constitutional Way, The Heritage
  Foundation:
  http://www.heritage.org/research/reports/2011/01/how-a-bill-
  becomes-a-law-the-constitutional-way
Madison's Notes on the Constitutional Convention, Avalon Project, Yale
  University:
  http://avalon.law.yale.edu/subject_menus/debcont.asp
Philip B. Kurland and Ralph Lerner, *The Founder's Constitution –*
  Volume Two - Preamble through Article I, Section 8, Clause 4;
  Indianapolis: Liberty Fund (1987)
Pocket Veto Glossary Term, United States Senate:
  www.senate.gov/reference/glossary_term/pocket_veto.htm
The Ten Most Important Things to Know About the U.S. Senate,
  CongressLink:
  http://www.congresslink.org/print_expert_tenthingssenate.htm

Chapter 9

Andrew M. Allison, Mr. Richard Maxfield, K. Delynn Cook, and W.
  Cleon Skousen, *The Real Thomas Jefferson*; New York: National
  Center for Constitutional Studies (2009).
Articles of Confederation, March 1, 1781;
  http://avalon.law.yale.edu/18th_century/artconf.asp
David McCullough, *John Adams*; New York: Simon and Schuster
  (2001).
Donald Porter Geddes, *Franklin Delano Roosevelt - A Memorial*; New
  York: Pitman Publishing Corporation (1945).
Ethan Pope, *America's Financial Demise*; Dallas: Intersect Press (2010).
James Madison, Federalist No. 41: General View of the Powers
  Conferred by The Constitution (addresses General Welfare
  Clause as well), *http://www.constitution.org/fed/federa41.htm*
James Madison, Federalist No. 42: The Powers Conferred by the

Constitution, *http://avalon.law.yale.edu/18th_century/fed42.asp*

James Madison, Veto of Federal Public Works Bill 1817; Constitution dot org: *http://www.constitution.org/jm/18170303_veto.htm*

Jay A. Parry, Andrew M. Allison, and W. Cleon Skousen, *The Real George Washington*; New York: National Center for Constitutional Studies (2010).

K. Daniel Glover, FDR's Court-Packing Fiasco; Enter Stage Right: *http://www.enterstageright.com/archive/articles/0799fdrcourt.ht m* (1999).

Larry Schweikart and Michael Allen, *A Patriot's History of the United States*; New York: Sentinel (2004).

Madison's Notes on the Constitutional Convention, Avalon Project, Yale University: *http://avalon.law.yale.edu/subject_menus/debcont.asp*

Philip B. Kurland and Ralph Lerner, *The Founder's Constitution – Volume Two - Preamble through Article I, Section 8, Clause 4*; Indianapolis: Liberty Fund (1987)

Philip B. Kurland and Ralph Lerner, *The Founder's Constitution – Volume Three - Article I, Section 8, Clause 5 to Article 2, Section 1*; Indianapolis: Liberty Fund (1987)

Robert Brown, Gold and Silver Coin or Paper Money?; The John Birch Society: *http://www.jbs.org/blog/gold-and-silver-coin-or-paper-money.html* (2010)

Thomas J. DiLorenzo, *Hamilton's Curse*; New York: Three Rivers Press (2008).

U.S. Code, Title 10, Subtitle A, Part 1, Chapter 13, § 311: Militia: composition and classes; *http://www.law.cornell.edu/uscode/html/uscode10/usc_sec_10_0 0000311----000-.html*

Chapter 10

Articles of Confederation, March 1, 1781; *http://avalon.law.yale.edu/18th_century/artconf.asp*

Larry Schweikart and Michael Allen, *A Patriot's History of the United States*; New York: Sentinel (2004)

Madison's Notes on the Constitutional Convention, Avalon Project, Yale University: *http://avalon.law.yale.edu/subject_menus/debcont.asp*

Philip B. Kurland and Ralph Lerner, *The Founder's Constitution – Volume Three - Article I, Section 8, Clause 5 to Article 2, Section 1*; Indianapolis: Liberty Fund (1987)

The Original 13th Article of Amendment; American Patriot Friend's
 Network: *http://www.apfn.org/apfn/13th.htm*
Thomas J. DiLorenzo, *Hamilton's Curse*; New York: Three Rivers Press
 (2008)

Chapter 11

21st-Century Militia: State Defense Forces and Homeland Security,
 Heritage Foundation:
 *http://www.heritage.org/Research/Reports/2010/10/The-21st-
 Century-Militia-State-Defense-Forces-and-Homeland-Security*
Madison's Notes on the Constitutional Convention, Avalon Project, Yale
 University:
 http://avalon.law.yale.edu/subject_menus/debcont.asp
Philip B. Kurland and Ralph Lerner, *The Founder's Constitution –
 Volume Three - Article I, Section 8, Clause 5 to Article II,
 Section 1*; Indianapolis: Liberty Fund (1987)
UNITED STATES v. COMSTOCK (No. 08-1224), Clarence Thomas
 Dissenting Opinion (State Sovereignty):
 http://www.law.cornell.edu/supct/html/08-1224.ZD.html (2010)

Chapter 12

Alexander Hamilton, The Law of Nations and the U.S. Constitution,
 http://east_west_dialogue.tripod.com/vattel/id4.html
Associated Press, "Hillary Clinton Calls for End to Electoral College,"
 CBS News (2009)
 *http://www.cbsnews.com/stories/2000/11/10/politics/main24864
 5.shtml*
Brian Stelter, "FCC Faces Challenges to Net Rules," New York Times,
 *http://query.nytimes.com/gst/fullpage.html?res=9801E6D91739
 F931A15751C1A9669D8B63*
George Washington, The First Inaugural Address of George Washington,
 The Avalon Project - Yale University (1789/2008)
 http://avalon.law.yale.edu/18th_century/wash1.asp
Joseph Andrews, *A Guide for Learning and Teaching The Declaration of
 Independence and The U.S. Constitution - Learning from the
 Original Texts Using Classical Learning Methods of the
 Founders*; San Marcos: The Center for Teaching the Constitution
 (2010).
Madison's Notes Constitutional Convention, Avalon Project, Yale
 University:

http://avalon.law.yale.edu/subject_menus/debcont.asp

Marjorie Kehe, "How George Washington racked up a $300,000 fine for overdue library books," Christian Science Monitor, *http://www.csmonitor.com/Books/chapter-and-verse/2010/0419/How-George-Washington-racked-up-a-300-000-fine-for-overdue-library-books*

Mark Drajem, "EPA Introduces First Greenhouse-Gas Limits for Power Plants," Bloomberg, *http://www.bloomberg.com/news/2012-03-27/epa-issues-first-greenhouse-gas-limit-for-u-s-power-plants-1-.html*

Mountain Publius Goat, "Law of Nations, 1758 law book defines Natural Born Citizen," Kerchner (2008) *http://www.kerchner.com/protectourliberty/goatsledge/20081212%20Law%20of%20Nations.pdf*

Naturalization Act of 1790, Harvard University: *http://pds.lib.harvard.edu/pds/viewtext/5596748?n=1&imagesize=1200&jp2Res=.25&printThumbnails=no*

Philip B. Kurland and Ralph Lerner, *The Founder's Constitution – Volume Three - Article I, Section 8, Clause 5 to Article II, Section 1*; Indianapolis: Liberty Fund (1987)

Philip B. Kurland and Ralph Lerner, *The Founder's Constitution – Volume Four – Article I I, Section 8, Clause 5 to Article VII*; Indianapolis: Liberty Fund (1987)

Ron Paul, "Hands Off The Electoral College," Lew Rockwell (2004) *http://www.lewrockwell.com/paul/paul226.html*

Ron Paul, "The Electoral College vs. Mob Rule," Lew Rockwell (2004) *http://www.lewrockwell.com/paul/paul214.html*

Sean Rooney, "The Death of President William Henry Harrison," Associated Content (2008) *http://www.associatedcontent.com/article/518591/the_death_of_president_william_henry.html?cat=37*

Vatell's Law of Nations: *http://www.constitution.org/vattel/vattel_01.htm*

Chapter 13

James Madison, Veto of Federal Public Works Bill 1817; Constitution.org: http://www.constitution.org/jm/18170303_veto.htm

Jon Roland, Meaning of "High Crimes and Misdemeanors"; Constitution Society: http://www.constitution.org/cmt/high_crimes.htm, (1999)

Joseph Andrews, *A Guide for Learning and Teaching The Declaration of Independence and The U.S. Constitution - Learning from the Original Texts Using Classical Learning Methods of the Founders*; San Marcos: The Center for Teaching the Constitution (2010).

Madison's Notes Constitutional Convention, Avalon Project, Yale University: *http://avalon.law.yale.edu/subject_menus/debcont.asp*

Officers of the United States Within the Meaning of the Appointments Clause; Justice.gov: http://www.justice.gov/sites/default/files/olc/opinions/2007/04/3 1/appointmentsclausev10.pdf

Philip B. Kurland and Ralph Lerner, *The Founder's Constitution – Volume Three - Article I, Section 8, Clause 5 to Article II, Section 1*; Indianapolis: Liberty Fund (1987)

Philip B. Kurland and Ralph Lerner, *The Founder's Constitution – Volume Four – Article I I, Section 8, Clause 5 to Article VII*; Indianapolis: Liberty Fund (1987)

Vincent Gioia, What is a 'Misdemeanor' Under the Constitution and Why is it Important?; Right Side News: http://www.rightsidenews.com/2010091511636/editorial/rsn-pick-of-the-day/what-is-a-misdemeanor-under-the-constitution-and-why-is-it-important.html, (2010)

Chapter 14

Draft of the Kentucky Resolutions (Jefferson's Draft), Avalon Project, Yale University: *http://avalon.law.yale.edu/18th_century/jeffken.asp*

John Jay to John Adams, Correspondence, January 2, 1801, The Founder's Constitution: *http://press-pubs.uchicago.edu/founders/documents/a3_1s18.html*

Madison's Notes Constitutional Convention, Avalon Project, Yale University: *http://avalon.law.yale.edu/subject_menus/debcont.asp*

Mark R. Levin, *Men in Black: How the Supreme Court is Destroying America*; Washington, D.C.: Regnery Publishing (2006)

Philip B. Kurland and Ralph Lerner, *The Founder's Constitution – Volume Four – Article I I, Section 8, Clause 5 to Article VII*; Indianapolis: Liberty Fund (1987)

Understanding Madison's Notes on Nullification, Tenth Amendment Center:

http://tenthamendmentcenter.com/2014/01/21/understanding-madisons-notes-on-nullification/
Virginia Resolution - Alien and Sedition Acts, Avalon Project, Yale University:
http://avalon.law.yale.edu/18th_century/virres.asp

Chapter 15

Doris Kearns Goodwin, *Team of Rivals: The Political Genius of Abraham Lincoln*; New York: Simon & Schuster Paperbacks (2005)
Hyatt v. People ex rel. Corkran, 188 U.S. 691 (1903) ("We are of opinion that, as the relator showed…he was not within the state of Tennessee at the times stated in the indictments found in the Tennessee court, nor at any time when the acts were, if ever, committed, he was not a fugitive from justice within the meaning of the Federal statute upon that subject…")
Joseph Andrews, *A Guide for Learning and Teaching The Declaration of Independence and The U.S. Constitution - Learning from the Original Texts Using Classical Learning Methods of the Founders*; San Marcos: The Center for Teaching the Constitution (2010).
Madison's Notes Constitutional Convention, Avalon Project, Yale University:
http://avalon.law.yale.edu/subject_menus/debcont.asp
Philip B. Kurland and Ralph Lerner, *The Founder's Constitution – Volume Four – Article II, Section 8, Clause 5 to Article VII*; Indianapolis: Liberty Fund (1987)
Thomas J. DiLorenzo, *The Real Lincoln: A New Look at Abraham Lincoln, His Agenda, and an Unnecessary War*; Roseville, California: Prima Publishing, a division of Random House (2002)

Chapter 16

Friends of the Article V. Convention: *http://foavc.com/*
G. R. Mobley, *We the People: Whose Constitution is it Anyway?*; Hobart, Washington: Mobius Strip Press (2013)
G. R. Mobley, *We the People: The Strategy to Convene a Convention for Republic Review*; Hobart, Washington: Mobius Strip Press (2014)
Joseph Andrews, *A Guide for Learning and Teaching The Declaration of*

Independence and The U.S. Constitution - Learning from the
Original Texts Using Classical Learning Methods of the
Founders; San Marcos: The Center for Teaching the Constitution
(2010).

Madison's Notes Constitutional Convention, Avalon Project, Yale
University:
http://avalon.law.yale.edu/subject_menus/debcont.asp

Mark R. Levin, *The Liberty Amendments: Restoring the American*
Republic; New York: Threshold Editions, a division of Simon &
Schuster (2013)

Philip B. Kurland and Ralph Lerner, *The Founder's Constitution –*
Volume Four – Article I I, Section 8, Clause 5 to Article VII;
Indianapolis: Liberty Fund (1987)

Chapter 17

John Taylor, *New Views of the Constitution of the United States*;
Washington City: By Way and Gideon (1823)

Joseph Andrews, *A Guide for Learning and Teaching The Declaration of*
Independence and The U.S. Constitution - Learning from the
Original Texts Using Classical Learning Methods of the
Founders; San Marcos: The Center for Teaching the Constitution
(2010).

Madison's Notes Constitutional Convention, Avalon Project, Yale
University:
http://avalon.law.yale.edu/subject_menus/debcont.asp

Philip B. Kurland and Ralph Lerner, *The Founder's Constitution –*
Volume Four – Article I I, Section 8, Clause 5 to Article VII;
Indianapolis: Liberty Fund (1987)

Sam Cornell, *The Other Founders: Anti-Federalism and the*
Dissenting Tradition in America, 1788-1828; Chapel Hill:
University of North Carolina Press (1999)

Chapter 18

Joseph Andrews, *A Guide for Learning and Teaching The Declaration of*
Independence and The U.S. Constitution - Learning from the
Original Texts Using Classical Learning Methods of the
Founders; San Marcos: The Center for Teaching the Constitution
(2010).

Madison's Notes Constitutional Convention, Avalon Project, Yale

University:
http://avalon.law.yale.edu/subject_menus/debcont.asp
Philip B. Kurland and Ralph Lerner, *The Founder's Constitution –
    Volume Four – Article I I, Section 8, Clause 5 to Article VII*;
    Indianapolis: Liberty Fund (1987)

Chapter 19

Joseph Andrews, *A Guide for Learning and Teaching The Declaration of
    Independence and The U.S. Constitution - Learning from the
    Original Texts Using Classical Learning Methods of the
    Founders*; San Marcos: The Center for Teaching the Constitution
    (2010).
Philip B. Kurland and Ralph Lerner, *The Founder's Constitution –
    Volume Five – Amendments 1-12*; Indianapolis: Liberty Fund
    (1987)
The Charters of Freedom: The Bill of Rights, National Archives and
    Records Administration:
    http://archives.gov/exhibits/charters/bill_of_rights.html

Chapter 20

14th Amendment to the U.S. Constitution: Civil Rights (1868), Our
    Documents dot gov:
    http://www.ourdocuments.gov/doc.php?flash=true&doc=43
Intent of the Fourteenth Amendment was to Protect All Rights (argument
    supporting incorporation of the Bill of Rights to the States),
    Constitution dot org (2000):
    http://www.constitution.org/col/intent_14th.htm
Joseph Andrews, *A Guide for Learning and Teaching The Declaration of
    Independence and The U.S. Constitution - Learning from the
    Original Texts Using Classical Learning Methods of the
    Founders*; San Marcos: The Center for Teaching the Constitution
    (2010).
Philip B. Kurland and Ralph Lerner, *The Founder's Constitution –
    Volume Five – Amendments 1-12*; Indianapolis: Liberty Fund
    (1987)
Richard L. Aynes, On Misreading John Bingham and the Fourteenth
    Amendment (1993):
    http://www.constitution.org/lrev/aynes_14th.htm
The Fourteenth Amendment and Incorporation, The Tenth Amendment
    Center (2010):

http://newyork.tenthamendmentcenter.com/2010/05/the-14th-amendment-and-incorporation/

To Whom Does The Bill Of Rights Apply?, Lew Rockwell dot com (2005): *http://www.lewrockwell.com/browne/browne27.html*

What is the Bill of Rights?, About dot com Civil Liberties (argument supporting incorporation of Bill of Rights to the States: *http://civilliberty.about.com/od/historyprofiles/f/what_is_bill.htm*

Chapter 21

Danbury Baptist Association's letter to Thomas Jefferson, October 7, 1801: *http://www.stephenjaygould.org/ctrl/dba_jefferson.html*

Jefferson's Final Letter to the Danbury Baptists, January 1, 1802: *http://www.loc.gov/loc/lcib/9806/danpre.html*

Joseph Andrews, *A Guide for Learning and Teaching The Declaration of Independence and The U.S. Constitution - Learning from the Original Texts Using Classical Learning Methods of the Founders*; San Marcos: The Center for Teaching the Constitution (2010).

Philip B. Kurland and Ralph Lerner, *The Founder's Constitution – Volume Five - Amendments I-XII*; Indianapolis: Liberty Fund (1987).

The Declaration and Resolves of the First Continental Congress declared on October 14, 1774, U.S. History dot org: *http://www.ushistory.org/Declaration/related/decres.htm*

Thomas Jefferson, The Virginia Act For Establishing Religious Freedom, 1786: *http://religiousfreedom.lib.virginia.edu/sacred/vaact.html*

Chapter 22

10 USC § 311 - Militia: Composition and Classes, Cornell University Law School: *http://www.law.cornell.edu/uscode/text/10/311*

McDonald v. City of Chicago, United States Supreme Court: *http://www.supremecourt.gov/opinions/09pdf/08-1521.pdf*

Noah Webster, An Examination of the Leading Principles of the Federal Constitution (Philadelphia 1787), The Federalist Papers: *http://www.thefederalistpapers.org/founders/noah-webster/noah-webster-an-examination-of-the-leading-principles-of-the-federal-constitution-philadelphia-1787*

The Tree of Liberty Quotation, Monticello - TH: Jefferson Encyclopedia: *http://wiki.monticello.org/mediawiki/index.php/The_tree_of_liberty...(Quotation)*

Washington, D.C. v. Heller, Supreme Court of the United States Blog:
http://www.scotusblog.com/case-files/cases/dc-v-heller/

Chapter 23

Joseph Andrews, *A Guide for Learning and Teaching The Declaration of Independence and The U.S. Constitution - Learning from the Original Texts Using Classical Learning Methods of the Founders*; San Marcos: The Center for Teaching the Constitution (2010).
Madison's Notes Constitutional Convention, Avalon Project, Yale University:
http://avalon.law.yale.edu/subject_menus/debcont.asp
Philip B. Kurland and Ralph Lerner, *The Founder's Constitution – Volume Five - Amendments I-XII*; Indianapolis: Liberty Fund (1987).
Quartering Act, U.S. Constitution Online:
http://www.usconstitution.net/quarteringact.html
The Declaration of Rights and Grievances, U.S. Constitution Online:
http://www.usconstitution.net/intol.html

Chapter 24

How Congress Has Assaulted Our Freedoms in the Patriot Act by Andrew P. Napolitano, Lew Rockwell.com:
http://www.lewrockwell.com/orig6/napolitano2.html
Joseph Andrews, *A Guide for Learning and Teaching The Declaration of Independence and The U.S. Constitution - Learning from the Original Texts Using Classical Learning Methods of the Founders*; San Marcos: The Center for Teaching the Constitution (2010).
Paul A. Ibbetson, *Living Under the PATRIOT Act: Educating a Society*; Bloomington, IN: Author House (2007)
Philip B. Kurland and Ralph Lerner, *The Founder's Constitution – Volume Five - Amendments I-XII*; Indianapolis: Liberty Fund (1987).

Chapter 25

Definition of Due Process, Family Rights Association:
http://www.familyrightsassociation.com/bin/definition_due_proc ess_.htm

Joseph Andrews, *A Guide for Learning and Teaching The Declaration of Independence and The U.S. Constitution - Learning from the Original Texts Using Classical Learning Methods of the Founders*; San Marcos: The Center for Teaching the Constitution (2010).

Philip B. Kurland and Ralph Lerner, *The Founder's Constitution – Volume Five - Amendments I-XII*; Indianapolis: Liberty Fund (1987).

U.S. Supreme Court case, Miranda v. Arizona, 384 US 436 (1966) *http://caselaw.lp.findlaw.com/scripts/getcase.pl?court=US&vol =384&invol=436*

Chapter 26

Joseph Andrews, *A Guide for Learning and Teaching The Declaration of Independence and The U.S. Constitution - Learning from the Original Texts Using Classical Learning Methods of the Founders*; San Marcos: The Center for Teaching the Constitution (2010).

Philip B. Kurland and Ralph Lerner, *The Founder's Constitution – Volume Five - Amendments I-XII*; Indianapolis: Liberty Fund (1987).

Chapter 27

Joseph Andrews, *A Guide for Learning and Teaching The Declaration of Independence and The U.S. Constitution - Learning from the Original Texts Using Classical Learning Methods of the Founders*; San Marcos: The Center for Teaching the Constitution (2010).

Philip B. Kurland and Ralph Lerner, *The Founder's Constitution – Volume Five - Amendments I-XII*; Indianapolis: Liberty Fund (1987).

Chapter 28

Joseph Andrews, *A Guide for Learning and Teaching The Declaration of Independence and The U.S. Constitution - Learning from the Original Texts Using Classical Learning Methods of the Founders*; San Marcos: The Center for Teaching the Constitution (2010).

Philip B. Kurland and Ralph Lerner, *The Founder's Constitution –*

Volume Five - Amendments I-XII; Indianapolis: Liberty Fund (1987).

Chapter 29

Alexander Hamilton, Federalist Paper #84, Avalon Project, Yale
University: *http://avalon.law.yale.edu/18th_century/fed84.asp*
Joseph Andrews, *A Guide for Learning and Teaching The Declaration of
Independence and The U.S. Constitution - Learning from the
Original Texts Using Classical Learning Methods of the
Founders*; San Marcos: The Center for Teaching the Constitution
(2010).
Philip B. Kurland and Ralph Lerner, *The Founder's Constitution –
Volume Five - Amendments I-XII*; Indianapolis: Liberty Fund
(1987).

Chapter 30

About the Tenth Amendment, Tenth Amendment Center:
*http://tenthamendmentcenter.com/about/about-the-tenth-
amendment/*
Definition of Enumerated, 1828 Webster's Dictionary:
http://1828.mshaffer.com/d/search/word,enumerate
Definition of Reserved, 1828 Webster's Dictionary:
http://1828.mshaffer.com/d/search/word,reserved
James Madison, The Federalist Papers #45, Avalon Project, Yale
University: *http://avalon.law.yale.edu/18th_century/fed45.asp*
Joseph Andrews, *A Guide for Learning and Teaching The Declaration of
Independence and The U.S. Constitution - Learning from the
Original Texts Using Classical Learning Methods of the
Founders*; San Marcos: The Center for Teaching the Constitution
(2010).
Philip B. Kurland and Ralph Lerner, *The Founder's Constitution –
Volume Five - Amendments I-XII*; Indianapolis: Liberty Fund
(1987).
Thirty Enumerated Powers, Tenth Amendment Center:
*http://tenthamendmentcenter.com/historical-documents/united-
states-constitution/thirty-enumerated-powers/*

Chapter 31

Chisholm v. Georgia, 2 Dall. 419 (1793), Cornell College - Politics:

http://cornellcollege.edu/politics/courses/allin/365-366/documents/chisholm_v_georgia.html
Jefferson's Draft of the Kentucky Resolutions - October 1798, Avalon
    Project, Yale University:
    http://avalon.law.yale.edu/18th_century/jeffken.asp
Joseph Andrews, *A Guide for Learning and Teaching The Declaration of
    Independence and The U.S. Constitution - Learning from the
    Original Texts Using Classical Learning Methods of the
    Founders*; San Marcos: The Center for Teaching the Constitution
    (2010).
Philip B. Kurland and Ralph Lerner, *The Founder's Constitution –
    Volume Five - Amendments I-XII*; Indianapolis: Liberty Fund
    (1987).
Virginia Resolution of 1798, Constitution.org:
    http://www.constitution.org/cons/virg1798.htm

Chapter 32

David McCollough, *John Adams;* New York: Simon and Schuster.
    (2002)
Edward J. Larson, *A Magnificent Catastrophe: The Tumultuous Election
    of 1800*; New York: Free Press (2007)
Joseph Andrews, *A Guide for Learning and Teaching The Declaration of
    Independence and The U.S. Constitution - Learning from the
    Original Texts Using Classical Learning Methods of the
    Founders*; San Marcos: The Center for Teaching the Constitution
    (2010).
Philip B. Kurland and Ralph Lerner, *The Founder's Constitution –
    Volume Five - Amendments I-XII*; Indianapolis: Liberty Fund
    (1987).

Chapter 33

Congressional Proposals and Senate Passage Harper Weekly. The
    Creation of the 13th Amendment. Retrieved Feb. 15, 2007
Joseph Andrews, *A Guide for Learning and Teaching The Declaration of
    Independence and The U.S. Constitution - Learning from the
    Original Texts Using Classical Learning Methods of the
    Founders*; San Marcos: The Center for Teaching the Constitution
    (2010).

Chapter 34

Congressional Globe, 39th Congress (1866) pg. 2890: Senator Jacob
     Howard States the Intent of the Fourteenth Amendment
     Published in the Congressional Record, May 30, 1866.
Civil Rights Act, The - April 9, 1866,
     http://www.tedhayes.us/CVR_civil_rights_act_of_1866.htm
Doris Kearns Goodwin, *Team of Rivals: The Political Genius of
     Abraham Lincoln*; New York: Simon & Schuster Paperbacks
     (2005)
Frank J. Williams, *Judging Lincoln*; Carbondale: Southern Illinois
University Press (2002)
John F. Marszalek, Sherman: *A Soldier's Passion for Order*; New York:
     Vintage Civil War Library (1993)
Joseph Andrews, *A Guide for Learning and Teaching The Declaration of
     Independence and The U.S. Constitution - Learning from the
     Original Texts Using Classical Learning Methods of the
     Founders*; San Marcos: The Center for Teaching the Constitution
     (2010).
Thomas J. DiLorenzo, *The Real Lincoln: A New Look at Abraham
     Lincoln, His Agenda, and an Unnecessary War*; Roseville,
     California: Prima Publishing, a division of Random House
     (2002)
William S. NcFeely, *Grant*; New York: W.W. Norton & Company
     (1981)

Chapter 35

Congressional Globe, 40th Cong., 3d Sess (1869) pg. 1318
Foner, Eric, *Reconstruction: America's Unfinished
     Revolution, 1863-1877;* New York: Harper Perennial Modern
     Classics (2002)
Gillette, William, *The Right to Vote: Politics and the Passage of the
     Fifteenth Amendment*; Baltimore: John Hopkins Press (1969)

Chapter 36

Abolish the Federal Reserve dot org: *http://abolishthefederalreserve.org/*
Bill Benson, The Law That Never Was:
     http://www.thelawthatneverwas.com/
Ethan Pope, *America's Financial Demise: Approaching the Point of No
     Return*; Dallas, TX: Intersect Press (2010)
G. Edward Griffin, *The Creature from Jekyll Island : A Second Look at*

the Federal Reserve; Appleton, WI: American Opinion
    Publishing (1994)
W. Cleon Skousen, History of the 16th Amendment, National Retail
    Sales Tax Alliance:
    http://www.salestax.org/library/skousen_16history.html

Chapter 37

Allison, Maxfield, Cook, Skousen, *The Real Thomas Jefferson*; New
    York: National Center for Constitutional Studies (1983).
David McCullough, *John Adams*; New York: Simon and Schuster
    (2001)
Devvy, 36 States Did Not Ratify The 17th Amendment: What Will States
    Do?; rense.com, *http://www.rense.com/general95/36_dev.htm*
Earl Taylor, Jr., The Seventeenth Amendment and the Destruction of
    Federalism; National Center for Constitutional Studies,
    *http://www.nccs.net/2013-03-seventeenth-amendment-and-the-
    destruction-of-federalism.php*
James Madison, Federalist Paper No. 45,
    http://avalon.law.yale.edu/18th_century/fed45.asp
Jon Wolverton, II, J.D., 17th Amendment Mudslinging; The New
    American (November, 2010)
    *http://www.thenewamerican.com/usnews/constitution/item/7826-
    17th-amendment-mudslinging*
Joseph Andrews, *A Guide for Learning and Teaching The Declaration of
    Independence and The U.S. Constitution - Learning from the
    Original Texts Using Classical Learning Methods of the
    Founders*; San Marcos: The Center for Teaching the Constitution
    (2010)
Larry Schweikart and Michael Allen, *A Patriot's History of the United
    States*; New York: Sentinel (2004).
Richard Aynes, On Misreading John Bingham and the Fourteenth
    Amendment; Yale Law Journal (October, 1993)
    http://www.constitution.org/lrev/aynes_14th.htm

Chapter 38

Joseph Andrews, *A Guide for Learning and Teaching The Declaration of
    Independence and The U.S. Constitution - Learning from the
    Original Texts Using Classical Learning Methods of the
    Founders*; San Marcos: The Center for Teaching the Constitution
    (2010)

Kobler, John, *Ardent Spirits The Rise and Fall of Prohibition*, New
    York: G.P. Putnam's Sons (1973)
The Temperance Movement, US History.com;
    http://www.u-s-history.com/pages/h1054.html
Steven Mintz, *Moralists & Modernizers: America's Pre-Civil War
    Reformers*; Baltimore: Johns Hopkins University Press (1995)

Chapter 39

Aaron Burr Biography, Essortment; *http://www.essortment.com/aaron-
    burr-biography-20550.html*
Abigail Adams urges husband to "remember the ladies", History.com;
    http://www.history.com/this-day-in-history/abigail-adams-urges-
    husband-to-remember-the-ladies
Andrew M. Allison, K. DeLynn Cook, M. Richard Maxfield, and W.
    Cleon Skousen, *The Real Thomas Jefferson*; New York: National
    Center for Constitutional Studies (2009)
David McCullough, *John Adams*; New York: Simon and Schuster (2001)
W. Cleon Skousen, The Role of Women in Healing America, Latter Day
    Conservative and The Constitution magazine, November 1985;
    *http://www.latterdayconservative.com/articles/the-role-of-
    women-in-healing-america/*

Chapter 40

Joseph Andrews, *A Guide for Learning and Teaching The Declaration of
    Independence and The U.S. Constitution - Learning from the
    Original Texts Using Classical Learning Methods of the
    Founders*; San Marcos: The Center for Teaching the Constitution
    (2010)
United States Senate, Lame Duck Session Definition:
    *http://www.senate.gov/reference/glossary_term/lame_duck_sessi
    on.htm*

Chapter 41

Andrew M. Allison, Jay A. Perry, and W. Cleon Skousen, *The Real
    George Washington*; New York: National Center for
    Constitutional Studies (2010)
Catherine Drinker Bowen, *Miracle at Philadelphia: The Story of the
Constitutional Convention, May to September 1787*; Boston: Atlantic
    Monthly Press (1966)

Donald Porter Geddes (ed.), *Franklin Delano Roosevelt - A Memorial*; New York: Pitman Publishing Corporation (1945)

James Srodes, On Dupont Circle: Franklin and Eleanor Roosevelt and the Progressives Who Shaped Our World; Berkeley: CounterPoint Press (2012)

James Thomas Flexner, *Washington: The Indispensible Man*; Boston: Back Bay Books (1969)

John Morton Blum, *The Progressive Presidents: Theodore Roosevelt, Woodrow Wilson, Franklin D. Roosevelt, Lyndon B. Johnson*; New York: W.W. Norton & Co. (1982)

Willard Sterne Randall, George Washington: A Life; New York: Henry Hold & Co. (1997)

Chapter 42

Joseph Andrews, *A Guide for Learning and Teaching The Declaration of Independence and The U.S. Constitution - Learning from the Original Texts Using Classical Learning Methods of the Founders*; San Marcos: The Center for Teaching the Constitution (2010)

Larry Schweikart and Michael Allen, *A Patriot's History of the United States*; New York: Sentinel (2004)

Smithsonian, Washington, D.C., History and Heritage, (2007)
http://www.smithsonianmag.com/travel/destination-hunter/north-america/united-states/east/washington-dc/washingtondc-history-heritage.html

Chapter 43

Congressional and Presidential Primaries: Open, Closed, Semi-Closed, and "Top Two", Fair Vote:
http://www.fairvote.org/congressional-and-presidential-primaries-open-closed-semi-closed-and-top-two#.T01VzPGPWHM

Joseph Andrews, *A Guide for Learning and Teaching The Declaration of Independence and The U.S. Constitution - Learning from the Original Texts Using Classical Learning Methods of the Founders*; San Marcos: The Center for Teaching the Constitution (2010)

Tom Spencer, American-style primaries would breathe life into European elections (2004):
http://www.europeanvoice.com/article/imported/american-style-

*primaries-would-breathe-life-into-european-
elections/49725.aspx*

Ware, Alan. The American Direct Primary: Party Institutionalization and
Transformation in the North (2002), the invention of primaries
around 1900:
http://www.questia.com/PM.qst?a=o&d=105149213

Chapter 44

Joseph Andrews, *A Guide for Learning and Teaching The Declaration of
Independence and The U.S. Constitution - Learning from the
Original Texts Using Classical Learning Methods of the
Founders*; San Marcos: The Center for Teaching the Constitution
(2010)

Understanding the 25th Amendment, Law.com,
*http://constitution.laws.com/american-
history/constitution/constitutional-amendments/25th-amendment*

United States Constitution and Citizenship Day: 25th Amendment,
http://www.usconstitutionday.us/p/25th-amendment.html

Chapter 45

Joseph Andrews, *A Guide for Learning and Teaching The Declaration of
Independence and The U.S. Constitution - Learning from the
Original Texts Using Classical Learning Methods of the
Founders*; San Marcos: The Center for Teaching the Constitution
(2010)

Larry Schweikart and Michael Allen, *A Patriot's History of the United
States*; New York: Sentinel (2004)

Old Enough to Fight, Old Enough to Vote, Nixon Foundation,
*http://blog.nixonfoundation.org/2014/06/old-enough-fight-old-
enough-vote/*

Repeal the 26th Amendment! by Anne Coulter, Townhall,
*http://townhall.com/columnists/anncoulter/2010/11/10/repeal_th
e_26th_amendment%21*

Youth Vote: Dems' Secret Weapon 40 Years in the Making? by Carl M.
Cannon, Real Clear Politics,
*http://www.realclearpolitics.com/articles/2011/03/25/youth_vote
_dems_delayed_time_release_capsule.html*

Chapter 46

Amendment XXVII: Congressional Compensation, United States History, *http://www.u-s-history.com/pages/h924.html*

Joseph Andrews, *A Guide for Learning and Teaching The Declaration of Independence and The U.S. Constitution - Learning from the Original Texts Using Classical Learning Methods of the Founders*; San Marcos: The Center for Teaching the Constitution (2010)

Members of Congress Haven't Had a Raise in Years, by Jesse Rifkin, USA Today, *http://www.usatoday.com/story/news/politics/2013/08/15/congress-pay-salaries/2660545/*

Notes on the 27th Amendment, Constitution of the United States "Charters of Freedom", *http://www.archives.gov/exhibits/charters/constitution_amendment_27.html*

Understanding the 27th Amendment, Laws.com, http://constitution.laws.com/american-history/constitution/constitutional-amendments/27th-amendment

Other Resources:

Andrew M. Allison, M. Richard Maxfield, W. Cleon Skousen, *The Real Benjamin Franklin*; Washington: National Center for Constitutional Studies (2009)

Arthur J. Stansbury, *Elementary Catechism on the Constitution of the United States*; Boston: Hilliard, Gray, Little, and Wilkins (1828) Reprinted by National Center for Constitutional Studies (2010)

Edmund Lindop, *Birth of the Constitution*; Hillside, New Jersey: Enslow Publishers (1987)

Francis Russell, *Adams: An American Dynasty*; Edison, New Jersey: Castle Books (1976)

Jon Kukla, *Mr. Jefferson's Women*; New York: Alfred A. Knopf (2007)

Kevin R. C. Gutzman, *James Madison and the Making of America*; New York: St. Martin's Press (2012)

Theodore P. Savas and J. David Dameron, *A Guide to the Battles of the American Revolution*; New York: Savas Beatie (2006)

William Kottmeyer, Our Constitution and what it means; St. Louis: Webster Publishing Co. (1961)

GLOSSARY

1559 Act of Uniformity - In Britain it was illegal not to attend Church of England services, with a fine imposed for each missed Sunday and holy day. Penalties for having unofficial services included arrest and larger fines.

3/5s Clause - Compromise in the Constitution that disallowed the northern states, or the southern states, to dominate the House of Representatives. 3/5 of a whole for the purposes of enumeration was decided upon so that both regions had about equal representation in the House of Representatives.

Activist Judge - A public officer charged with applying the law in order to administer justice, but also interprets the law, and modifies the law according to his opinion; a judge who legislates from the bench.

Adjourn - Suspend proceedings to a later time and/or place.

Advise and Consent Powers - Treaties, appointments, and other executive functions, though executed by the President, requires the advise by, and the approval of, the Senate.

Affirmation - A solemn sworn declaration, or promise, to fulfill a pledge.

American Civil War - See War Between the States.

Americanism - A philosophy of freedom that actively seeks less government and more personal responsibility.

Anarchy – Zero government. Supporters of anarchy believe that from chaos rises order. They seek to destroy the old system so that a new political system may rise up from the rubble. Anarchy is a transitional state of governance, transitioning whatever it destroys into oligarchy, or a similar centralized system, where the powerful few rule over the many.

Annapolis Convention - Titled by the participants: Proceedings of the Commissioners to Remedy Defects of the Federal Government,

Annapolis in the State of Maryland, September 14, 1786; a regional meeting of five States originally intended to discuss ways of improving navigation on the Potomac River. The participating delegates determined they could not deal effectively with national commercial problems without changes in the Articles of Confederation, and called for a convention of all the states to meet eight months later in Philadelphia, where the Constitution of the United States was ultimately drafted.

Anti-Federalists - Opposed to formation of a federal government, particularly by adoption of the Constitution of the United States.

Arms - Weapons, firearms; a gun that may be used for protection of property or as part of a militia.

Article V. Convention - A convention for the proposal of constitutional amendments applied for by the States and called by Congress.

Articles of Confederation - Agreement between the thirteen original states establishing the terms under which they agreed to participate in an organized, central form of government, adopted November 15, 1777, during the American Revolutionary War.

Atlantic Slave Trade - Started by the Portuguese, but soon dominated by the English, the Atlantic Slave Trade was the sale and exploitation of African slaves by Europeans that occurred in and around the Atlantic Ocean from the 15th century to the 19th century.

Bailey Bill - Income Tax introduced in April 1909 by Senator Joseph W. Bailey, a Democrat from Texas, designed to embarrass conservative Republicans when they voted against it. The introduction of the bill was one of the factors that led to the proposal of the 16th Amendment.

Bankruptcy - A legal condition recognizing a financial failure, allowing a debtor to have their debts discharged upon the satisfaction of certain requirements.

Bicameral - Having two branches or chambers (regarding a legislative body).

Bill of Rights - The first ten amendments of the U.S. Constitution; a formal summary of those rights and liberties considered essential to a people or group of people.

Bills of Attainder - When a legislature declares the guilt of a person or group of persons, and punishes them without due process.

Bills of Credit - Paper banknotes, promissory notes, bonds or bills issued exclusively on the credit of the issuing government, and for the payment of which the faith of the issuing government only is pledged.

Black Codes - Laws put in place in the United States after the Civil War with the effect of limiting the basic human rights and civil liberties of blacks.

Bribery - The exchange of money, promises, or other things, with someone in office, in order to influence that person's views or conduct.

Cap and Trade - Emissions trading; a regulatory approach to control pollution by providing economic incentives for achieving reductions in the emissions of pollutants; central control limit of amount of pollutants that can be emitted (cap), and companies are permitted to sell the unused portion of their limits to other companies who are struggling to comply (trade).

Capital Crime - A crime for which the punishment is death. Punishment for a Capital Crime is called Capital Punishment.

Capitalism - An economic system characterized by private or corporate ownership of capital goods, by investments that are determined by private decision, and by prices, production, and the distribution of goods that are determined mainly by competition in a free market.

Capitation - Head tax; a direct tax on each person.

Carte Blanche - Unrestricted power to act at one's own discretion; unconditional authority; derived from "blank cheque."

Caucuses - A meeting of the members of a legislative body who are members of a particular political party, to select candidates or decide policy.

Censure - Procedure for publicly reprimanding a public official for inappropriate behavior. There are normally no legal consequences.

Censure is not mentioned in the Constitution, but is a procedure devised by the legislature as a tool for formal condemnation of a member of the congressional body.

Census - A required head count to be taken once every ten years in order to determine the enumeration for establishing the number of Representatives each state would receive.

Central Government - Nationalistic government; a government system that is typically a characteristic of a unitary state.

Charter - A document issued by a sovereign, legislature, or other authority, creating a public or private corporation, such as a city, college, or bank, and defining its privileges and purposes; a written grant from the sovereign power of a country conferring certain rights and privileges on a person, a corporation, or a people.

Checks and Balances - An internal system in government where each part of government can counter the actions or decisions of the other parts. This arrangement ensures transparency, and prevents domination of the government by any part.

Civic Activities - Participating in community events, donating time for society, i.e. donating blood, and charity events.

Civil War - See War Between the States.

Closed Primary - A primary election in which only party members may select candidates for a general election.

Collective Right - Rights held by a group, rather than its members separately.

Collectivism - The theory that giving a group priority over each individual in it provides for the greater good, practice of the ownership of land and the means of production by the state in the name of equity and justice.

Collusion - Conspire together.

Commercial Center - A central location of commercial activity; an environment for commerce, or business activity.

Common Law - The part of English law that is derived from custom and judicial precedent rather than statutes, able to be changed by the whims of the governed, or their representatives.

Communism - Socialism realized; theory of social organization based on principles of common ownership, ownership and possessions being ascribed to the community as a whole, or to the state. System in which all economic and social activity is controlled by a dominant government, administered by the ruling elite of a single, and self-perpetuating, political party.

Communitarianism - A society where the good of the community outweighs the good of the individual; a common good conception of justice; a well ordered society without rulers that uses pluralism as the guiding principle.

Concurrent Powers – Government powers shared by the State and the federal government.

Confederation - An association of sovereign member states that, by treaty or other agreement, have delegated some of their powers to a common institution in order to coordinate policies, without constituting a new state on top of the member states.

Congress - A legislative body granted the authority of legislative powers. In the United States, the Congress is the only part of government granted the authority of legislative powers.

Congress of the United States - The legislative branch of the federal government which consists of two houses; a Senate and House of Representatives. The Congress is the only part of the federal government granted the authority of legislative powers.

Constitutional Amendment - Changes made to an existing constitution.

Constitutional Republic - Government that adheres to the rule or authority of the principles of a constitution. A representative government that operates under the rule of law.

Consultative Assembly - A legislative body that advises a ruler on matters of law, policy, and foreign affairs. Consultative assemblies lack the lawmaking power of traditional legislatures, and often exist only to give the appearance of giving the people a voice, when in reality they provide no real check against the central government, or the head of state. Consultative assemblies are normally just a rubber stamp for the ruling party, or head of state. Members can be elected, or appointed.

Corruption of Blood - Punishment inherited or passed down, all inheritable qualities are destroyed.

Declaration of Independence - The unanimous formal Declaration of the thirteen united States of America declaring their freedom from Great Britain, dated July 4, 1776.

Declaration of Rights - See English Bill of Rights.

Democracy - A form of government in which all citizens have an equal say in the decisions that affect their lives. Such a system includes equal participation in the proposal, development and passage of legislation into law.

Direct Election - Direct vote.

Direct Taxation - A government levy on the income, property, or wealth of people or companies. A direct tax is borne entirely by the entity that pays it, and cannot be passed on to another entity.

Direct Vote - Citizens vote themselves; popular vote.

Divided Allegiance/Divided Loyalties - A condition in which a person carries allegiances, or loyalties, to more than one country, a condition met with disapproval by the Founding Fathers for fear that person could be manipulated by foreign influences.

Divine Providence - The care and superintendence which God exercises over His creatures.

Double Jeopardy - The act of putting a person through a second trial for an offense for which he or she has already been prosecuted or convicted.

Dry Counties - Counties in the United States whose government forbids the sale of alcoholic beverages within the county.

Due Process - The essential elements of due process of law are notice, an opportunity to be heard, the right to defend in an orderly proceed, and an impartial judge. It is founded upon the basic principle that every man shall have his day in court, and the benefit of the general law which proceeds only upon notice and which hears and considers before judgment is rendered. In short, due process means fundamental fairness and substantial justice.

Duties - A tax levied by a government on the import or export of goods.

Electoral College - A body of electors chosen by the voters in each State to elect the President and Vice President of the United States.

Electors - A qualified voter in an election; a member of the Electoral College of the United States.

Eminent Domain - The power to take private property for public use by a State, municipality, or private person or corporation authorized to exercise functions of public character, following the payment of just compensation to the owner of that property.

English Bill of Rights - Enacted in 1689, the English Bill of Rights is one of the fundamental documents of English constitutional law, marking a fundamental milestone in the progression of English society from a nation of subjects to a nation of free citizens with God-given rights. The evolution began with the Magna Carta in 1215.

Enumerated - Counted or told, number by number; reckoned or mentioned by distinct particulars.

Equal Protection Under the Law - Laws must treat an individual resident or citizen in the same manner.

Ex post facto law - Retroactive law, a law that retroactively changes the legal consequences (or status) of actions committed or relationships that existed prior to the enactment of the law.

Exceptionalism - The condition of being exceptional or unique; the theory or belief that something, especially a nation, does not conform to a pattern or norm.

Excise - Tax on the manufacture, sale, or consumption of goods, or upon licenses to pursue certain occupations, or upon corporate privileges.

Exclusive Powers - Sole authority over a particular power, be it for the States within their own territorial boundaries, or sole federal powers. Also known as Reserved Powers.

Executive Branch - The branch of government responsible for executing, or carrying out, the laws. An executive in government can be a president, or a governor.

Executive Order - An order issued by the President of the United States that may be a proclamation, or an order to change the processes within the Executive Branch.

Express Powers - Powers granted to the federal government by enumerated authorities expressly granted in the United States Constitution.

Extradite - The surrender of a person charged with a crime by one state or country to another state or country.

Fascism - A governmental system that regiments all industry and commerce through heavy regulatory controls. Characteristics of fascism include the forced suppression of all opposition and criticism, aggressive nationalism, class warfare, and racial division.

Federal Government - System of government in which power is distributed between central authority and constituent territorial units.

Federal Reserve - A privately owned corporation owned by a secret group of international bankers. The federal reserve holds a monopoly on the creation of money in the United States. Whenever the U.S. Government needs money it borrows the money from the federal reserve, thus creating a national debt.

Federalism - Government in which the central government's power and authority is limited by local government units, and where each unit is delegated a sphere of power and authority only it can exercise, while other powers must be shared. The term federalism comes from the Latin root *foedus*, which means "formal agreement or covenant." It includes the interrelationships between the states as well as between the states and the federal government.

Federalist Papers - Series of essays written by John Jay, James Madison, and Alexander Hamilton defending, and explaining the principles of, the Constitution in order to encourage the New York Ratifying Convention to decide to ratify the Constitution.

Felony - Offense of graver character than misdemeanors, especially those commonly punished in the U.S. by imprisonment for more than a year. Felonies may include Capital Crimes and Infamous Crimes.

Fiat Money - Money that derives its value from government regulation or law, but is not backed by any tangible collateral; money that lacks any intrinsic value.

Foreign Entanglements - Unnecessary involvement with other nations.

Freeman - A person who is not a slave, indentured servant, or serf.

Free Market - Market economy in which the exchange of goods and services, and the fluctuation of prices, are free from intervention by government; an economic system governed by competition among private businesses, and the forces of supply and demand.

Full Faith and Credit - Requiring all States in the U.S. to recognize and give effect to the legislation, public records, and judicial decisions of other States in the United States. Full Faith and Credit also means: An unconditional commitment to pay interest and principal in debt, usually issued or guaranteed by the U.S. Treasury or another government entity.

General Welfare - A general sense of Welfare throughout the republic; the founders tasked the federal government with the duty of ensuring there was Welfare throughout the nation in a general manner; an atmosphere in general that is one of "Welfare," or "all's well."

Grand Jury - A group of citizens convened in a criminal case to consider the prosecutor's evidence and determine whether probable cause exists to prosecute a suspect for a felony. At common law, a group of persons consisting of not less than twelve nor more than twenty-four who listen to evidence and determine whether or not they should charge the accused with the commission of a crime by returning an indictment. The number of members on a grand jury varies in different States.

Granted - To confer, give, or bestow. A gift of legal rights or privileges, or a recognition of asserted rights, as in treaty. To legally transfer.

Great Depression - A severe worldwide economic depression in the decade preceding World War II.

Habeas Corpus - Latin for "You may have the body;" a writ that releases a prisoner from unlawful detention.

High Crimes - Punishable offenses that only apply to high persons, meaning "public officials," or those who, because of their official status, are under special obligations that ordinary persons are not under.

House of Representatives - Representatives of the people, directly voted into office by voters of the district the statesman represents. The members of the House of Representatives are divided among the States proportionally.

Ideology - A set of political or economic ideas that forms the basis of economic or political theory and policy.

Impeachment - To charge with misconduct. Formal process that may lead to removal of an official accused of unlawful activity; impeachment does not mean the removal from office, though removal from office is often the result of impeachment proceedings.

Implied Law - Legal concept serving as a legal substitute for authorities expressly granted by the United States Constitution; an agreement created by actions of the parties involved, but it is not written or spoken, because they are assumed to be logical extensions or implications of the other powers delegated in the Constitution.

Implied Powers - Legal or governmental authority not expressly stated by the U.S. Constitution, but considered to be logical extensions or implications of the other powers delegated in the Constitution. The concept of Implied Powers is often defended by the Necessary and Proper Clause (Article I, Section 8, Clause 18).

Imposts - A tax, especially an import duty; Import Duty is a tariff paid at a border or port of entry to the relevant government to allow a good to pass into that government's territory.

Incorporation of the Bill of Rights - The process through court rulings based on the interpretation of the 14th Amendment to apply the Bill of Rights to the States.

Indentured Servants - Colonists serving under indenture contracts which paid for their passage to America and lasted for a term of years (usually seven years) generally ending with a lump sum payment in money or goods, a plot of land, and freedom.

Indirect Taxation - An indirect tax is contrasted with a direct tax which is collected directly by the government from the people. An indirect tax, for example, may increase the price of a good so that consumers are actually paying the tax by paying more for the products. Another example of indirect tax is for one entity to tax another entity, and then the second entity taxing the people to recoup the taxes it paid (federal government taxes the State, and the State taxes the people).

Indirect Vote - Representatives of Electors vote instead of the citizens. The indirect vote may be based on criteria that includes the will, or portions of the will, of the citizens; before the 17th Amendment, United States Senators were chosen by an indirect vote of the people, in which State representatives who attained their office by a direct vote of the people appointed U.S. Senators to represent their State in Congress; the President is elected by an indirect vote of the people through electors who traditionally follow the popular vote of their State, but have the choice to change that vote if believed to be necessary, and a President may be elected based on an Electoral majority that does not reflect the national popular vote.

Individual Right - Rights held by individuals within a particular group.

Infamous Crime - A crime which works infamy in the person who commits it. Infamous crimes tend to be classified as treason, felonies, and any crime involving the element of deceit.

Inflation - A sustained, rapid increase in prices, over months or years, and mirrored in the correspondingly decreasing purchasing power of the currency.

Intolerable Acts - A series of laws passed by the British Parliament against the American Colonies in March of 1774. The British Parliament referred to these laws as the Coercive Acts. The acts were primarily designed to punish the colony of Massachusetts for defying British policies, and more specifically, for the Boston Tea Party. The Intolerable Acts caused outrage among the Americans, which led to the calling of the First Continental Congress in September of 1774. Among the actions taken by this united Congress was a boycott of British goods. The Intolerable Acts were called "impolitic, unjust, and cruel," and included the Boston Port Act, the Massachusetts Government Act, the Quartering Act, the Quebec Act, and the Administration of Justice Act.

Joint Resolution - A joint resolution is a legislative measure requiring approval by the Senate and the House and then is presented to the President for approval or disapproval. There is generally no legal difference between a joint resolution and a bill. Laws enacted by virtue of a joint resolution are not distinguished from laws enacted by a bill. Constitutional amendments are passed by joint resolutions, which are instead presented to the States for ratification. Resolutions are often temporary in nature.

Judicial Activism - When judges violate the Separation of Powers through their rulings; when a judge rules legislatively by modifying or striking down a law using the unconstitutional authority of judicial review.

Judicial Branch - The branch of the United States Government responsible for the administration of justice; a central judiciary that is limited to federal authorities, and separated from the will of the central leadership.

Judicial Review - The unconstitutional authority of the federal courts to review law, interpret the Constitution regarding laws, and then determine the constitutionality of laws.

Jurisdiction - Full loyalty, a condition in which all foreign allegiances have been released; not owing allegiance to anybody else.

Jury Nullification - The ability of a jury to nullify an unjust law.

Just Compensation - The value of a property deemed to be just by the property owner.

Lame Duck Congress - A lame duck session of Congress in the United States occurs whenever one Congress meets after its successor is elected, but before the successor's term begins.

Leftism - Progressivism; a political philosophy that advocates popular control of government, in order to ultimately establish an oligarchy.

Legislative Authority - See Legislative Powers.

Legislative Branch - Congress; the branch of the federal government that is vested with all legislative powers and consists of two Houses, the House of Representatives, and the United States Senate.

Legislative Powers - The ability to make law, modify law, repeal law, and anything else that has to do with affecting law.

Leveling - Moving money from one group of people to another by raising and lowering taxes accordingly in an effort to achieve economic equity in society.

Limited Government - A government that acts within the limitations granted to it; a governmental system that is restrained by an enumerated list of authorities; a limited government is the essence of liberty.

Line of Succession - The order in which individuals are expected to succeed one another in some official position.

Magna Carta - The Great Charter of the Liberties of England; the first document that limited the power of government by subjecting it to the rule of law; signed in June 1215 between the barons of Medieval England and King John.

Maladministration - Inefficient or dishonest administration; mismanagement.

Mercantilism - The use of protectionism to control trade and commerce, while generating wealth for a government through the accumulation of profitable balances.

Midnight Judges - In pursuance of the Judiciary Act of 1801, President John Adams, during the final 19 days of his administration, quickly filled as many of the new circuit judgeships created by the Act as possible in an attempt to completely reorganize the American court system. Thomas Jefferson was appalled by the actions of President John Adams, calling the appointment of the midnight judges evidence of the "Federalists retir[ing] into the judiciary as a stronghold . . . and from that battery all the works of Republicanism are to be beaten down and destroyed." After his inauguration in 1801, Jefferson refused to deliver the remaining appointments that John Adams had not gotten to, which ultimately led to the *Marbury v. Madison* case in 1803.

Military Districts - Districts created in the seceded states (not including Tennessee, which had ratified the 14th Amendment and was readmitted to the Union), headed by a military official empowered to appoint and remove state officials.

Militia - An army composed of ordinary citizens rather than professional soldiers; a military force that is not part of a regular army and is subject to call for service in an emergency; the whole body of physically fit civilians eligible by law for military service.

Mineral Rights - Federal government must purchase properties to be considered federal land, and do so with the consent of the State Legislature. All property within a State's boundaries belong to the State, including mineral rights. Mineral Rights is the ownership of mineral interest in real property. It is the right of the owner to exploit, mine, and/or produce any or all of the minerals lying below the surface of the property. The mineral estate of the land includes all unusual organic and inorganic substances forming a part of the soil which possess a useful property giving them special value. An exception would be sand, gravel, limestone, subsurface water, etc. which are normally considered part of the surface estate.

Miranda Rights - A warning given advising the accused of their right to remain silent, their right to an attorney, and the right to an appointed attorney if they are unable to afford counsel - prior to conducting a custodial interrogation.

Misdemeanors - In the Constitution the definition is bad behavior including, but not limited to, gross incompetence, gross negligence, or outright distasteful actions which clearly show "malevolence toward this country and constitution, which is unabated"; maladministration.

Mob-Rule - A government ruled by a mob or a mass of people; the intimidation of legitimate authorities; the tyranny of the majority; pure democracy without due process.

Monarch - A hereditary ruler, head of state, such as a king, queen, or emperor. A monarch reigns over a kingdom, or empire. Monarchs are sole, and absolute, rulers.

National Bank - In the United States, a bank chartered by the federal government authorized to issue notes that serve as currency; a bank owned and administered by the government, as in some European countries.

National Government - Any political organization that is put in place to maintain control of a nation; a strong central government that does not recognize the individualism or local authorities of the smaller parts, such as states, of the nation.

Nationalism - Political ideology which involves a strong identification of a group of individuals with a political entity defined in national terms. There are various strands of nationalism. The ideology may dictate that citizenship in a state should be limited to one ethnic, cultural or identity group. Nationalism may also include the belief that the state is of primary importance, which becomes the unhealthy love of one's government, accompanied by the aggressive desire to build that governmental system to a point that it is above all else, and becomes the ultimate provider for the public good.

Nationalist - An advocate of Nationalism.

Natural Born Citizen - A person born as a citizen of a country whose parents were both citizens at the time of the person's birth.

Natural Law - Unchanging moral principles regarded as a basis for all human conduct; observable law relating to natural existence; birthright law.

Natural Rights - Rights that exist by virtue of natural law; God-given rights; unalienable rights endowed by the Creator. Rights that exist, according to John Locke, as a result of the Laws of Nature. Rights, as described in the first paragraph of the Declaration of Independence, as being of the "Laws of Nature and of Nature's God."

Nullification - State power to ignore unconstitutional federal law.

Nullify - See Nullification.

Oath - A solemn sworn declaration, or promise, to a deity (God), to fulfill a pledge.

Officers of the United States – All persons holding office under the government; any appointee exercising significant authority pursuant to the laws of the United States.

Oligarchy - Government by a few powerful persons, over the many. A state governed by a few persons.

Open Primary - A primary election in which voters, regardless of party may select candidates from any party for a general election.

Organized Crime - Transnational, national, or local groupings of highly centralized enterprises run by criminals for the purpose of engaging in illegal activity, most commonly for monetary profit.

Organized Militia - A well trained militia that is in good order that operates under the authority of Congress, able to be called into actual service by the executive authority of a State, or by the Congress of the United States; National Guard, Naval Militia, State Militias.

Original Authority - Principal agent holding legal authority; initial power to make or enforce laws; the root authority in government.

Original Intent - Original meaning of the United States Constitution as intended by the framers during the Federal Convention of 1787, and the subsequent State Ratification Conventions.

Original Jurisdiction - In the Constitution the United States Supreme Court has original jurisdiction on some cases, which means the case must proceed directly to the United States Supreme Court, and the high court must accept the case.

Originalist view of the Constitution - View that the Constitution as written should be interpreted in a manner consistent with what was meant by those who drafted and ratified it.

Parliament – May consist of a single legislature, or function as a legislature that consists of two, or more, houses. In a parliament, the members make law, modify law, and repeal law. The leading party, or political organization that holds the voting majority, serves as the head of state, or executive branch. In a parliament, there is no separation of powers between the legislative and executive branches of government.

Patriotism - Wholesome, constructive love of one's land and people.

Perjury - Lying under oath, violation of one's oath (or affirmation).

Plausible Deniability - Circumstances where denial of responsibility or knowledge of wrongdoing cannot be proved as true or untrue due to a lack of evidence proving the allegation; when high ranking officials deny responsibility for or knowledge of wrongdoing by lower ranking officials; any act that leaves little or no evidence of wrongdoing or abuse.

Pocket Veto - The Constitution grants the president 10 days to review a measure passed by the Congress. If the president has not signed the bill after 10 days, it becomes law without his signature. However, if Congress adjourns during the 10-day period, the bill does not become law.

Police State - A system where the government exercises rigid and repressive controls through strong law enforcement or military control.

Political Spectrum - A broad range of political philosophies; the level of control of government over a society.

Poll Tax - A tax levied on people rather than on property, often as a requirement for voting.

Preamble - Introduction of the U.S. Constitution, holds no legal authority; the Preamble serves to establish who is granting the authority to create a new federal government, and the reasons for the decision.

President pro tempore - Second highest ranking official of the United State Senate. The Vice President is President of the Senate and the highest ranking official of the Senate despite not being a member of the body. During the Vice President's absence, the president pro tempore presides over its sessions or appoints another senator to do so. The president pro tempore is elected by the Senate and is customarily the most senior senator in the majority party.

Primary Election - An election in which party members or voters select candidates for a general election.

Prime Minister - Chief servant; agent appointed to manage business under the authority of another; one to whom a king or prince entrusts the direction of the affairs of state; as minister of state; an executive officer. In modern government, where the monarch is only a figurehead, the prime minister is the chief magistrate. In a parliamentary system, the prime minister is also a part of the legislature, usually the head of the majority party.

Privateer - A ship owned and operated by private individuals, but holding a government commission authorizing the vessel for use in service of the issuing government, especially in wartime, and for capture of enemy merchant shipping.

Pro Forma Session - A session in either house of the United States Congress at which no formal business is expected to be conducted, so as to fulfill the obligation "that neither chamber can adjourn for more than three days without the consent of the other." Pro forma sessions are also used to prevent the President from pocket-vetoing bills, calling the Congress into a special session, and to prevent the President from making recess appointments.

Profiteer - A person who seeks exorbitant profits.

Progressive Taxation - A tax where the tax rate increases as the taxable base amount increases.

Progressivism - Philosophy that views progress as seeking change in approaches to solving economic, social, and other problems, often through government sponsored programs.

Prohibition - Period in United States history during which the manufacture and sale of alcohol was prohibited. Drinking alcohol itself was never illegal, and there were always exceptions for medicinal and religious uses.

Protectionist Tariffs - Heavy taxation on imports designed, in theory, to foster or develop domestic industries, protecting them from foreign competition. Historically, these policies reduce domestic innovation and quality.

Protestant Reformation - Movement of the Church Reform begun in 1517 that was influenced by Martin Luther's critiques of the Roman Catholic Church. The movement led to the formation of the Protestant Christian groups.

Public Debt - National debt; the financial obligations of a national government resulting from deficit spending.

Quartering Act of 1765 - Act passed by the British Parliament in 1765 that stated that British troops in America would be housed in barracks and in public houses unless and until the number of troops overwhelmed the facilities, at which time, the troops could be housed in private commercial property, such as inns and stable, and in uninhabited homes and barns. The quartering would be without compensation and, in fact, owners would be required to provide soldiers with certain necessities such as food, liquor, salt, and bedding, also without compensation.

Quorum - Minimum number of members of an assembly necessary to conduct the business of that group.

Recess Appointment - The appointment of a senior federal official (department head, judge, etc.) by the President while the U.S. Senate is in recess.

Reciprocity - Mutuality; mutual exchange or recognition of privileges between states, nations, businesses or individuals.

Reconstruction Period - Period following the American Civil War during which the United States government began to rebuild the States that had seceded from the Union to form the Confederacy, lasting from 1865-1877. During Reconstruction, the federal government proposed a number of plans and committed large amount of resources, to the readmittance to the union, and the rebuilding, of the defeated Confederate States.

Regulated - To make regular; to put in good order.

Regulatory Agencies - Agencies within the Executive Branch tasked with executing the laws of the nation; the enforcement arm of the Executive Branch.

Republic - Form of government that uses the rule of law through a government system led by representatives and officials voted in by a democratic process. The United States enjoys a Constitutional Republic.

Republic Review - A convention of delegates representing the several States in order to audit the laws, actions, and composure of the United States federal government; a review of unconstitutional characteristics of the federal government based on the amendment ratification concept that if it takes three-quarters of the States to ratify an amendment, a quarter (plus one) of the States determining a law, action or department of the federal government to be unconstitutional allows the States to nullify the item.

Republicanism - Rule by law through a government system led by representatives and officials voted in by a democratic process. The United States enjoys a Constitutional Republic.

Reserved - Kept for another or future use; retained.

Reserved Powers - Sole authority over a particular power, be it for the States within their own territorial boundaries, or sole federal powers. Also known as Express Powers.

Resulting Powers - Powers that exist as a result of any action the government takes. These "resulting powers" are considered to be de facto constitutional by virtue of the fact that the action by the federal government occurred in the first place. Constitutionalists that adhere to the original intent of the Constitution reject resulting powers, and consider them to be unconstitutional.

Rule of Law - The restriction of the arbitrary exercise of power by subordinating it to well-defined and established laws; Laws of Nature and of Nature's God; self-evident standard of conduct and law.

Rule of Man - The unrestricted exercise of power by a ruling elite who adjust the law based on the whims of society, or the interpretation of the law by ruling class, or judicial class; a living breathing system of law.

Saxbe Fix - Salary rollback. A mechanism by which the President of the United States can avoid restrictions by the United States Constitution which prohibits the President from appointing a current or former member of Congress to a position that was created, or to an office position for which the pay and/or benefits were increased, during the term for which that member was elected until the term has expired. First used in 1909 without being named, the Saxbe Fix was later named for William Saxbe, a Senator appointed Attorney General by Nixon in 1973.

Search Warrant - The Search Warrant specifically requires that the government demonstrate to a judge the existence of probable cause of criminal activity on the part of the person whose property the government wishes to search. The Fourth Amendment commands that only a judge can authorize a search warrant.

Seat of Government - The location of the government for a political entity. The seat of government is usually located in the capital.

Secession - The action of withdrawing formally from membership of a federation or body, especially a political state.

Sectionalism - Loyalty to the interests of one's own region or section of the country, rather than to the country as a whole; loyalty to a political agenda or ideology rather than to the country as a whole.

Securities - A contract that can be assigned a value so that it may be traded, like a bond.

Separate But Equal - Various laws designed to undermine the 14th Amendment requirement that former slaves be treated equally under the law, contending that the requirement of equality could be met in a manner that kept the races separate. The result of these laws was a generally accepted doctrine of segregation throughout The South.

Separation of Church and State - Distance in the relationship between organized religion and the nation state.

Separation of Powers - A division of governmental authority into three branches: legislative, executive, and judicial; division of powers between the States and federal government.

Separatists - Pilgrims were a group not in connection with the Church of England. The Puritans kept their membership in the Church of England, while the Separatists though their differences with the Church of England were so severe that their worship should be organized independently.

Shays' Rebellion - An uprising led by a former militia officer, Daniel Shays, which broke out in western Massachusetts in 1786 over the economic hardship of the Revolutionary War veterans as a result of a poor economic climate, and the pay of the militiamen with worthless U.S. Government paper money.

Social Contract - An implicit agreement among the members of a society to cooperate for social benefits.

Socialism - An economic system in which good and services are provided through a central system of cooperative and/or government ownership rather than through competition and a free market system.

Socialist - A person who supports socialism.

Standing Army - A professional permanent army composed of full-time career soldiers who are not disbanded during times of peace.

State of the Union address - A speech about the state of the union addressed to Congress by the President.

State Sovereignty - The individual autonomy of the several states; strong local government was considered the key to freedom; a limited government is the essence of liberty.

States' Rights - The authorities of the States over local issues, and other issues, that are not directly related to the preservation of the union or are considered as federal issues.

Statism - A system in which the concentration of economic controls and planning are consolidated in the hands of a highly centralized government. These controls, in a system of statism, often extend to government ownership, or heavy regulation by the government, of private industry.

Statist - An advocate of statism, which is a system in which the concentration of economic controls and planning in the hands of a highly centralized government often extend to government ownership of industry.

Statists - Individuals that hold that government should control the economic and social policies of the system it serves.

Supremacy Clause - Clause in the Constitution that indicates that all federal laws, and treaties, passed under the authorities granted by the Constitution, are the Supreme Law of the Land.

Tax - A compulsory monetary contribution to the revenue of an organized political community, levied by the government of that political entity.

Temperance Movement - A social movement urging the reduced use of alcoholic beverages during the 19th and early 20th centuries.

Theocracy - Form of government in which a state is as governed by religion, or by clergy who believes they are under immediate divine guidance.

Totalitarian Government - Absolute control by a highly centralized government.

Treason - Levying war against the States, or adhering to the enemies of the States, giving aid and comfort to the enemy.

Two-Party System - A form of political system where two major political parties dominate voting in nearly all elections, at every level; a political system consisting chiefly of two major parties, more or less equal in strength.

Tyranny - Arbitrary, or despotic, exercise of power; the exercise of power over subjects and others with a rigor not authorized by law or justice, or not requisite for the purposes of government. Hence tyranny is often synonymous with cruelty and oppression; a cruel government.

Unalienable Rights - Incapable of being alienated; Incapable of being sold or transferred. You cannot surrender, sell or transfer unalienable rights, they are a gift from the Creator to the individual and cannot under any circumstances be surrendered or taken. All individuals have unalienable rights.

Unitary State - A system of government governing a state as one single unit, in which all power is derived from a supreme, central government. Any administrative divisions, or subnational units, exercise only powers the central government chooses to delegate. A majority of states in the world are governed under a unitary system of government.

United States are - These States that are united; a group of sovereign member States in America voluntarily united into a republic.

United States Constitution - Document that establishes the United States federal system of government; written May 14 through September 17, 1787 in Philadelphia, Pennsylvania. The convention was called with the intention to amend the Articles of Confederation. The Constitution was the product of political compromise after long debates over issues like States' rights, consent of the governed through representation, and slavery.

United States is - Nation of the United States containing a number of States similar to provinces ruled over by a centralized federal government.

United States Senate - The House of Congress in which each State enjoys equal suffrage of representation, with two Senators per State. The appointment of Senators was originally by their State legislatures, creating a natural check and balance between the House of Representatives, and the U.S. Senate. The appointment of Senators was changed to the popular vote of the people by the 17th Amendment in 1913.

Unorganized Militia - Able-bodied citizens of the United States, or those who have made a declaration of intention to become citizens of the United States, who are members of the militia who are not members of the National Guard or the Naval Militia.

Vatell's Law of Nations - A written work concerning natural law that served as the foundation of internationally recognized political philosophies. The volume was written by Swiss born Emer de Vattel, published in 1758. Vattel strove to integrate the commonly understood and internationally accepted political and legal definitions of the day into a single source.

Vested - Legally transferred, secured in the possession of, assigned.

Veto - The power of a chief executive to reject a bill passed by the legislature in order to prevent or delay its enactment into law.

Volstead Act - Officially The National Prohibition Act; the law that was the enabling legislation for the Eighteenth Amendment which established prohibition in the United States.

War Between the States - The Civil War was fought from 1861 to 1865 after Seven Southern slave States seceded from the United States, forming the Confederate States of America. The "Confederacy" grew to include eleven States. The war was fought between the States that did not declare secession, known as the "Union" or the "North", and the Confederate States. The war found its origin in the concept of State's Rights, but became largely regarding the issue of slavery after President Abraham Lincoln delivered the Emancipation Proclamation. Over 600,000 Union and Confederate soldiers died, and much of the South's infrastructure was destroyed. After the War, Amendments 13, 14, and 15 were proposed and ratified to abolish slavery in the United States, and to begin the process of protecting the civil rights of the freed slaves.

War Power - Power exercised in the prosecution of war.

Women's Suffrage - The right of women to vote and to run for office. The expression is also used for the economic and political reform movement aimed at extending these rights to women without any restrictions or qualifications such as property ownership, payment of tax, or marital status.

Writs of Assistance - British search warrants that were very broad and general in their scope. British agents, once obtaining these writs, could search any property they believed might contain contraband goods.

INDEX

Made in the USA
Columbia, SC
03 May 2021